TRANSPORTATION

AMERICA'S LIFELINE

TRANSPORTATION
AMERICA'S LIFELINE

Donna Lawrence

INFORMATION PLUS® REFERENCE SERIES
Formerly published by Information Plus, Wylie, Texas

GALE GROUP
™
THOMSON LEARNING

Detroit • New York • San Diego • San Francisco
Boston • New Haven, Conn. • Waterville, Maine
London • Munich

TRANSPORTATION: AMERICA'S LIFELINE

Donna Lawrence, *Author*

The Gale Group Staff:

Editorial: Ellice Engdahl, *Series Editor*; John F. McCoy, *Series Editor*; Charles B. Montney, *Series Editor*; Andrew Claps, *Series Associate Editor*; Jason M. Everett, *Series Associate Editor*; Michael T. Reade, *Series Associate Editor*; Heather Price, *Series Assistant Editor*; Teresa Elsey, *Editorial Assistant;* Debra M. Kirby, *Managing Editor*; Rita Runchock, *Managing Editor*

Image and Multimedia Content: Barbara J. Yarrow, *Manager, Imaging and Multimedia Content* ; Robyn Young, *Project Manager, Imaging and Multimedia Content*

Indexing: Susan Kelsch, *Indexing Supervisor*

Permissions: Lori Hines, *Permissions Specialist*; Maria Franklin, *Permissions Manager*

Product Design: Michelle DiMercurio, *Senior Art Director and Product Design Manager*; Michael Logusz, *Cover Art Designer*

Production: Evi Seoud, *Assistant Manager, Composition Purchasing and Electronic Prepress*; NeKita McKee, *Buyer*; Dorothy Maki, *Manufacturing Manager*

Cover photo © Digital Stock.

TABLE OF CONTENTS

PREFACE

Transportation: America's Lifeline is one of the latest volumes in the Information Plus Reference Series. Previously published by the Information Plus company of Wylie, Texas, the Information Plus Reference Series (and its companion set, the Information Plus Compact Series) became a Gale Group product when Gale and Information Plus merged in early 2000. Those of you familiar with the series as published by Information Plus will notice a few changes from the 1999 edition. Gale has adopted a new layout and style that we hope you will find easy to use. Other improvements include greatly expanded indexes in each book, and more descriptive tables of contents.

While some changes have been made to the design, the purpose of the Information Plus Reference Series remains the same. Each volume of the series presents the latest facts on a topic of pressing concern in modern American life. These topics include today's most controversial and most studied social issues: abortion, capital punishment, care for the elderly, crime, health care, the environment, immigration, minorities, social welfare, women, youth, and many more. Although written especially for the high school and undergraduate student, this series is an excellent resource for anyone in need of factual information on current affairs.

By presenting the facts, it is Gale's intention to provide its readers with everything they need to reach an informed opinion on current issues. To that end, there is a particular emphasis in this series on the presentation of scientific studies, surveys, and statistics. These data are generally presented in the form of tables, charts, and other graphics placed within the text of each book. Every graphic is directly referred to and carefully explained in the text. The source of each graphic is presented within the graphic itself. The data used in these graphics is drawn from the most reputable and reliable sources, in particular the various branches of the U.S. government and major independent polling organizations. Every effort has been made to secure the most recent information available. The reader should bear in mind that many major studies take years to conduct, and that additional years often pass before the data from these studies is made available to the public. Therefore, in many cases the most recent information available in 2001 is dated from 1998 or 1999. Older statistics are sometimes presented as well, if they are of particular interest and no more recent information exists.

Although statistics are a major focus of the Information Plus Reference Series, they are by no means its only content. Each book also presents the widely held positions and important ideas that shape how the book's subject is discussed in the United States. These positions are explained in detail and, where possible, in the words of their proponents. Some of the other material to be found in these books includes: historical background; descriptions of major events related to the subject; relevant laws and court cases; and examples of how these issues play out in American life. Some books also feature primary documents, or have pro and con debate sections giving the words and opinions of prominent Americans on both sides of a controversial topic. All material is presented in an even-handed and unbiased manner; the reader will never be encouraged to accept one view of an issue over another.

HOW TO USE THIS BOOK

Modern American society relies on a vast and complicated transportation network for its very existence. Aircraft, ships, railroads, and especially cars and trucks transport hundreds of millions of Americans around the country every day, not to mention millions of tons of goods. Each type of transportation is explored in detail in this book. Their particular advantages and drawbacks are discussed, and their importance to America is made clear.

Transportation: America's Lifeline consists of eight chapters and three appendices. Each chapter is devoted to a particular segment of the U.S. transportation system. For a summary of the information covered in each chapter, please see the synopses provided in the Table of Contents at the front of the book. Chapters generally begin with a history of the chapter's topic and an overview of basic facts and background information, then proceed to examine sub-topics of particular interest. For example, Chapter 4: Automobiles begins by describing how automobiles came to dominate personal transportation in the United States during the mid-twentieth century, a trend that has continued to the present day. The chapter then provides detailed statistics on the number of automobiles built, sold, and used in the United States, and in the rest of the world. The chapter moves on to examine a number of auto-related issues. Highlights include: the costs of purchasing, driving, and maintaining an automobile; the relative safety of different types of automobiles; the annual numbers and types of automobile accidents in America, and their causes; alternative fuel automobiles; and much more. Readers can find their way through a chapter by looking for the section and sub-section headings, which are clearly set off from the text. Or, they can refer to the book's extensive index if they already know what they are looking for.

Statistical Information

The tables and figures featured throughout *Transportation: America's Lifeline* will be of particular use to the reader in learning about this issue. These tables and figures represent an extensive collection of the most recent and important statistics on transportation in the United States and related issues—for example, the amount and source of highway construction funding, the size of the U.S. and world merchant shipping fleets, the average fuel economy of cars and light trucks, a map of the nation's "hub" airports, and mass transit usage in the twentieth century. Gale believes that making this information available to the reader is the most important way in which we fulfill the goal of this book: to help readers understand the issues

and controversies surrounding transportation in the United States and reach their own conclusions.

Each table or figure has a unique identifier appearing above it, for ease of identification and reference. Titles for the tables and figures explain their purpose. At the end of each table or figure, the original source of the data is provided.

In order to help readers understand these often complicated statistics, all tables and figures are explained in the text. References in the text direct the reader to the relevant statistics. Furthermore, the contents of all tables and figures are fully indexed. Please see the opening section of the index at the back of this volume for a description of how to find tables and figures within it.

In addition to the main body text and images, *Transportation: America's Lifeline* has three appendices. The first is the Important Names and Addresses directory. Here the reader will find contact information for a number of government and private organizations that can provide information on transportation. The second appendix is the Resources section, which can also assist the reader in conducting his or her own research. In this section, the author and editors of *Transportation: America's Lifeline* describe some of the sources that were most useful during the compilation of this book. The final appendix is the index. It has been greatly expanded from previous editions, and should make it even easier to find specific topics in this book.

COMMENTS AND SUGGESTIONS

The editors of the Information Plus Reference Series welcome your feedback on *Transportation: America's Lifeline*. Please direct all correspondence to:

Editor
Information Plus Reference Series
27500 Drake Rd.
Farmington Hills, MI, 48331-3535

ACKNOWLEDGEMENTS

Permission to use the following quotes, photographs, illustrations, figures, charts, and tables appearing in Information Plus Transportation 2001 *was received from the following sources:*

Air Transport Association of America, Inc. From tables in *Air Transport Association 2000 Annual Report.* Courtesy of the Air Transport Association of America, Inc., Washington, DC, 2000.

American Public Transportation Association (formerly known as the American Public Transit Association). From tables in *APTA 2001 Public Transportation Fact Book.* American Public Transportation Association. *Public Transportation Fact Book,* American Public Transit Association, Washington, DC, 2001. Reproduced by permission.

American Trucking Associations. From tables and figures in *American Trucking Trends.* Courtesy of the American Trucking Associations, Alexandria, VA, 2000. From a table in *Trucks and Clean Air: Meeting the Challenges of the Future.* American Trucking Association. Reproduced by permission.

AP/Wide World Photos. Photograph of Regional Transportation District light rail train, Denver, 1997. AP/Wide World Photos. Reproduced by permission. Photograph of EV1. AP/Wide World Photos. Reproduced by permission.

Association of American Railroads. From figures and tables in *Railroad Facts, 2000 Edition.* Courtesy of the Association of American Railroads, Washington, DC, 2000.

Bureau of Labor Statistics. From a table in *Issues in Labor Statistics.* Courtesy of the Bureau of Labor Statistics, Washington, DC, 1999.

DuPont Automotive. From a table accessible at http://www.dupont.com/automotive/news/ hires/color00.jpg. Courtesy of DuPont Automotive, MI. Accessed on May 17, 2001.

Eno Transportation Foundation. From a chart in *Transportation in America.* Eno Transportation Foundation, 1998. Reproduced by permission.

Federal Aviation Administration. From a table in *Aviation Safety Statistical Handbook.* Courtesy of the Federal Aviation Administration, Washington, DC, 1999. From a table in *FAA Aerospace Forecasts, Fiscal Years 1999–2010.* Courtesy of the Federal Aviation Administration, Washington, DC, 1999. From a table in *FAA Aerospace Forecasts, Fiscal Years 2000–2011.* Courtesy of the Federal Aviation Administration, Washington, DC, 2000.

Gallup Organization. From a table in "Many Teens Have Cars Using Air Bags: Fewer Use Bike Helmets," *YOUTHviews,* 1999. Copyright © 1999 by The Gallup Organization. Reproduced by the permission of The Gallup Organization.

General Aviation Manufacturers Association. From tables and figures in *General Aviation 2000 Statistical Databook.* Courtesy of the General Aviation Manufacturers Association, Washington, DC, 2000.

Minneapolis Star Tribune. From "Tracking Light Rail: How Other Cities are Faring," *Minneapolis Star Tribune,* March 29, 1998. Reproduced by permission.

The Motorcycle Industry Council. Tables. © The Motorcycle Industry Council, 1999. Reproduced by permission.

Motorcycle Safety Foundation. From a chart in *What You Should Know About Motorcycle Helmets.* Motorcycle Safety Foundation. Reproduced by permission.

National Academy Press and the Office of Technology Assessment. From a table in

Replacing Gasoline: Alternative Fuels for Light-Duty Vehicles. Courtesy of the National Academy Press and the Office of Technology Assessment, Congress of the United States, Washington, DC, 1990.

National Bicycle Dealer's Association. From a table in *2000 STATPAK.* Courtesy of the National Bicycle Dealer's Association, Newport Beach, CA, 2000.

National Safety Council. From tables and figures in *Injury Facts, 1999 Edition.* Courtesy of the National Safety Council, Itasca, IL, 1999.

Penton Media. From a table in *Air Transport World.* Courtesy of Penton Media, Cleveland, OH, 2000.

Phototake. Photograph of moving Grand Vitesse train, France. Phototake. Reproduced by permission.

Recreational Vehicle Industry Association. From a table titled "RV Shipments Data." Courtesy of the Recreational Vehicle Industry Association, Reston, VA, 2001. From a table available at http://www.rvia.org/ consumers/recreationvehicles/types.htm. Recreational Vehicle Industry Association, Reston, VA. Reproduced by permission.

U.S. Census Bureau. From a table in *The Statistical Abstract of the United States: 2000.* Courtesy of the U.S. Census Bureau, Washington, DC, 2000.

U.S. Department of Transportation. From tables and figures in *1999 Status of the Nation's Surface Transportation: Conditions and Performance Report.* Courtesy of the U.S. Department of Transportation, Washington, DC, 1999. From a figure in *The Changing Face of Transportation.* Courtesy of the U.S. Department of Transportation, Washington, DC, 2000. From a table in *Condition and Performance: 1995 Status of the Nation's Surface Transportation.* Courtesy of the U.S. Department of Transportation, Washington, DC, 1995. From a table in *Condition and Performance: 1997 Status of the Nation's Surface Transportation System.* Courtesy of the U.S. Department of Transportation, Washington DC, 1997. From a table in *Fatality Analysis Reporting System (FARS).* Courtesy of the U.S. Department of Transportation, National Highway Traffic Safety Administration, Washington, DC, 1999. From a table in *Merchant Fleets of the World.* Courtesy of the U.S. Department of Transportation, Maritime Administration, Maritime Statistics, Washington, DC, 2001. From a table in *National Bridge Inventory, June 30, 1996.* Courtesy of the U.S. Department of Transportation, Federal Highway Administration, Washington, DC, June 30, 1996. From a table in *National Intelligent Transportation Systems Program.* Courtesy of the U.S. Department of Transportation, Federal Highway Administration, Washington, DC, 1996. From a table in *National Strategic Planning Study.* Courtesy of the U.S. Department of Transportation, Washington, DC, 1990. From a table in *National Transportation Strategic Planning Study.* Courtesy of the U.S. Department of Transportation, Federal Highway Administration, Washington, DC, 1990. From tables and figures in *Our Nation's Highways, Selected Facts and Figures.* Courtesy of the U.S. Department of

Transportation, Federal Highway Administration, Washington, DC, 1998. From a chart in *Outlook for the U.S. Shipbuilding and Repair Industry, 1998.* Courtesy of the U.S. Department of Transportation, Maritime Administration, Washington, DC, 1999. From tables in *A Report to Congress on the Status of the Public Ports of the United States 1996–1997.* Courtesy of the U.S. Department of Transportation, Maritime Administration, Washington DC, 1997. From tables and figures in *Traffic Safety Facts 1998: Overview.* Courtesy of the U.S. Department of Transportation, National Highway Traffic Safety Administration, Washington, DC. From tables and figures in *Traffic Safety Facts, 1999.* Courtesy of the U.S. Department of Transportation, National Highway Traffic Safety Administration, Washington, DC, 2000. From tables and figures in *Transportation Statistics Annual Report 1999.* Courtesy of the U.S. Department of Transportation, Bureau of Transportation Statistics, Washington, DC, 1999. From tables in *Twenty-Fourth Annual Report to Congress, 1999.* Courtesy of the U.S. Department of Transportation, National Highway Traffic Safety Administration, Washington, DC, 1999.

U.S. Department of Justice, Bureau of Justice Statistics. From a table in *Carjackings in the United States, 1992–96.* Courtesy of the

U.S. Department of Justice, Bureau of Justice Statistics, 1999.

U.S. General Accounting Office. From a table in *Air Traffic Control: Status of FAA's Modernization Program.* Courtesy of the U.S. General Accounting Office, Washington, DC, 1998. From a figure in *Intercity Passenger Rail, Assessing the Benefits of Increased Federal Funding for Amtrak and High-Speed Passenger Rail Systems.* Courtesy of the U.S. General Accounting Office, Washington, DC, 1999. From a table in *Intercity Passenger Rail: Outlook for Improving Amtrak's Financial Health.* Courtesy of the U.S. General Accounting Office, Washington, DC, 1998. From a table in *Surface Infrastructure: High-Speed Rail Projects in the United States.* Courtesy of the U.S. General Accounting Office, Washington, DC, 1999.

Ward's Communications. From tables and figures in *Ward's Automotive Yearbook, 1999.* Courtesy of Ward's Communications, Southfield, MI, 1999.

Waterborne Commerce Statistics Center, U.S. Army Corps of Engineers. From tables and figures in *Waterborne Commerce of the United States, Part 5, 1999.* Courtesy of the Waterborne Commerce Statistics Center, U.S. Army Corps of Engineers, New Orleans, LA.

CHAPTER 1
SHIPS—TRAVELING THE WATERWAYS

Shipping played a major role in the early growth and development of the United States. The first European settlers made their way to the New World by boat. Slaves were packed into the holds of slave ships and brought over to work the fields of the growing colonies. The very existence of the colonies and later of the young republic depended on the flow of passengers and vital goods on both inland and oceanic waterways. For almost two hundred years after the arrival of those first settlers, ships were the country's primary mode of transporting both passengers and commercial cargo. From the mid-1800s through the early 1900s, ships brought millions of European and Asian immigrants to American shores.

All of this spawned the development of thousands of ocean, Great Lakes, and inland waterway (river) ports. Together, the waterways, lakes, oceans, harbors, and ports form the network of the national waterborne transportation system. The waterborne transportation system provides the link for the exchange of goods and passengers between land and water. It includes ships, piers and wharves, cargo handling equipment, storage facilities, and connections to other types of transportation. This system plays a vital role in the nation's trade and economy, providing jobs, income, tax revenues, and a magnet for other industries.

U.S. SHIPPING OVER THE YEARS

For thousands of years, the movement of ships depended on sails and oars. The first European settlers in what would become the United States all arrived on sailing ships. Without modern technology like radios and aircraft, or even good maps and roads, these early settlers depended on ships for trade and communication with the rest of the world. Population and development tended to concentrate near major ports and rivers.

A Revolutionary Technology

In 1787, the same year that the U.S. Constitution was drafted, Robert Fitch, an explorer, mapmaker, and survey-or by profession, launched the first fully operational steamboat. By 1790, one of his steamboats was regularly carrying passengers and freight between Philadelphia and Burlington, New Jersey. Fitch took out patents in the United States and France for his invention, but he could not capture the interest of the American public. He lost financial backing for his enterprise and died in 1798. A few years later, Robert Fulton was able to popularize the steamboat and begin a dramatic transformation of U.S. and world shipping. Fulton's steamship, the *Clermont*, cruised up the Hudson River in 1807 to instant success and a place in the history of navigation. The potential for steamships—unlike sailing ships—to move upstream or downstream, with or against the currents, independent of the direction of the wind or the strength of oars, was finally recognized. On May 22, 1819, the steam-powered *SS Savannah* crossed the Atlantic Ocean.

The steamboat is now perhaps most closely associated with the mighty Mississippi River. The well-dressed riverboat gambler, who traveled the river on paddlewheel steamboats, is as familiar a folk figure as the cowboy riding the range. Even more significantly, however, steam power made the process of navigating ships across oceans much more predictable and dependable, as they were not at the complete mercy of the weather and currents. As engines gradually became more powerful, steamships became faster and more efficient, capable of carrying large amounts of passengers or cargo at consistently high speeds. Steam powered many of the large ships that plied the oceans of the world throughout the nineteenth and twentieth centuries, gradually driving sailing ships out of commercial shipping. As the twentieth century dawned, however, both types of ships carried people, raw materials, and finished products across the oceans. They brought generations of immigrants to this country, carried agricultural products—cotton, tobacco, wheat—to markets overseas, and hauled imported goods from Europe and Asia. Shipping, which required ports and harbors, stimulated the growth of cities adjacent to harbors. As the industrial age began, dependable shipping connected the world.

The Canal Age

At about the same time as steam ships were first powering across oceans and up rivers, new cross-country shipping routes were being sought, from the East Coast to the largely unsettled West. People wanted economical ways to connect lakes and rivers in order to link large portions of the country. Settlers and merchants were eager to go westward. Yet travel by water remained by far the best way to move large amounts of goods and people.

In 1817, the New York State Legislature authorized the construction of a canal as a watercourse between the Hudson River at Albany and Lake Erie at Buffalo. During its construction, opponents derisively called it "Clinton's Big Ditch" (after Governor DeWitt Clinton), but the canal became a tremendous success once completed. Financed, built, and operated solely with state funds, the waterway returned its $8 million construction cost within seven years of its completion in 1825. By using the 338-mile canal rather than overland routes, the cost of hauling a ton of freight between Buffalo and New York City dropped from $100 to $10, and travel time was reduced from 26 to 6 days. As it became relatively easy to travel to Ohio, Michigan, Indiana, and the rest of the Midwest, the region became a destination for farmers seeking new land to cultivate, who needed efficient transportation to carry crops to the major marketplaces in the east.

While several canals had been constructed earlier, the success of the Erie Canal prompted other states with navigable waterways to make serious commitments to canal building. Unfortunately, many of the new canals were not as successful as the Erie. Lack of capital for construction and maintenance, mismanagement, corruption, and overbuilding created huge debts that many states were never able to pay off. Nevertheless, the canals filled an important transportation need.

Domestic Shipping Begins to Fade

Soon after the Civil War (1861–65), the railroads were connected across the country and trains rapidly became the dominant means of transporting people and goods from coast to coast and points in between. As railroad routes proliferated across the country at the turn of the twentieth century, and the auto industry also rose to prominence, shipping declined somewhat. In addition, an economic depression and a five-month United Mine Workers strike in 1901 made the procurement of coal for steamships difficult.

Despite the shipping industry's slump and declining use of the Erie Canal and other waterways, however, shipping traffic on major rivers and in the Great Lakes continued to be essential to the transport of goods across the nation. In 1900, the Chicago Sanitary and Ship Canal opened, connecting Lake Michigan (and the other Great Lakes) with the Des Plaines River, and ultimately with the Mississippi River and the Gulf of Mexico.

International shipping also received a boost in 1901, when the U.S. Congress and President Theodore Roosevelt decided to proceed with construction of the Panama Canal. The Canal would enable ships to travel from the Atlantic to the Pacific without the long and arduous trip around the southern tip of South America. That same year, U.S. Steel executive Charles M. Schwab founded the United States Shipbuilding Company.

World War I

As World War I approached, the American shipping industry was still strong, if in decline. The shipbuilding industry was in somewhat worse shape. As industrialization spread, the industry faced more and more foreign competitors, some of whom could produce ships at a lower price than U.S. shipyards. The onset of World War I (1914–18), however, generated a surge in shipbuilding in the U.S. The federal government had, up to this time, shown little interest in the shipping industry. As the nation moved towards war in Europe, however, federal officials realized that the country was practically without ships for transporting arms and troops to the fighting fronts in Europe. To correct the situation, Congress passed the Shipping Act of 1916. The new law authorized the creation of the Emergency Fleet Corporation, which built 2,318 vessels between 1918 and 1922. Most of these ships, however were delivered too late to serve in the war, and were often so poorly designed and constructed that they could not be used for any other purpose.

To stimulate its shipping industry, Congress soon passed another significant piece of maritime legislation, the Merchant Marine Act of 1920, known as the Jones Act. Under the Jones Act, U.S. owners were not permitted to buy less expensive foreign-made ships. By law, all waterborne goods between ports throughout the United States and its territories had to be carried on ships built and registered in America and owned by U.S. citizens.

The Merchant Marine Act Of 1936

The Great Depression of the 1930s created another slump in shipbuilding and transport. In response, Congress passed the Merchant Marine Act of 1936, declaring it national policy to foster the creation of a merchant marine fleet capable of handling domestic and foreign commerce and of serving in time of war. The fleet was to be owned and operated "insofar as practicable" by private U.S. concerns. The federal government would provide subsidies to private companies to make up the difference between the cost of building and operating ships in the United States and the often much lower costs of these activities in for-

FIGURE 1.1

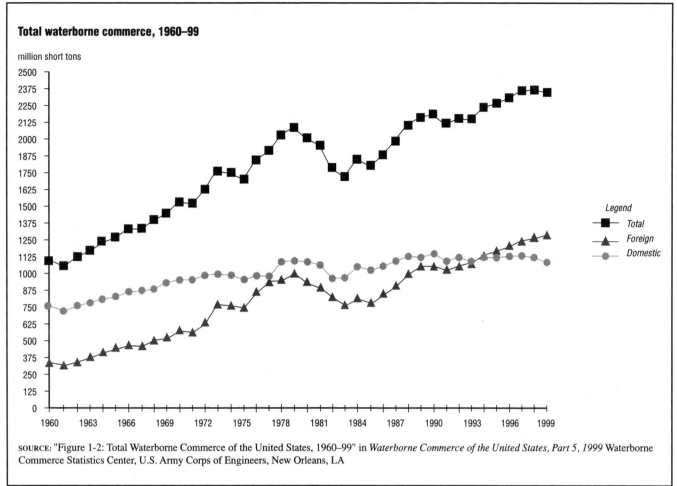

Total waterborne commerce, 1960–99

million short tons

SOURCE: "Figure 1-2: Total Waterborne Commerce of the United States, 1960–99" in *Waterborne Commerce of the United States, Part 5, 1999* Waterborne Commerce Statistics Center, U.S. Army Corps of Engineers, New Orleans, LA

eign countries. Freight rates and trade routes were placed under federal jurisdiction. A Maritime Commission was formed to survey the state of the merchant marine fleet and develop a long-range program to meet future needs.

World War II

Within five years of the passage of the Merchant Marine Act of 1936, the United States was again at war. This time, however, the country's maritime fleet was in much better condition. Under the newly created War Shipping Administration, the federal government took full control of almost all shipping operations. Between 1942 and 1945, 5,592 merchant ships were built, half of which were the mass-produced, cheaply made Liberty ships, often derisively referred to as "tin cans." These new ships, along with those acquired from private owners, were instrumental in securing an Allied victory.

After the war ended, the War Shipping Administration was dissolved and merchant fleets returned to private control. The government sold off excess ships, for a total of almost $2 billion, while retaining some vessels in reserve fleets for emergency use. These reserve fleets were called into action in both the Korean and Vietnam wars.

The Maritime Administration (MARAD)

In 1950, the Maritime Commission was disbanded and replaced with the Federal Maritime Board and the Maritime Administration (MARAD) under the U.S. Department of Transportation. The Maritime Administration was assigned many functions that it continues to carry out in the present day. Most significantly, it maintains the National Defense Reserve Fleet, administers government subsidies to ship builders and operators, promotes and provides technical assistance for the development of port facilities and intermodal transportation systems, and operates the U.S. Merchant Marine Academy at Kings Point, New York.

The Post-War Era

It was not long after the end of World War II that the development of long-distance passenger air travel and a national network of highways made passenger travel by ship effectively obsolete. Shipping remained the most practical method for moving large amounts of heavy goods from place to place, however, especially over long distances. Nevertheless, the U.S. merchant fleet declined greatly after World War II. The cause was the increasing number of ships registered in "flag of convenience" coun-

TABLE 1.1

Waterborne commerce in the United States, 1960–99

In short tons of 2000 pounds

Year	Total	Foreign	Domestic
1960	1,099,850,431	339,277,275	760,573,156
1961	1,062,155,182	329,329,818	732,825,364
1962	1,129,404,375	358,599,030	770,805,345
1963	1,173,766,964	385,658,999	788,107,965
1964	1,238,093,573	421,925,133	816,168,440
1965	1,272,896,243	443,726,809	829,169,434
1966	1,334,116,078	471,391,083	862,724,995
1967	1,336,606,078	465,972,238	870,633,840
1968	1,395,839,450	507,950,002	887,889,448
1969	1,448,711,541	521,312,362	927,399,179
1970	1,531,696,507	580,969,133	950,727,374
1971	1,512,583,690	565,985,584	946,598,106
1972	1,616,792,605	629,980,844	986,811,761
1973	1,761,552,010	767,393,903	994,158,107
1974	1,746,788,544	764,088,905	982,699,639
1975	1,695,034,366	748,707,407	946,326,959
1976	1,835,006,819	855,963,909	979,042,910
1977	1,908,223,619	935,256,813	972,966,806
1978	2,021,349,754	946,057,889	1,075,291,865
1979	2,073,757,628	993,444,963	1,080,312,665
1980	1,998,887,402	921,404,000	1,077,483,402
1981	1,941,558,947	887,102,150	1,054,456,797
1982	1,776,740,579	819,730,983	957,009,596
1983	1,707,661,011	751,140,194	956,520,817
1984	1,836,020,619	803,338,133	1,032,682,486
1985	1,788,434,822	774,323,283	1,014,111,539
1986	1,874,416,280	837,223,503	1,037,192,777
1987	1,967,458,261	890,980,045	1,076,478,216
1988	2,087,993,484	976,220,985	1,111,772,499
1989	2,140,442,372	1,037,910,213	1,102,532,159
1990	2,163,854,373	1,041,555,740	1,122,298,633
1991	2,092,108,462	1,013,557,036	1,078,551,426
1992	2,132,095,154	1,037,466,130	1,094,629,024
1993	2,128,221,188	1,060,041,217	1,068,179,971
1994	2,214,754,086	1,115,742,828	1,099,011,258
1995	2,240,393,059	1,147,357,782	1,093,035,277
1996	2,284,065,249	1,183,386,621	1,100,678,628
1997	2,333,142,046	1,220,615,132	1,112,526,914
1998	2,339,500,081	1,245,388,049	1,094,112,032
1999	2,322,557,251	1,260,770,656	1,061,786,595

Note: Beginning in 1996, fish was excluded for internal and intraport domestic traffic.

SOURCE: "Table 1-1: Total Waterborne Commerce of the U.S., 1960–99" in *Waterborne Commerce of the United States, Part 5, 1999* Waterborne Commerce Statistics Center, U.S. Army Corps of Engineers, New Orleans, LA

tries such as Panama or the Bahamas, where laws are favorable to shippers and labor relatively cheap. The shipbuilding industry suffered even more, as it lost almost all of its business to foreign shipyards that could produce ships at low cost.

THE MODERN U.S. FLEET

In 1955, America's ports were handling about one billion tons of freight. At the end of the 1970s, the ports handled just over two billion tons of cargo each year, divided almost equally between foreign and domestic commerce. In 1983, in the midst of a recession, total U.S. tonnage dropped to a low of 1.7 billion tons and then rose again in 1990 to 2.16 billion tons. By 1997, tonnage rose to 2.3 billion tons, with the cargo fairly evenly divided between domestic and foreign traffic. It maintained this approxi-

mate level through 1999, although domestic cargo declined slightly while foreign cargo increased. (See Table 1.1 and Figure 1.1.)

In 1994, experts projected that U.S. oceanborne trade would grow at an average annual rate of 4.5 percent up to 2005. By 2005, U.S. oceanborne trade is projected to be over 130 million long tons. (A long ton is 2,240 pounds, the same as a gross ton.) Because the demand for shipping capacity is largely a function of the volume of international oceanborne trade, the demand for shipping services is expected to increase. (See Figure 1.2.)

What Is Carried?

The advantage of shipping by water is that ships can hold large amounts of heavy goods. It should not be surprising, then, that coal and oil account for over half of those commodities carried by water between U.S. ports and sources both domestic and foreign. Food and farm products also account for a significant percentage, as do crude raw materials (such as iron or copper ore). (See Figure 1.3.)

The Domestic Fleet

The U.S. domestic fleet (the fleet of ships that primarily carries goods from one part of the United States to another) is made up of cargo ships with a combined capacity of 67 million short tons. (A short ton equals 2,000 pounds.) The dry cargo barge, which carries dry materials, is the main vessel in this fleet. The Great Lakes fleet consists almost entirely of dry bulk vessels, most of which transport ores and grains. Also included in the fleet are tank barges, which carry liquid bulk cargo. Towboats and tugboats, as their names imply, push and pull dumb (non-self-propelled) vessels and rafts. They are considered part of the fleet, but do not carry cargo.

The U.S. Oceangoing Fleet

There are two components to the U.S. ocean-going fleet. The domestic deep-sea fleet travels offshore along the nation's coasts, as well as to Alaska, Hawaii, and the U.S. territories of Guam, Puerto Rico, Wake and Midway Islands, and the Virgin Islands. As of 1999, 159 ships operated in domestic ocean trade. Tankers carrying American petroleum products and coal make up the bulk of the domestic fleet. Less cargo is being hauled by the domestic

FIGURE 1.2

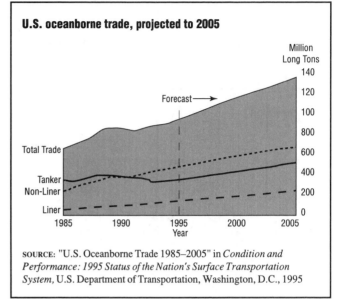

U.S. oceanborne trade, projected to 2005

SOURCE: "U.S. Oceanborne Trade 1985–2005" in *Condition and Performance: 1995 Status of the Nation's Surface Transportation System,* U.S. Department of Transportation, Washington, D.C., 1995

FIGURE 1.3

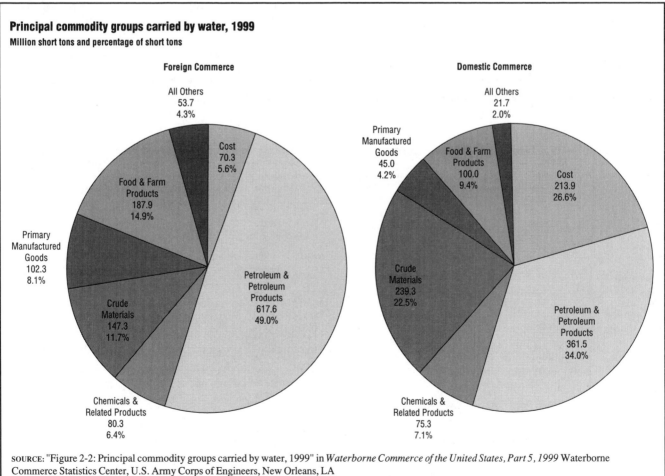

Principal commodity groups carried by water, 1999
Million short tons and percentage of short tons

SOURCE: "Figure 2-2: Principal commodity groups carried by water, 1999" in *Waterborne Commerce of the United States, Part 5, 1999* Waterborne Commerce Statistics Center, U.S. Army Corps of Engineers, New Orleans, LA

ocean fleet due to the decline in production and shipments of crude oil from the Alaska North Slope. In 1997, 263 million tons moved in the domestic ocean fleet—a 20 percent decline from 1988 tonnage. The foreign trade fleet carries goods between U.S. and foreign ports and is in direct competition with all other international fleets. Figure 1.4 shows the primary foreign trade routes.

As of October 1, 2000, there were 461 oceangoing U.S. vessels (counting both privately owned and govern-ment owned ships) registered in the United States, with a carrying capacity of about 16.1 million deadweight tons, or DWT (weight of a vehicle without a load). However, 159 of these ships were primarily involved in domestic trade. Each of these ships weighs 1,000 gross tons or more. (A gross ton is 2,240 pounds.) (See Table 1.2.) Eighty percent of the privately owned vessels are actively engaged in commerce. Most of the federally owned vessels are in long-term storage, held in MARAD custody in case they are needed during a national emergency.

The U.S. fleet plays a very minor role in international shipping. In 1999, the world fleet of ocean-going ships weighing 1,000 tons or more consisted of 28,087 ships. The U.S. fleet made up less than 2 percent of this figure, down from 8 percent in 1970 and 17 percent in 1960. (See Table 1.2.) The U.S. Coast Guard estimated in 2000 that 95 percent of all ships visiting U.S. ocean ports are foreign-owned and operated.

Compared to other nations' merchant fleets, the United States is at a distinct disadvantage for several reasons. Most international operators use lower-cost foreign ship-yards for maintenance and repairs. They also save on fuel costs because they usually use more modern, efficient ships. Foreign operators can use smaller crews than U.S. collective bargaining and safety requirements allow. Furthermore, they can employ low-priced labor from Third World nations. Total employment expenditures per day on

FIGURE 1.4

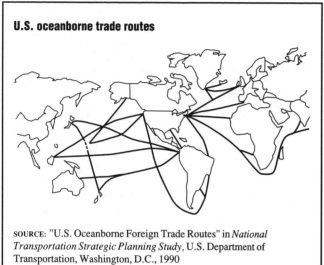

U.S. oceanborne trade routes

SOURCE: "U.S. Oceanborne Foreign Trade Routes" in *National Transportation Strategic Planning Study,* U.S. Department of Transportation, Washington, D.C., 1990

TABLE 1.2

Number of self-propelled oceangoing vessels weighing 1,000 gross tons or more, as of October 1, 2000, by country

	Total		Tanker		Dry bulk carrier		Full container		Other*	
	Number	Deadweight	Number	Deadweight	Number	Deadweight	Number	Deadweight	Number	Deadweight
Panama	4,615	165,028	1,084	56,123	1,368	80,446	504	14,388	56	1,217
Liberia	1,480	77,242	582	42,821	372	23,236	227	6,578	1,659	14,071
Malta	1,407	45,870	362	21,730	437	18,063	54	901	299	4,607
Bahamas	1,023	45,107	263	28,088	139	8,107	56	1,567	554	5,176
Greece	696	43,204	280	26,309	263	14,388	44	1,645	565	7,345
Cyprus	1,310	36,199	174	7,900	463	20,091	131	2,870	109	861
Singapore	888	34,531	401	19,110	130	8,691	175	4,139	542	5,337
Norway(NIS)	661	27,755	309	17,349	89	6,695	5	102	182	2,591
China	1,439	22,052	258	3,529	327	10,804	108	1,789	258	3,609
United States	461	16,137	147	8,738	15	604	60	1,260	209	3,737
Japan	623	15,751	254	8,378	155	5,649	24	739	190	985
Hong Kong	322	15,470	34	1,225	188	11,672	49	1,482	51	1,092
Marshall Islands	179	14,363	89	10,723	56	2,774	23	710	11	156
India	295	10,445	102	5,209	116	4,538	8	131	69	567
Philippines	458	9,718	64	277	168	7,733	7	80	219	1,628
Italy	400	9,530	220	4,195	40	3,500	22	696	118	1,139
Bermuda	106	9,409	27	4,840	28	3,699	17	506	34	363
Saint Vincent	749	9,394	97	1,126	131	4,508	27	175	494	3,585
Turkey	539	9,362	92	1,277	156	6,335	22	222	269	1,528
Korea (South)	471	8,492	125	1,370	100	5,116	50	1,002	196	1,004
All other flags	9,965	145,837	2,096	56,871	884	32,081	1,000	26,400	6,705	36,997
Total all flags	28,087	770,894	7,060	327,187	5,625	278,729	2,613	67,382	12,789	97,597

(Tonnage in thousands)

*Roll-on/roll-off, passenger, breakbulk ships, partial containerships, refrigerated cargo ships, barge carriers and specialized cargo ships.

SOURCE: "Self-Propelled Oceangoing Vessels of 1,000 Gross Tons and Over" in *Merchant Fleets of the World,* Maritime Statistics, Maritime Administration, U.S. Department of Transportation, Washington, D.C., 2001

FIGURE 1.5

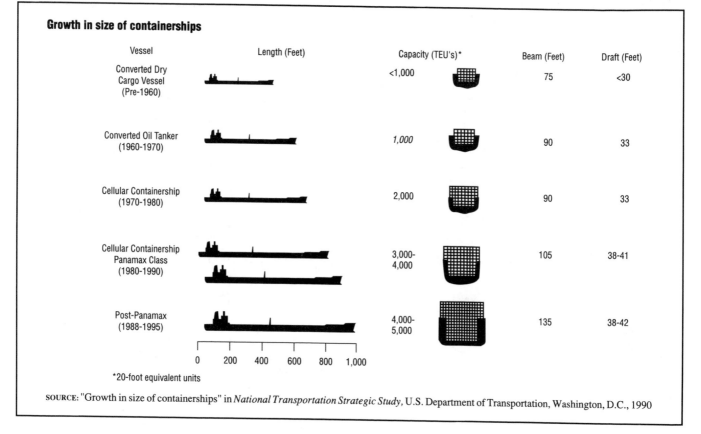

Growth in size of containerships

Vessel	Length (Feet)	Capacity (TEU's)*	Beam (Feet)	Draft (Feet)
Converted Dry Cargo Vessel (Pre-1960)		<1,000	75	<30
Converted Oil Tanker (1960-1970)		1,000	90	33
Cellular Containership (1970-1980)		2,000	90	33
Cellular Containership Panamax Class (1980-1990)		3,000-4,000	105	38-41
Post-Panamax (1988-1995)		4,000-5,000	135	38-42

0   200   400   600   800   1,000

*20-foot equivalent units

SOURCE: "Growth in size of containerships" in *National Transportation Strategic Study,* U.S. Department of Transportation, Washington, D.C., 1990

a foreign ship with a non-U.S. crew are only 15 to 20 percent of the total cost for crew wages on an American ship of the same size and number of crew members. It is for this reason that many privately owned vessels belonging to U.S. citizens or corporations are registered in other countries. The practice of registering a ship in a country where the laws are less restrictive and costs cheaper is known as carrying a "flag of convenience."

TYPES OF SHIPS. The ocean transportation system is devoted almost entirely to freight shipping. There are three categories of service: general cargo, dry bulk, and liquid bulk. General cargo, primarily finished products, is usually carried on regularly scheduled ocean freighters, often in large boxes on container ships. Dry bulk cargoes, such as grain, coal, and fertilizer, are shipped in specialized vessels under contract. Liquid bulk cargoes, mainly petroleum products, are handled by tankers and tank barge fleets. Most of the ocean-going liquid bulk cargo ships are tankers.

Over the years, freight ships have grown dramatically in size, and so has their carrying capacity. Figure 1.5 illustrates the growth in the size and capacity of the nation's ocean-going container ships over the past 40 years. Oil tankers are also bigger than ever before. In 1945, the largest tanker held 16,500 tons of oil; today's supertankers carry more than 550,000 tons. The age and vessel sizes of all ocean-going fleets vary considerably by vessel

type, but all the newer ships are larger and more fuel-efficient and have smaller crews.

WHERE THE LAND AND SEA MEET

Ports and Harbors

The U.S. port system consists of two basic components: harbor works and port facilities. By definition, harbors provide ships and boats shelter from wind, high waves, and storms. The U.S. Army Corps of Engineers maintains 757 commercial harbors, most of which are located on the nation's four major shorelines—Atlantic, Gulf, Pacific, and Great Lakes. Ports, on the other hand, allow the loading and unloading of both freight and passengers. Not all harbors have port facilities. While Congress has declared that every town and city located on federally improved harbors and waterways should have at least one public port terminal for shipping, port development has traditionally relied on local and private initiative.

The United States has the world's largest port system. According to MARAD, there are 4,970 port berths and other ship facilities. There are 3,158 major U.S. seaport berths, and 1,812 river port berths located in 21 states on the U.S. inland waterway system. The East Coast maintains 35.1 percent of the U.S. seaport berths, followed by the Gulf Coast with 24.9 percent and the West Coast with 24.7 percent. The Great Lakes have 15.1 percent of the berths. (See Table 1.3.) The Mississippi River system has

TABLE 1.3

U.S. seaport terminals by type of berth and region, 1997

Berth Type	Berth Total		North Atlantic		South Atlantic		Gulf		Coastal Region South Pacific		North Pacific		Great Lakes	
	No.	%	No.	%	No.	%	No.	%	No.	%	No.	%	No.	%
General Cargo Berths:	1,185	37.5%	264	34.7%	204	58.5%	264	33.6%	208	50.2%	149	40.8%	96	19.9%
General Carge	560		135		78		193		63		56		35	
Container	163		46		19		12		66		20		—	
Lash/Seabee	3		—		1		2		—		—		—	
Ro-Ro	35		6		19		3		4		3		—	
Automobile	32		17		4		—		9		2		—	
General/Container	42		16		12		2		1		10		1	
General/Ro-Ro	52		13		9		14		6		6		4	
General/Passenger	21		—		11		4		—		6		—	
General/Dry Bulk	155		19		15		20		26		24		51	
General/Liquid Bulk	77		9		8		2		11		11		—	
Container/Ro-Ro	41		9		8		2		11		11		—	
Container/Dry Bulk	4		1		1		1		—		—		1	
Dry Buld Berths:	692	21.9%	96	12.6%	48	13.8%	163	20.7%	51	12.3%	74	20.3%	260	53.8%
Coal	50		11		2		12		—		2		23	
Grain	87		9		1		28		5		10		34	
Ore	58		7		3		6		—		5		37	
Loga	14		—		—		—		1		13		—	
Wood Chips	12		—		—		—		1		11		—	
Cement	46		10		5		7		2		4		18	
Chemical	76		9		6		47		3		4		7	
Dry Bulk - Other	280		39		23		46		23		16		133	
Dry Bulk/Liquid Bulk	69		11		8		17		16		9		8	
Liquid Bulk Berths:	610	19.3%	188	24.7%	51	14.6%	182	23.2%	73		71	19.5%	45	9.3%
Crude Petroleum	60		8		—		37		10		5		—	
Refined Petroleum	279		109		28		37		31		41		33	
Petroleum-Crude/Refined	161		29		15		64		28		20		5	
LPG	7		1		1		5		—		—		—	
LNG	5		3		—		1		—		1		—	
Liquid Bulk - Other	98		38		7		38		4		4		7	
Passenger Berth:	87	2.8%	19	2.5%	24	6.9%	10	1.3%	18	4.3%	10	2.7%	6	1..2%
Passenger	66		13		24		10		18		—		1	
Ferry	21		6		—		—		—		10		5	
Other Berths:	584	18.5%	194	25.5%	22	6.2%	167	21.2%	64	15.6%	61	16.7%	76	15.8%
Barge	354		126		11		133		33		36		15	
Mooring	124		39		7		19		9		20		30	
Inactive	96		29		4		13		14		5		31	
Other	10		—		—		2		8		—		—	
Total	3,158	100.1%	761	100.0%	349	100.0%	786	100.0%	414	100.0%	365	100.0%	%483	100.0%

SOURCE: "Table 17: U.S. Seaport Terminals by Berth Type and Constal Region" in *A Report to Congress on the Status of the Public Ports of the United States 1996-1997*, Maritime Administration, Department of Transportation, Washington D.C., 1997

by far the largest number of river port terminals, at 1,748. (See Table 1.4) Figure 1.6 illustrates the distribution of ports, both river ports and seaports, in the United States.

Naturally, the states involved to the greatest degree in waterborne commerce are those located on major waterways. Table 1.5 shows the waterborne commerce of the various states in 1999. Louisiana and Texas led the 50 states in the amount of waterborne commerce, followed by California, Ohio, Florida, Illinois, Pennsylvania, Washington, and New York.

THE INTERMODAL PROCESS. The United States developed intermodal shipping systems, which plan and execute the movement of goods from point of departure to final destination, using containerized vessels, port terminals, computerized technology, and inland delivery systems, including trucking and rail. (See Figure 1.7.) This process not only reduces transportation and inventory costs, but reduces damage and theft as well.

Container ships carry cargo in pre-loaded, standard-size containers, making loading and unloading faster and easier, and enabling more efficient transportation of cargo to and from the port area. One example of the container ship is the Roll-on/Roll-off ship, or RO/RO. Vehicles such as trucks and trailers that carry cargo can drive directly on and off a RO/RO ship. Most experts expect intermodal ships to continue to grow in size and DWT capacity.

LARGER U.S. SEAPORTS. Global trade is expanding, and every major port in the country is spending or proposing to spend large amounts of money to attract more cargo. Nationwide, ports are expected to spend a record $9 billion between 1999 and 2003 on expansion and infrastructure projects, according to the American Association of Port Authorities.

TABLE 1.4

U.S. inland and riverport shipping terminal facilities by state, 1997

State	Number of Terminals	General Cargo	Dry Bulk Cargo				Liquid Bulk Cargo			Multi-Purpose
			Grain	Coal	Ore	Other	Petrol	LPG	Other	
Alabama	137	8	16	21	–	41	21	–	15	15
Arkansas	84	2	26	–	–	24	7	–	6	19
Illinois	267	6	64	18	1	70	37	–	42	29
Indiana	60	2	8	14	1	16	9	–	2	8
Iowa	75	–	16	9	–	17	8	–	11	14
Kansas	8	–	4	–	–	1	–	–	2	1
Kentucky	175	3	13	48	–	49	32	1	15	14
Louisiana	66	1	8	2	–	12	19	1	14	9
Minnesota	55	1	10	–	–	20	8	–	7	9
Mississippi	69	1	16	–	–	13	16	1	6	16
Missouri	133	2	22	6	–	59	14	–	18	12
Nebraska	17	1	7	–	–	4	–	–	4	1
Ohio	132	6	7	21	2	43	23	–	19	11
Oklahoma	27	3	5	–	–	9	4	–	2	4
Pennsylvania	145	9	–	41	2	49	18	–	18	8
Tennessee	129	6	21	7	1	47	23	–	12	12
West Virginia	149	9	–	47	1	52	21	1	15	3
Wisconsin	20	1	1	4	–	7	3	–	2	2
Mississippi System Sub-total	**1,748**	**61**	**244**	**238**	**8**	**533**	**263**	**4**	**210**	**187**
Idaho	4	1	2	–	–	1	–	–	–	–
Oregon	24	3	7	–	–	12	–	–	1	1
Washington	36	5	18	–	–	5	2	–	4	2
Columbia/Snake Sub-total	**64**	**9**	**27**	**–**	**–**	**18**	**2**	**–**	**5**	**3**
Total	**1,812**	**70**	**271**	**238**	**8**	**551**	**265**	**4**	**215**	**190**

SOURCE: "Table 18: U.S. Inland/Riverport Terminal Facilities by State," in *A Report to Congress on the Status of the Public Ports of the United States 1996–1997*, U.S. Department of Transportation, Maritime Administration, Washington, D.C., 1997

The funds will be spent on dredging for deep-draft ships, and construction of modern berths, huge cranes, rail lines, and roads to handle interface with the huge post-Panamax vessels—1,000-foot cargo ships that require harbors at least 50 feet deep. (They are called post-Panamax vessels because they are too large to pass through the Panama Canal.) Some of the port cities planning expansion include:

- New Orleans, Louisiana—Construction has begun on the $50 million first phase of what is estimated to be a $1 billion Millennium Port complex on the Mississippi River, to accommodate an expected sixfold increase in container cargo through 2030.

- Savannah, Georgia—A $70 million container berth with two enormous cranes was completed in 1998, and construction on an eighth container berth is set to begin in 2001. Port officials have launched extensive environmental review to determine whether they can proceed with a plan to deepen the Savannah River to 48 feet to accommodate large container ships. There is also a proposed $20 million, 150-acre rail yard, which would allow four trains to be loaded each day.

- New York and New Jersey—The Port of New York and New Jersey, the largest port in the eastern United States, has committed $1.8 billion to port redevelop-

ment projects during the period 2001 to 2006, including deepening major channels to 45 feet from their current 40 feet.

- Houston, Texas—A 720-acre Bayport intermodal container complex is planned, to expand the port facilities at Houston. In addition, a 375-acre port terminal is planned at nearby Texas City.

- Long Beach, California—The Port of Long Beach, the largest container port in the United States, is in the process of building a mega-terminal that will offer 5,000 linear feet of wharf, 50-foot water depths, a dockside rail yard, and as many as 16 huge cranes capable of unloading post-Panamax size ships. The second phase of this terminal is expected to be completed by 2003.

Inland Waterways

The United States has a total 11,703 miles of commercially navigable inland waterways. More than half are on the Mississippi River system and its tributaries (6,651 miles), with most of the rest running along the coasts of the Gulf of Mexico and the Atlantic ocean. The fleet of barges and tugboats that navigate these waters consists of over 36,000 vessels. (See Figure 1.6 for an illustration of the nation's major waterways.)

FIGURE 1.6

Major waterways of the United States, 1999

SOURCE: "Figure 1-1: Major waterways of the United States, 1999" in *Waterborne Commerce of the United States, Part 5, 1999* Waterborne Commerce Statistics Center, U.S. Army Corps of Engineers, New Orleans, LA

FIGURE 1.6

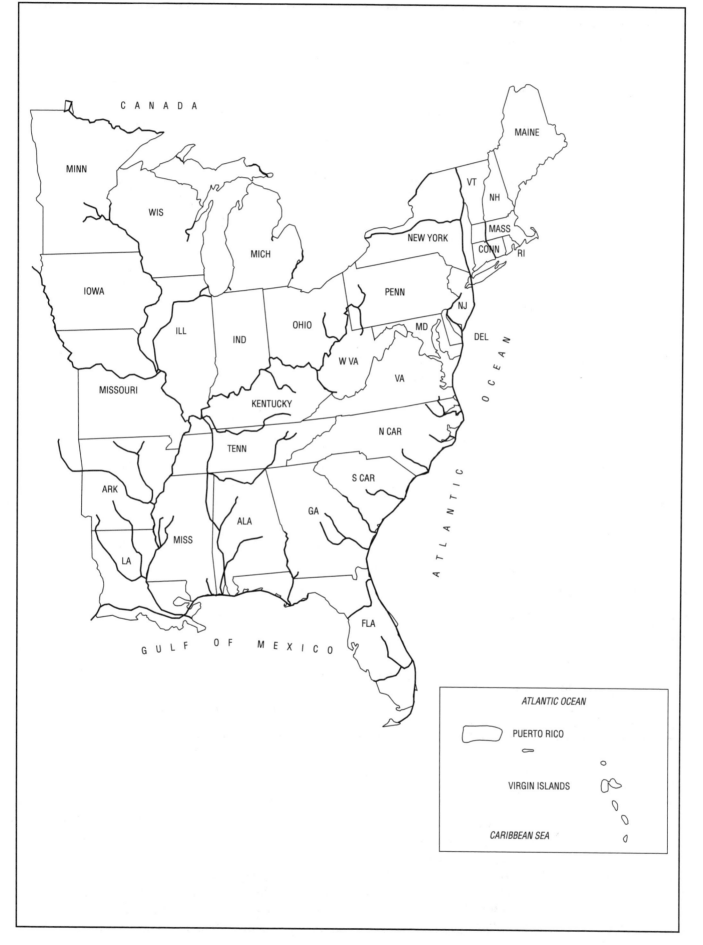

TABLE 1.5

Waterborne commerce by state, 1999

In thousands of short tons

State	Total*	Shipping		Receiving		
		Domestic	Foreign	Domestic	Foreign	Intrastate
Total	2,322,558	751,560	399,996	751,798	860,775	309,989
Louisiana	499,752	109,472	105,510	132,387	112,661	39,723
Texas	406,166	42,928	55,763	20,975	236,490	50,010
California	171,819	5,453	38,290	32,719	82,721	12,635
Ohio	129,095	25,038	18,057	63,691	5,789	16,519
Florida	128,633	12,958	19,792	59,484	31,506	4,891
Illinois	120,500	86,107	747	19,339	5,167	9,141
Pennsylvania	115,471	19,650	556	35,312	38,653	21,300
Washington	111,774	12,367	33,669	27,333	20,328	18,077
New York	107,645	20,619	4,415	20,911	45,847	15,852
New Jersey	95,171	27,622	4,450	22,841	35,494	4,764
Kentucky	90,218	50,854	—	27,766	—	11,597
Michigan	81,363	27,196	8,121	22,944	7,630	15,472
West Virginia	75,756	45,281	—	18,062	—	12,412
Indiana	72,852	14,991	28	54,465	—	3,368
Alaska	71,170	51,839	11,174	2,614	1,375	4,167
Alabama	68,039	10,430	8,580	20,212	15,488	13,329
Virginia	64,745	11,856	30,409	4,552	11,510	6,418
Other	61,606	7,095	1,536	7,712	45,255	7
Minnesota	54,247	39,374	4,595	7,020	694	2,563
Tennessee	47,769	6,557	—	36,928	—	4,283
Mississippi	46,327	13,642	2,853	11,666	16,868	1,298
Virgin Island	44,727	19,120	866	—	24,359	381
Maryland	44,315	5,911	7,735	9,432	16,438	4,798
Wisconsin	41,703	23,521	8,368	7,639	1,359	817
Missouri	35,537	16,872	—	9,465	—	9,199
Oregon	35,110	3,108	14,288	8,995	4,842	3,876
Puerto Rico	29,690	2,112	1,200	8,409	15,652	2,317
Massachusetts	28,148	915	647	10,821	13,799	1,966
Delaware	27,500	13,650	537	1,736	9,881	1,695
Maine	23,719	225	383	3,315	19,700	95
South Carolina	21,481	255	6,709	4,594	9,711	213
Hawaii	21,310	1,164	609	5,136	6,548	7,852
Georgia	20,746	859	6,892	2,064	10,619	312
Iowa	17,022	11,805	—	3,850	—	1,367
Connecticut	16,849	952	137	11,209	3,203	1,347
North Carolina	12,308	73	2,926	2,933	3,687	2,689
Arkansas	12,263	5,207	—	4,425	—	2,632
Rhode Island	8,773	258	121	4,365	3,992	38
New Hampshire	4,556	11	30	1,008	3,507	—
Oklahoma	4,159	2,087	—	2,036	—	36
Idaho	1,665	1,118	—	18	—	529
Kansas	767	701	—	66	—	—
District of Columbia	760	—	—	760	—	—
Nebraska	292	196	—	94	—	3
Guam	282	31	—	250	—	—
Pacific Islands	238	77	—	160	—	—
Trans-Shipment**	83	—	—	83	—	—
Vermont	—	—	—	—	—	—

*Excludes duplication.

** Ports and offshore anchorages where cargo is moved from one vessel to another. These are St. Lucia, Virgin Islands, Heald Bank off LA-TX coast, Cherique Grande, Panama, Puerto Amuelles, Panama and Hondo Platform-Pacific Ocean.

SOURCE: "Table 4-2: Waterborne Commerce by States, 1999, Ranked by Total Tons" in *Waterborne Commerce of the United States, Part 5, 1999* Waterborne Commerce Statistics Center, U.S. Army Corps of Engineers, New Orleans, LA

THE MODERN U.S. SHIPBUILDING INDUSTRY— NEW HOPE

In the twentieth century, the U.S. fleet experienced significant growth only during the World Wars. After World War II, new shipbuilding decreased sharply as naval ship orders declined. During the 1950s and 1960s, U.S. commercial shipping persisted, but with little growth. As a result of the suspension of federal construction assistance, the U.S. shipbuilding industry's commercial orderbook fell from 77 vessels in the mid-1970s to zero by 1990. This was the lowest activity level for the industry since before World War II. (See Figure 1.8.)

Additionally, a global economic recession during the 1980s and an excess inventory of ships, particularly oil tankers, contributed to a continuing decline of the shipbuilding industry worldwide. Major shipbuilders in Europe and Japan also faced serious drops in demand, but were able to turn to their governments for support. At the

FIGURE 1.7

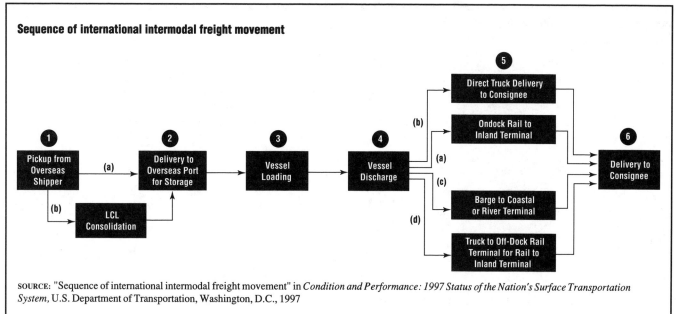

Sequence of international intermodal freight movement

SOURCE: "Sequence of international intermodal freight movement" in *Condition and Performance: 1997 Status of the Nation's Surface Transportation System,* U.S. Department of Transportation, Washington, D.C., 1997

same time, however, the U.S. government was ending its own subsidies for the U.S. shipbuilding industry. As a result, Japan and Korea are now the leading merchant ship builders, with a combined 64 percent share based on DWT. In 1998, the United States ranked 26th in terms of its shipbuilding orderbook.

U.S. shipyards delivered only one privately owned ocean-going merchant vessel of 1,000 gross tons or larger in the fiscal years 1988–1993. In 1998, however, five privately owned new vessels were delivered. By that time, 13 privately owned commercial ships (all tankers) were under construction or on order. Two ships were delivered in 1999, and nine were under contract in 2000. (See Table 1.6.)

National Shipbuilding and Shipyard Conversion Act

The increase in U.S. shipbuilding orders closely followed the passage of legislation to encourage shipbuilding in the United States. In 1993, the National Shipbuilding and Shipyard Conversion Act (PL 103-160) was passed, and U.S. shipyards began to compete once again in the domestic and foreign commercial shipbuilding markets. The National Shipbuilding and Shipyard Conversion Act includes a five-point revitalization plan:

- Extension of government guarantees to finance vessels purchased in U.S. shipyards by foreign owners, through the existing domestic loan guarantee program (Title XI).

- Efforts to ensure fair international competition.

- Improvement of commercial competitiveness.

- Elimination of unnecessary government regulation.

- Assistance in international marketing.

FIGURE 1.8

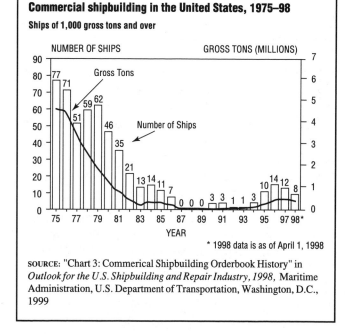

Commercial shipbuilding in the United States, 1975–98

Ships of 1,000 gross tons and over

SOURCE: "Chart 3: Commerical Shipbuilding Orderbook History" in *Outlook for the U.S. Shipbuilding and Repair Industry, 1998,* Maritime Administration, U.S. Department of Transportation, Washington, D.C., 1999

The act also funded research and development projects under MARITECH (short for "maritime technology"), which focuses on market penetration and longer-term technology development. The original MARITECH program ended in 1999, and MARITECH ASE (advanced shipbuilding enterprise) took its place.

The Title XI loan guarantee program allows MARAD to guarantee private sector debt financing, up to 87.5 percent of the cost of the vessel. The construction or reconstruction must be done in U.S. shipyards and includes both U.S.- and foreign-flag vessels. This program extends

TABLE 1.6

Statistics on private U.S. shipyards, 1980–2000

Item	Unit	1980	1985	1990	1995	1996	1997	1998	1999	2000 [1]
Employment [2]	1,000	178.0	138.3	130.8	105.0	100.4	98.6	104.4	99.1	98.1
Production workers	1,000	138.8	101.2	93.6	77.8	73.5	70.8	74.9	67.7	67.6
Building activity:										
Merchant vessels: [3]										
Under construction [4]	Number	69	10	—	3	10	14	12	5	9
Ordered	Number	7	—	3	8	5	6	1	6	—
Delivered	Number	23	3	—	1	1	4	5	2	—
Cancelled	Number	4	—	—	—	—	4	3	—	—
Under contract [5]	Number	49	7	3	10	14	12	5	9	9
Naval vessels: [3]										
Under construction [4]	Number	99	100	95	57	46	46	42	50	44
Ordered	Number	11	11	7	6	11	4	20	—	2
Delivered	Number	19	26	15	17	11	8	12	6	—
Under contract [5]	Number	91	85	87	46	46	42	50	44	46
Unfinished work: [4]										
Commercial ships	Mil. dol	2,070	450	—	93.4	365.4	572.1	746.5	594.6	1917.0
Naval ships	Mil. dol	7,107	12,091	24,495	20,768	17,734	20,116	19,097	22,385.6	21,589.5

- Represents zero. [1] As of June 1. [2] Annual average of monthly data. [3] Vessels of 1,000 tons or larger. [4] As of Jan. 1. [5] As of Dec. 31.

SOURCE: "No 1090. Private Shipyards—Summary: 1980–2000" in *The Statistical Abstract of the United States: 2000*, U.S. Census Bureau, Washington, D.C., 2000

to U.S. shipyard modernization and improvement projects as well.

A Dilemma

For many years the merchant marine had faced a dilemma related to shipbuilding. Under Section 27 of the Jones Act, U.S. owners were not permitted to buy less expensive foreign-made ships. Since 1920, the law had required all waterborne shipping between ports throughout the United States and its territories to be carried on ships built and registered in this country and owned by U.S. citizens. This put U.S. shippers at a disadvantage in the competitive shipping industry abroad.

Realizing the extent of the financial problem facing the merchant marine, Congress passed and President Clinton signed the Maritime Security Act of 1996 (MSA) ordering an annual appropriation of $100 million to maintain a U.S.-flag presence in international trade and a U.S. shipbuilding capability. The program gives limited assistance to the U.S. merchant marine involved in U.S.-foreign commerce, in an effort to help that industry become more competitive internationally.

In return, participating carriers would be required to enroll in an Emergency Preparedness Program to provide intermodal sealift support (a system for transporting persons or cargo by ship) in time of war or national crisis. Vessel owners would be required to provide ships, intermodal equipment, terminal facilities, and management services. This partnership would provide the government with cost-effective sealift capability, using commercial vessels to complement U.S. Department of Defense sealift programs.

CHAPTER 2
RAILROADS

While the ship was a major factor in the birth of the United States, the railroad played a dominant role in its growth and development. It contributed to westward expansion and allowed access to the land's vast resources. California was bound to the Union as a result of the physical and commercial ties provided by the railroad, which opened the continent from ocean to ocean.

Railways offered some distinct advantages over canals, which had previously provided the major routes for inland transportation. They were cheaper to construct, offered faster service, and did not freeze in winter. By no means were railroads problem-free: timetables reflected more wishful thinking than actual times of arrivals and departures, breakdowns were frequent, and the lack of standard-gauge tracks (gauge is the distance between the rails of a track) could mean numerous transfers from line to line. Moreover, trains were dangerous. Soft roadbeds, broken rails, collapsed bridges, and almost nonexistent brakes led to frequent and often serious wrecks. Nonetheless, the technology was well suited to the pioneering spirit and economic needs of a young and growing nation.

UNITING THE COUNTRY

In 1830, only 23 miles of railroad track existed in the United States. The advantages of rail transport were becoming obvious, however, and the industry experienced rapid growth. Congress designated the nation's railways as postal routes in 1838, and the postmaster general ordered them to be used for all reasonable transportation of the mail. Track mileage increased to 30,000 miles by 1860, and Chicago was the terminal for 11 major railroads.

Railroads exacerbated the strained relationship between the northern and southern states before the Civil War (1861–65). Most lines ran east-west, connecting the major cities and the seacoasts to the Mississippi River. Virtually all southern railroads served southern river port cities, with almost no ties to the North. Different size track gauges, a problem throughout a nation that still had 12 different track sizes in 1860, was most apparent in the South. The inability to run southern trains on northern tracks (and vice-versa) further separated the two segments of the country. The superior railroads of the North contributed to the Union victory during the Civil War, providing the North with a formidable means of transporting millions of men, arms, and supplies to strategic locations.

Go West

Even during the Civil War, the federal government was looking toward California and the western territories. The government wanted to make sure that this rich land remained a part of the Union, even though an entire continent separated it from the centers of government and commerce. The solution was to connect west to east with thousands of miles of railroad tracks. This not only created a physical link to the West, but also provided a means of exploiting its vast commercial potential. As an incentive to build railroads in the largely unsettled and sometimes hostile expanse between the Mississippi River and California, the government offered financial support, as well as land grants, to those who would build the railroads.

In 1862, Congress passed legislation to promote a transcontinental railway. The legislation granted the Central Pacific and the Union Pacific Railroads direct subsidies of:

- $16,000 for each mile of track laid on smooth ground

- $32,000 per mile through uneven regions

- $48,000 per mile through mountainous regions

- A substantial right-of-way on lands on either side of the tracks.

A virtual explosion of railroad building followed the Civil War. The dream of uniting the country by rail was realized on May 10, 1869, when the tracks laid by the Union Pacific, building from the east, and the Central Pacific, building from the west, met at Promontory Point, Utah. The momentous occasion was celebrated by driving the Gold Spike uniting the two tracks. For their efforts, the two companies received between 10 and 20 square miles of public land for every mile of track.

The 1880s saw 166,000 miles of track completed, and, by 1893, five transcontinental railroads were transporting huge quantities of agricultural, forestry, and mining products, along with settlers, adventurers, and businessmen. The railroad companies owned 12 percent of all the land west of the Mississippi—130 million acres—received in land grants from state and federal governments.

Time Zones

With the development of improved tracks and equipment, timetables began to reflect reality. This led to service complications, for the railways had to contend with almost 100 local times observed in different parts of the country. In order to provide scheduling uniformity, the railroad established, on November 18, 1883, the four time zones that are still used today—Eastern, Central, Mountain, and Pacific. While these time standards quickly came into general use, it was not until the Uniform Time Act of 1918 that they became national law.

STEAM TO DIESEL—BUT NOT ELECTRICITY

In 1895, the nation's first electrified train service began on the Nantasket Branch of the New York, New Haven, and Hartford Railroad. The first mainline electrification was through the 3.6-mile Baltimore Tunnel of the Baltimore and Ohio Railroad in 1895. However, despite early inroads, electric locomotives were largely replaced by steam locomotives. This was due in part to the extremely high start-up and maintenance costs for electric railroads, especially with long distances to cover. In addition, coal for fuel was abundant in the United States at the time of the rapid growth of railroads. In Europe, where distances are shorter and coal harder to get, most railroads are electrified.

While steam remained the major source of locomotive power for many years, diesel slowly began making inroads. In 1925, a diesel switch locomotive went into service for the Central Railroad of New Jersey. In 1934, the Chicago, Burlington, and Quincy Railroad put the first diesel locomotive into mainline service, and in 1940, the Santa Fe Railroad began using diesels in regular freight service. Gradually, the industry turned to diesel locomotives, and the last steam locomotive was retired in the 1950s.

GOVERNMENT REGULATION

As the railroad industry flourished, so did its abuses. Excessive rates, internal price wars, fraudulent investment schemes, and scandalous behavior became so widespread that eventually the government and the public reacted. In response to public pressure, many states formed commissions to control rates. But while states were granted the right to regulate businesses within their own state boundaries, the Supreme Court ruled that they could not control rates on interstate commerce. This set the stage for controls at the federal level. In 1887, Congress passed the Act to Regulate Commerce, which resulted in the formation of the Interstate Commerce Commission (ICC). The Elkins Act (1903) and the Hepburn Act (1906) gave the ICC further authority to regulate rates. On January 1, 1996, the Surface Transportation Board superseded the ICC.

FADING GLORY

Like the shipping industry, railroads could not maintain their monopoly on moving the people and products of an entire nation when they were themselves faced with new competitive forms of transportation: the car, the truck, and the airplane. Several factors contributed to the decline of the railroads. As is often the case, success led to excess. In 1916, 254,000 miles of railway line crisscrossed the nation. The supply of tracks and equipment had outstripped the demand for their use. Multiple lines served the same routes, reducing the market share for each operator and making it difficult for any of them to turn a profit.

It was under these conditions that the railroads faced dramatic changes in the U.S. transportation market. Railroads recorded almost 34 billion revenue passenger-miles (one paid passenger traveling one mile) in 1929, as three out of four Americans traveling the United States took the train. For the vast majority of people, railroads were the only way to travel long distances over land. After that peak, however, passenger miles and revenue began to drop off, as automobiles became more affordable and popular with Americans. After World War II (1941–45) Americans were richer than ever before, and automobile ownership surged. The building of a nationwide network of interstate highways in the 1950s meant that one could now drive almost anywhere in the United States. Perhaps even worse for railroads was the development of passenger air travel. As early as 1939, airplanes accounted for 2 percent of all revenue passenger-miles in the United States, and air travel developed rapidly. Long-distance travel by air was faster than by train and only slightly more expensive, making it almost impossible for railroads to compete.

During this same period, railroads faced a changing freight market. The U.S. economy was shifting from manufacturing toward services and technology, reducing the requirement for large quantities of bulk commodities, the mainstay of the railroad's freight business. Industrial centers sprang up all across the South, Southwest, and West, so that the need for long-haul transport of commodities from the Northeast to the rest of the country was diminished. Industry and population were also moving from the central cities into the suburbs. This made many older railroad routes obsolete, but financing for new tracks was often unavailable. Trucks saw dramatic increases in size and power, allowing them to haul goods that could only have been transported by train or by ship in the past.

CRISIS IN THE INDUSTRY

By the 1970s, the railroad industry was in serious trouble. Unable to compete effectively with aircraft and automobiles and burdened by price regulations, their profits had disappeared or greatly diminished. Tracks, equipment, and facilities deteriorated. Many lines went bankrupt, including the Penn-Central Transportation Company. The bankruptcy of this, the nation's largest railroad, shook the financial world and brought the poor condition of the nation's rail system to the public's attention. Congress decided to intervene. Its goals were to shore up the freight industry, which still served a vital role in transporting bulk goods and employed tens of thousands of people, as well as to reestablish a national passenger rail network.

Conrail

Congress established the United States Railroad Association (USRA) under the Regional Rail Reorganization Act of 1973 (PL 93-236) to plan and finance the restructuring of the Penn-Central and seven smaller bankrupt railways in the northeastern United States. The 3R Act, as amended by the Railroad Revitalization and Regulatory Reform (4R) Act of 1976 (PL 94-210), also created the Consolidated Rail Corporation, known as Conrail, which was to eventually become a "for profit" railroad. Conrail carried only freight, not passengers.

Conrail began operating on April 1, 1976, with a $2.1 billion congressional authorization to repair, upgrade, and replace track, equipment, and facilities. Later legislation added more monies, for a total of $3.3 billion in federal operating subsidies. Conrail slashed staff, phased out unprofitable routes, rebuilt many of the deteriorating roadbeds and tracks, and used modern technology to help run the railroad more efficiently. By the time the company was sold to the public in 1987, it was profitable. In 1993, Conrail had 11,831 miles of track, 64,834 rail cars, and 24,728 employees. Many other freight railroads followed Conrail's example and, with government assistance, were able to remain in business and return to profitability.

Amtrak

To fill the gap left by the decline in available passenger service, Congress passed the Railroad Passenger Service Act of 1970 (PL 91-518), creating the National Railroad Passenger Corporation, better known as Amtrak, a private/public corporation to operate on a "for-profit

basis." Amtrak was given three mandates from Congress. First, to provide modern, efficient intercity rail passenger service; second, to help alleviate the overcrowding of airports, airways, and highways; and third, to give Americans an alternative to private automobiles and airplanes to meet their transportation needs.

Amtrak's beginnings could be described as shaky at best. Amtrak began managing a national transportation system in May 1971 with a motley assortment of 20-year-old railway passenger cars from a variety of railroads. Ticketing and reservations were mostly handwritten. These limitations, coupled with poor on-time performance and lack of on-board amenities (no food service), did nothing to lure customers away from other forms of transportation, and the corporation steadily lost money. (It should be noted that even with the extensive, modern passenger systems in other countries, notably the high-speed lines in Germany, France, and Japan, no passenger service line in the world returns a profit.)

Realizing that Amtrak would probably not make a profit and would require government subsidy, Congress eventually ordered it to operate on an "as-for-profit" (rather than "for-profit") basis. The passage of the Regional Rail Reorganization Act (the 3R Act, PL 93-236) in 1973 and the Railroad Revitalization and Regulatory Reform Act of 1976, commonly called the 4R Act (PL 94-210), gave Amtrak the authority to take over 621 miles of rail from the bankrupt Penn-Central Railroad, which included the vital Northeast Corridor (NEC) between Washington and Boston. The Amtrak Reorganization Act of 1979 (PL 95-73) required that the company cover 50 percent of its annual costs by 1985.

DEREGULATION AND MODERNIZATION

In 1980, at the same time that deregulation was taking place in the airline and trucking industries, Congress passed the Staggers Rail Act (PL 96-448). After decades of close supervision by the ICC, this legislation permitted the railroads greater freedom in setting their rates, although, in many cases, they were required to justify rate hikes. The railways were also allowed to contract with other shippers to offer special services at special rates, a practice previously prohibited.

Rail deregulation, however, was not as comprehensive as air or trucking deregulation, and the Federal Railroad Administration (FRA) still plays a significant role in monitoring the railroads. It approves mergers and abandonment of rail lines, establishes standards for evaluating the financial condition of railroads, performs evaluations of a railroad's financial condition, and resolves rate and service disputes between railroads and shippers.

With the help of deregulation, freight railroads were able to increase their revenues and secure stronger financial backing in the 1980s. In many cases they used this money to modernize their systems. Older rail lines and trains were sold off or shut down, to be replaced with new equipment. New control centers featuring high levels of computerization were also developed. This increasing efficiency strengthened freight railroads financially, and made the U.S. freight railroad system one of the most modern in the world.

At the same time that the freight industry was being deregulated, Amtrak came under attack. In 1981, the incoming Reagan administration listed Amtrak among the government agencies that it wanted to severely cut back, if not eliminate. The administration felt that Amtrak should be forced to sustain itself through its own revenues or be allowed to fail. In virtually every budget proposal, the administration tried to either sharply cut or completely eliminate Amtrak, but ran into resistance from members of Congress representing the Northeast Corridor, where Amtrak was most successful and popular. The program continued to receive public funds, but also continued to be criticized as a waste of public money.

A GLOBAL PASSENGER RAIL REVIVAL?

Some critics believe that rail is poised to make a comeback in much of the world. Indeed, in many places rail never faltered as it did in the U.S. The United States is unusual in that trains play such a small role in transporting passengers. Airlines in Europe are now lobbying for more rail service to free overloaded terminals of short-trip passengers. The high-speed French TGV train has captured 80 percent of former air passengers on the Paris-Lyon route. In Japan, the bullet train has almost eliminated air travel between Nagoya and Tokyo.

Trains offer a vital alternative to people who cannot afford a car or airline ticket or are physically unable to drive or fly. Only an estimated 10 percent of the world's people can afford a car. Rail offers many advantages over highway or air transport, according to Worldwatch Institute, an environmental activist group, including:

- Greater energy efficiency

- Less dependence on oil

- Reduced air pollution

- Lower emissions of greenhouse gases

- Less air and road congestion

- Fewer injuries and deaths

- Less paved land area

- Local economic development

- Sustainable land use patterns

- Greater social equity

Despite these advantages, Americans began to use rail less as automobile use grew. Western European countries, however, never abandoned their passenger rail systems when the automobile became popular—intercity trains, metros, and new light rail systems have been an established part of the landscape and lifestyle and formed an integral part of their transportation system. The national railways, the largest employers in several countries, represent some of the most comprehensive rail networks in the world. Japan is notable for maintaining high train ridership even as cars have become widespread. All of this demonstrates that railroads play an important passenger transportation role in much of the world, and presumably could do the same in the United States. However, it would not come without a substantial cost. Even the most successful rail systems in other countries require government subsidies, just as Amtrak does in the United States.

Adequate funding is hard to find for all infrastructure—rail included—and critics of federal and state subsidies for rail ask where the money will come from. Supporters of rail contend that funding problems exist because national policymakers channeled billions of dollars into other transport modes, particularly highways. Contrary to popular belief, car and truck drivers do not pay their own way through user fees, but are heavily subsidized. According to the American Public Transit Association (APTA) in its *1999 Transit Fact Book* (Washington, DC), the public pays $2 to $3 trillion annually for highways and motor vehicle use, but only 53 percent to 68 percent of that amount is paid by users. The costs for building, maintaining, and operating highways are mostly paid by all citizens through taxes not directly related to use of an automobile.

TRANSPORTATION EQUITY ACT FOR THE TWENTY-FIRST CENTURY

In 1998, President Bill Clinton signed the Transportation Equity Act for the Twenty-first Century (TEA-21; PL 105-178). TEA-21 includes several programs for the rail industry. A total of $60 million was authorized for fiscal years (FYs) 1999–2001 to fund projects to determine whether transportation systems using magnetic levitation (Maglev) are both possible and safe. Of this amount, $15 million will be used for research and development of low-speed superconductivity Maglev technology in urban areas.

High-speed rail development will receive $40 million for corridor planning and $100 million for technology improvements. As this capital will come out of the General Fund, appropriations from Congress will be needed to finance the program.

A new program was created to fund light-density rail line pilot projects. It provides funding for capital improvements and rehabilitation of publicly and privately owned rail line structures. TEA-21 authorized $105 million for

TABLE 2.1

Industry total, by type of railroad, 2000

Railroad	Number	Miles Operated	Employees	Freight Revenue ($000)
Class 1	9	120,986	177,557	$32,680,081
Regional	36	21,250	11,372	1,764,646
Local	510	28,422	12,454	1,448,508
Total	**555**	**170,658**	**201,383**	**$35,893,235**

SOURCE: "Industry Total, by Type of Railroad, 2000" in *Railroad Facts, 2000 Edition,* Association of American Railroads, Washington, D.C., 2000

FYs 1998–2003, and the capital will come from the General Fund, requiring Congress to appropriate the finances.

The Alaska Railroad will receive $31.5 million for FYs 1998–2003 for capital rehabilitation and improvements to passenger services from the General Fund. In addition, transit formula grant funding totaling $29.1 million for FYs 1998–2003 will be available for capital improvements to the Alaska Railroad's passenger operations. Most (80 percent) of this funding will come from the Mass Transit Account, and 20 percent will come from the General Fund.

TEA-21 also authorizes a new Railroad Rehabilitation and Improvement Financing program to provide credit assistance. This aid will consist of direct loans and loan guarantees to public or private sponsors of intermodal (using different modes of transportation in the shipment of goods from point of departure to final destination) and rail projects. TEA-21 does not provide a set amount of funds for this program, but authorizes future appropriations to fund the credit assistance. The total amount of loans and guarantees that may be made under this program is $3.5 billion, with $1 billion reserved for projects primarily benefiting freight railroads other than Class I carriers.

TODAY'S FREIGHT SYSTEM

America's railroads are currently categorized into three types: Class I, regional, and local. As of 1999, Class I railroads were those with a reported annual operating revenue of $258.5 million or above. Only Class I railroads are required to report operating and financial data to the FRA. Table 2.1 shows that although the nine Class I railroads make up only 1.6 percent of the total number of railroads in the nation, in 1999, they accounted for the vast majority of miles operated (71 percent), railroad employees (88 percent), and freight revenue (91 percent).

The Association of American Railroads (AAR), the industry trade organization, pointed out that studies by both the General Accounting Office (GAO) and the FRA showed that freight rates fell significantly after the Staggers Rail Act was passed in 1980 (see above). In 1997, the railroads

FIGURE 2.1

Freight revenue

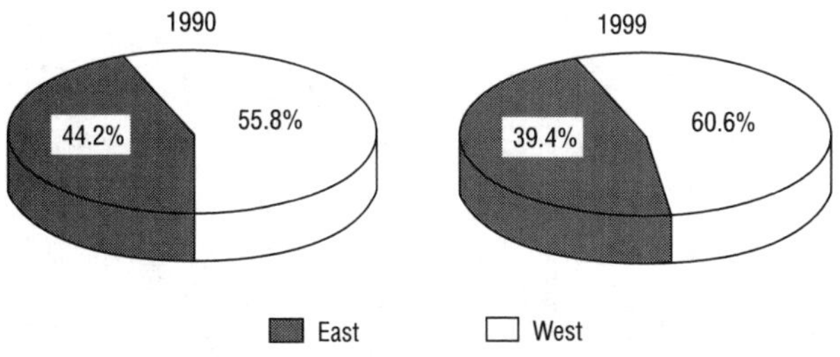

Year	United States	East	West
1929	$ 4,825,622	$ 2,948,430	$ 1,877,192
1939	3,251,096	2,000,183	1,250,913
1944	6,998,615	3,991,867	3,006,748
1947	7,041,185	4,114,802	2,926,383
1955	8,538,286	4,828,871	3,709,415
1960	8,025,423	4,361,581	3,663,842
1965	8,835,958	4,797,206	4,038,752
1970	10,921,813	5,834,402	5,087,411
1975	15,389,809	7,804,519	7,585,2901
1980	26,349,565	12,186,170	14,163,395
1985	26,687,652	12,444,633	14,243,019
1990	27,470,520	12,132,224	15,338,296
1991	26,949,280	11,701,307	15,247,973
1992	27,507,607	11,882,595	15,625,012
1993	27,990,562	11,986,218	16,004,344
1994	29,930,893	12,724,535	17,206,358
1995	31,355,593	12,973,711	18,381,883
1996	31,888,529	13,147,213	18,741,316
1997	32,322,291	13,407,206	18,915,085
1998	32,247,277	13,423,803	18,823,474
1999	32,680,081	12,872,027	19,808,054

SOURCE: "Freight Revenue" in *Railroad Facts, 2000 Edition,* Association of American Railroads, Washington, D.C., 2000

received 2.40 cents in revenue per ton-mile (the movement of one ton of freight the distance of one mile). Two particularly interesting points to note are the differences in revenue from freight over the years between the East and West sections of the country, and the steady increase in revenue since 1991, passing $32.6 billion in 1999. (See Figure 2.1 for the revenues from freight since 1929.)

American railroads handled 1.034 trillion ton-miles of freight traffic in 1990 and reached a record high of 1.433 trillion ton-miles in 1999. (See Figure 2.2.) AAR attributes this gain to an increase in the average length of haul.

In 1997, the average length of haul hit an all-time high of over 851 miles, compared to 616 in 1980 and only 334 in 1929. That average declined slightly in 1998 and 1999 (See Figure 2.3). Total tonnage shipped in 1999 increased to 1.72 billion tons. Coal accounted for 43.7 percent of all railroad tonnage, chemicals and allied products accounted for 9.0 percent, and farm products (8.1 percent) made up much of the rest (See Figure 2.4 and Table 2.2).

FIGURE 2.2

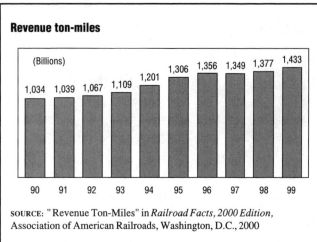

Revenue ton-miles

SOURCE: "Revenue Ton-Miles" in *Railroad Facts, 2000 Edition,* Association of American Railroads, Washington, D.C., 2000

FIGURE 2.3

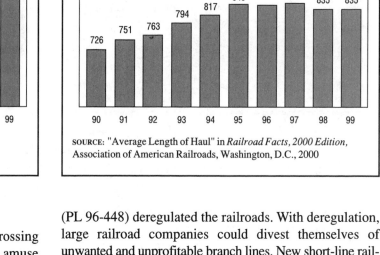

Average length of haul

SOURCE: "Average Length of Haul" in *Railroad Facts, 2000 Edition,* Association of American Railroads, Washington, D.C., 2000

Equipment

As anyone who has ever waited at a railroad crossing knows, a freight train can be very long. Those who amuse themselves by counting the number of cars on the train would have counted an average of 48 cars in 1929. The average number of cars grew steadily until 1985, when there were about 71 cars; in 1999, there was an average of 69 cars on a freight train. Today's average freight car is longer, larger, and carries almost twice as much freight as the old railroad cars. In 1999, the average car capacity was 91.4 tons (Figure 2.5), nearly twice the tonnage of 70 years ago. The average train carries about 2,947 tons of freight today, compared to an average trainload of only 804 tons in 1929. Figure 2.6 shows the types and percentages of cars in service in 1999.

Operating Expenses

There are four basic categories of operating expenses for the railroad industry. By far the largest is transportation expenses (mainly train crews and fuel), which accounted for 44 percent of all operating costs in 1999. Other expenses include the maintenance of train equipment (27 percent), maintenance of tracks and rail yards (18 percent), and general and administrative costs (11 percent).

Financial Report

In 1999, the U.S. freight railroad industry posted one of its strongest financial results since World War II, reflecting the eighth consecutive annual increase in revenues. Class I operating revenue rose 1.1 percent in 1999 to $33.5 billion, up from $33.2 billion in 1998. Operating expenses rose only 0.3 percent to $28 billion, up from $27.9 billion in 1998.

SHORT-LINE RAILROADS AND REGIONAL CARRIERS

A new segment of the railroad industry, short-line railroads, began to develop in 1980, when the Staggers Rail Act

(PL 96-448) deregulated the railroads. With deregulation, large railroad companies could divest themselves of unwanted and unprofitable branch lines. New short-line railroad enterprises began to buy up the available properties.

Of the 555 U.S. railroads, 510, or nearly 92 percent, are short-line or local carriers. Short-line railroads account for only about 17 per cent of all rail route miles, employ 6.2 percent of all rail workers, and generate approximately 4 percent of all rail revenues. There are also about 36 regional railroads in the U.S. They are similar to, but significantly smaller than, Class I companies and operate about the same number of miles as short-line railroads. In 1999, regional railroads employed 11,372 people and reported revenues of $1.76 billion, approximately 5 percent of all rail revenues. (See Table 2.1). These carriers are divided into two categories—linehaul and switching/terminal. Linehaul railroads operate like Class I railroads but on a much smaller scale. Switching and terminal railroads operate in large cities and simplify the interchange of rail shipments among the railroads (usually Class I railroads) in their area. Frequently, Class I companies own carriers of this type.

The three top short-line railroad companies are RailTex, with 3,800 miles in North America, RailAmerica, with over 2,300 miles, and Genesee & Wyoming, Inc., with more than 1,500 miles. The companies buy old locomotives and maintain the tracks only to the level needed for the speeds at which their trains travel—sometimes a mere 20 miles per hour. Short-line railroads move freight and pursue the small shipper.

Supporters of short-line railroads believe the large-railroad mergers should create new opportunities for the short-lines to keep on growing, as Class I railroads continue to divest themselves of unwanted lines. They see the smaller carriers being able to create profitable, more customer-oriented operations, because of their lower operating costs. On the other hand, some opponents warn

FIGURE 2.4

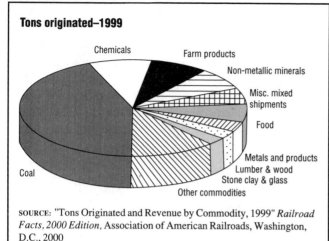

Tons originated–1999

Chemicals

Farm products

Non-metallic minerals

Misc. mixed shipments

Food

Metals and products

Lumber & wood

Stone clay & glass

Other commodities

Coal

SOURCE: "Tons Originated and Revenue by Commodity, 1999" *Railroad Facts, 2000 Edition,* Association of American Railroads, Washington, D.C., 2000

FIGURE 2.5

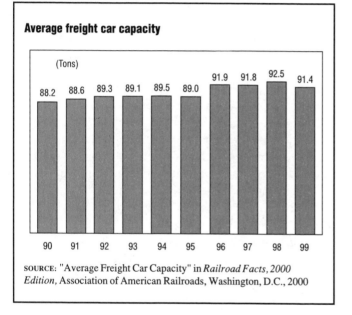

Average freight car capacity

(Tons)

| 88.2 | 88.6 | 89.3 | 89.1 | 89.5 | 89.0 | 91.9 | 91.8 | 92.5 | 91.4 |
| 90 | 91 | 92 | 93 | 94 | 95 | 96 | 97 | 98 | 99 |

SOURCE: "Average Freight Car Capacity" in *Railroad Facts, 2000 Edition,* Association of American Railroads, Washington, D.C., 2000

TABLE 2.2

Tons originated and revenue by commodity—1999

Commodity Group	Tons Orginated (000)	% of Total	Revenue (millions)	%of Total
Coal	750,814	43.7%	$7,739	21.8%
Chemicals & allied prod.	155,365	9.0	4,664	13.2
Farm products	138,988	8.1	2,720	7.7
Non-metallic minerals	125,066	7.3	955	2.7
Misc. mixed shipment	95,609	5.6	4,685	13.2
Food & kindred products	92,200	5.4	2,400	3.7
Metals & products	57,123	3.3	1,327	3.7
Lumber & wood products	50,288	2.9	1,528	4.3
Stone, clay & glass prod.	47,414	2.8	1,089	3.1
Waste & scrap materials	39,724	2.3	689	1.9
Petroleum & coke	38,689	2.3	932	2.6
Motor vehicles & equipment	37,469	2.2	3,453	9.7
Pulp, paper & allied prod.	35,445	2.1	1,457	4.1
Metallic ores	29,062	1.7	336	0.9
All other commodities	23,601	1.4	1,465	4.1
Total	**1,716,859**	**100.0%**	**35,441**	**100.0%**

SOURCE: "Tons Originated and Revenue by Commodity, 1999" in *Railroad Facts, 2000 Edition,* Association of American Railroads, Washington, D.C., 2000

FIGURE 2.6

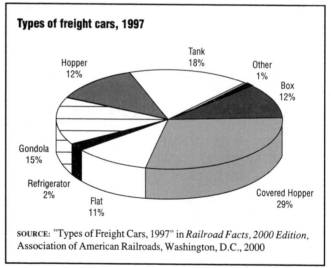

Types of freight cars, 1997

Tank 18%

Other 1%

Box 12%

Hopper 12%

Gondola 15%

Refrigerator 2%

Flat 11%

Covered Hopper 29%

SOURCE: "Types of Freight Cars, 1997" in *Railroad Facts, 2000 Edition,* Association of American Railroads, Washington, D.C., 2000

that short-line railroads are in a risky business. After all, the large railroad companies did not want these lines because they could not make money from them. They fear the short lines may find it hard to be profitable.

TODAY'S PASSENGER SYSTEM—AMTRAK

Amtrak, created by Congress with the Railroad Passenger Service Act of 1970, is the only significant long-distance passenger railroad left in the United States. By 1990, Amtrak looked very different from the fledgling passenger railroad started in the early 1970s (see above for Amtrak's early history). The system had progressed from trains heated by steam and purchased from 20 different bankrupt railroads, to a major transportation company with 24,037 employees. Amtrak operates approximately 220 intercity trains and 459 commuter trains each day, which cover 25,000 miles and serve 535 destinations in 45 states.

Several factors contributed to these successes. Amtrak improved service, reduced costs, and implemented an aggressive marketing campaign, pointing out the benefits and pleasures of train travel. In addition, the increased cost of air travel, coupled with the well-publicized stories of delays at the nation's airports, led some travelers to choose the train. While trains will never equal the speed of airplanes, some travelers with the time and with the desire to see America on ground level, without the stresses inherent in car travel, have chosen to travel by rail.

Struggling Again

In 1992, for the first time in over a decade, Amtrak revenues and passenger miles declined, due to the national

FIGURE 2.7

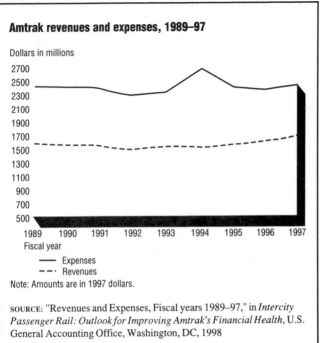

Amtrak revenues and expenses, 1989–97

Dollars in millions

Note: Amounts are in 1997 dollars.

SOURCE: "Revenues and Expenses, Fiscal years 1989–97," in *Intercity Passenger Rail: Outlook for Improving Amtrak's Financial Health,* U.S. General Accounting Office, Washington, DC, 1998

economic recession of the early 1990s. During those weak economic times, both business and discretionary travel fell, hurting all carriers. In addition, the airline industry responded with reduced fares, further undermining Amtrak ridership. Several important events occurred during 1992, however. After years of negotiations, agreements were reached with nearly all of Amtrak's 14 labor organizations. The year also began the transition to a new generation of train cars and locomotives that were delivered in 1993 and 1994. This allowed Amtrak to retire most of its original fleet of 40-year-old Heritage cars and worn-out locomotives.

Amtrak also took steps to ensure its future as a viable carrier. The Department of Transportation and Related Agencies Appropriations Act (PL 102-388), approved in 1993, provided $700.1 million in federal funds to Amtrak for fiscal year 1993, of which $331 million was for operating purposes, and the balance for capital acquisitions and improvements. That infusion of funds, however, wasn't enough. Like other major national intercity rail services in the world, Amtrak operates at a loss, and it has always relied on government subsidies. Despite an improving economy, financial difficulties for Amtrak worsened to the point that, in 1995, Congress studied Amtrak's future and debated its long-term viability. Two years later it passed the Amtrak Reform and Accountability Act of 1997 (PL 105-103). As part of the Department of Transportation's (DOT) surface transportation reauthorization bill, it approved $3.5 billion in federal funds for Amtrak's capital program over six years. Included in the act were incentives designed to encourage Amtrak to eliminate its dependence on federal operating subsidies. The act also established an

Amtrak Reform Council to evaluate Amtrak's performance and to make recommendations to Amtrak for financial reforms, further cost containment, and productivity improvements. The DOT would increase Amtrak's funds if it concluded that Amtrak was cutting spending and raising enough revenue to become self-sufficient by 2002, when subsidies are due to end. If Amtrak does not reach operational self-sufficiency by then, it must submit a plan to Congress for its own liquidation.

Amtrak's financial condition continued to deteriorate. It reduced its net losses (total expenses less total revenues) from about $892 million in fiscal year (FY) 1994 (in 1997 dollars) to about $762 million in 1997. (See Figure 2.7.) The loss would have been $63 million higher had there not been a one-time increase in revenue from the sale of real estate and telecommunications access rights in the Northeast Corridor.

Although Amtrak has reduced its net losses, it has not been able to close the gap between total revenues and expenses. For example, in 1997, intercity passenger-related revenues grew by about 4 percent, while intercity passenger-related expenses grew by about 7 percent. Most of Amtrak's 40 routes were losing money. Figure 2.8 shows Amtrak's route system. The Metroliner service between Washington, DC, and Boston, Massachusetts, made a profit of about $5 per passenger. All other trains on that route lost money. Amtrak lost an average of $53 per passenger on each of its remaining 39 routes, and more than $100 per passenger on 14 of those routes. Only 5 routes covered their train costs in FY 1997. In March 1998, Amtrak estimated that its net loss for FY 1998 would be about $845 million, about $56 million more than budgeted. Losses continued through 2000. In a Government Accounting Office (GAO) report to Congress on March 21, 2001, it was deemed unlikely that Amtrak would become self-sufficient by its deadline of 2002.

Nevertheless, still looking to the future, Amtrak plans to expand mail and express freight service (delivery of higher-value, time-sensitive goods), and in November 2000, it instituted high-speed rail service between New York City and Boston. The high-speed trains, called Acela, a combination of "acceleration" and "excellence," cut travel time between the two cities from the previous four-and-one-half hours to three hours by traveling at 150 miles-per-hour. The time gains were made possible through a $2 billion program that included electrifying the entire 470-mile stretch between Washington and Boston and straightening curves in the tracks. Moreover, 20 new trains have "tilt technology," enabling them to glide around corners by gently tilting into the bend. The ride is smooth and relatively quiet.

Acela has business-class and first-class seats with electric outlets for laptop computer use, audio jacks, cars with conference tables, upgraded food and food service,

FIGURE 2.8

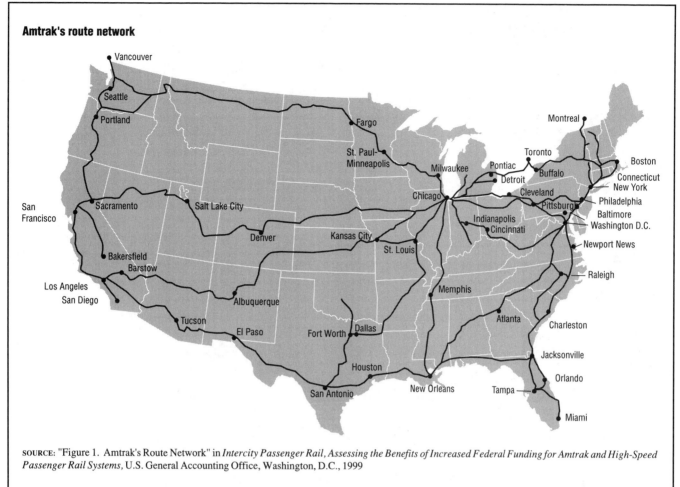

Amtrak's route network

SOURCE: "Figure 1. Amtrak's Route Network" in *Intercity Passenger Rail, Assessing the Benefits of Increased Federal Funding for Amtrak and High-Speed Passenger Rail Systems,* U.S. General Accounting Office, Washington, D.C., 1999

and beer on tap. All this comes with a price, however. The new one-way fare between New York and Boston is $120; New York to Washington runs $143. This is still less than the walk-up airplane fare for these routes.

Amtrak expects Acela to increase its market share in the Northeast Corridor from 12 to 15 percent annually—about 14.3 million passengers total. Amtrak believes Acela should generate $180 million in new profits in its first full year of service. If Acela is successful, similar high-speed Amtrak trains will enter service in the Great Lakes, Gulf Coast, California, and Pacific Northwest regions.

Amtrak and the federal government face difficult choices. The goal is for Amtrak to be free of federal operating support by 2002 by increasing revenues, controlling costs, and providing riders with quality service. Although Amtrak's business plans have helped to reduce net losses, significant challenges remain. It seems likely that Amtrak will continue to need federal assistance in terms of operations and capital well into the foreseeable future.

HIGH-SPEED TRAINS

The future of passenger rail will likely lie in high-speed trains, which could reduce travel time, relieve con-

gestion in increasingly crowded skies and cities, and win a portion of the air travel market. High-speed trains would be most practical for distances between 150 and 500 miles. For shorter distances, automobiles are preferred; for longer distances, airplanes would hold the advantage. Even at medium distances, trains would have to compete with airplanes, and, to keep fares low enough to compete, subsidies would probably be needed.

High-density corridors, where heavy passenger traffic occurs between several cities, are particularly well suited to high-speed train service. Prior to the introduction of Acela in 2000, the fastest U.S. train in service was Amtrak's Metroliner, which reached a maximum speed of about 125 miles an hour in its run between Washington and New York. Most Amtrak trains are much slower. The high-speed trains that are usually discussed for the American market could be either sophisticated wheeled vehicles that operate up to 200 miles per hour or futuristic trains driven on magnetic cushions at even higher speeds. Most analysts agree that federal grants would be needed for research into magnetic levitation, or Maglev, technology for the fastest possible trains. Maglev uses powerful electromagnets that lift passenger cars about six inches above a guideway and then propel

Railroads form a much more important part of the transportation system in Europe and Japan than they do in the United States. France's à Train Grand Vitesse, or TGV, are the fastest trains in the world, capable of traveling up to 320 miles an hour. *(Phototake: Reproduced by permission)*

them at speeds up to 300 miles per hour. More conventional technologies are available that would require less research before being built. For example, Amtrak's high-speed rail Acela program reduced the travel time between Washington, New York, and Boston by electrification, tilt technology, and straighter tracks.

Fast Trains in Other Countries

EUROPE. Much of the technology and information about high-speed trains has come from Europe. Rail systems like the French TGV (*Train à Grand Vitesse*) have been in use for many years. The primary reason for the popularity of high-speed rail in Europe is the severe congestion on Europe's roads and in the skies, a situation that America is also facing in its busiest metropolitan hubs. In European cities, short-distance flights are extremely expensive. The train costs less, takes only slightly longer, and carries passengers from downtown to downtown. (See Figure 2.9.)

The TGV holds the world speed record at over 320 miles per hour, and the trains average about 185 miles per hour in regular service. Italy, Sweden, and Germany also use high-speed trains. Each system is being supported to some degree by its government. Discussions are underway among the 12 European nations to link their high-speed systems into one network that will span the continent, expanding 1,800 miles of lines into 18,000 and

enabling average speeds of over 150 miles an hour. The 250-mile trip from Paris to London, using the Channel Tunnel (Chunnel), has been in operation since the mid-1990s and takes about three hours, often less than that of an air flight if ground time for the traveler is included.

Unfortunately, many technical obstacles remain to delay the European plan for a rail network. The many nationalities, economic and political differences, diverse electrical systems, various languages, and different visual rail signals currently reflect the generalized lack of unity on the continent. Obtaining agreement among so many nations is an awesome obstacle.

JAPAN. Japan has had great success with its 34-year-old bullet-train system. Its newest bullet train, the Shinkansen Asama 502, travels the 141 miles between Nagano and Tokyo in just 104 minutes, cutting commuters' travel time in half. The Nagano to Tokyo train costs $65 one way, carries 630 passengers, and can reach speeds of 160 miles per hour.

The Shinkansen, which means "new trunk line," was begun in 1964 between Tokyo and Osaka and carried 100 million passengers in its first 1,016 days of operation. Today, the bullet trains generally run between 6 a.m. and midnight and are always crowded. In 1964, the train traveled at 125 miles per hour; in 1997, a prototype test train

FIGURE 2.10

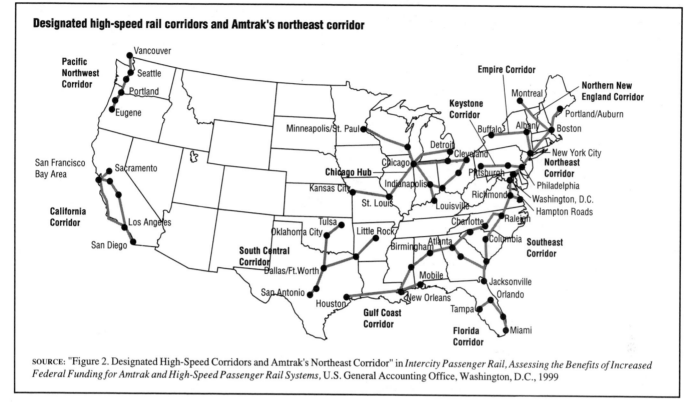

Designated high-speed rail corridors and Amtrak's northeast corridor

SOURCE: "Figure 2. Designated High-Speed Corridors and Amtrak's Northeast Corridor" in *Intercity Passenger Rail, Assessing the Benefits of Increased Federal Funding for Amtrak and High-Speed Passenger Rail Systems,* U.S. General Accounting Office, Washington, D.C., 1999

was clocked at 227 miles per hour. The Shinkansen Asama 502 can span the length of the country in a day. Nevertheless, despite its success as a method of transportation, the Japanese rail system has had chronic, severe financial problems.

High-Speed Rail Projects in the United States

In 1999, there were 11 corridors in the United States in various stages of developing high-speed rail projects. (See Table 2.3 and Figure 2.10.) There were 12 corridors until January 1999, when Florida Governor Jeb Bush halted plans for a high-speed train intended to link the cities of Orlando, Tampa, and Miami. Bush said the project posed too much financial risk for taxpayers.

According to a 1999 General Accounting Office (GAO) study, *Surface Infrastructure: High-Speed Rail Projects in the United States,* most of the corridors are in the early stages of planning. Two exceptions are Amtrak's Northeast Corridor (see above) and the Pacific Northwest Corridor. Officials in the Northeast Corridor have been upgrading the system for several years, and officials in the Pacific Northwest Corridor, between Vancouver, British Columbia, and Eugene, Oregon, have bought high-speed rail trains and have obtained funding to upgrade track.

Ten of the corridors, including the Northeast corridor, plan to upgrade their systems gradually, by making

a series of improvements to existing rail infrastructure (underlying foundation, such as tracks and communications systems) or equipment. The projects will improve track, signals, and safety systems along present rail lines by updating switches, replacing wooden railroad ties with concrete ties, and creating additional track capacity. New and improved signal and collision avoidance systems will also be needed to handle faster, increased traffic. California, on the other hand, is considering the development of an entirely new high-speed rail system that would use new technology able to reach speeds up to 310 miles per hour.

Federal funding for these projects may be obtained through various programs, including the High-Speed Rail program, the Magnetic Levitation Transportation Technology Deployment program, the Railroad Rehabilitation and Improvement Financing program, and the finance provisions under the Transportation Infrastructure Finance and Innovation Act of 1998 (TIFIA; PL 105-178) program. TIFIA helps large infrastructure projects costing at least $100 million by using federal funds to leverage significant private investment. To accomplish this, TIFIA authorizes the Secretary of Transportation to make secured loans, loan guarantees, and lines of credit available to eligible projects that will repay either all or part of the money from passenger fares.

TABLE 2.3

Scope, approach, and costs for 11 high-speed rail corridors

Dollars in millions

Corridor	Scope	Approach	Estimated cost
California	Sacramento/San Francisco to San Diego (676 miles)	Considering new high-speed rail (220 mph) or maglev (310 mph)	$21,000-$29,000
Chicago-St. Louis	Chicago, Ill., to St. Louis, Mo. (282 miles)	Incremental (110 mph)	350
Chicago-Detroit	Chicago, Ill., to Detriot, Mich. (279 miles)	Incremental (110 mph)	800
Chicago-Milwaukee	Chicago, Ill., to Milwaukee, Wis. (85 miles)	Incremental (110 mph)	471
Wisconsin-Illinois-Minnesota	Chicago, Ill., to Minneapolis, Minn. (418 miles)	Incremental (speed unknown)	To be determined
Empire (N.Y.)	Buffalo to Albany to New York City (431 miles)	Incremental (125 mph)	315
Pacific Northwest	Vancouver, B.C, to Eugene, Oreg. (466 miles)	Incremental (125 mph)	1,865
Southeast	Washington, D.C., to Charlotte, N.C. (390 miles)	Incremental (110 mph)	To be determined
Keystone (Pa.)	Philadelphia to Harrisburg (104 miles)	Incremental (110 mph)	To be determined
Northeast corridor	Washington, D.C., to Boston, Mass. (457 miles)	Incremental (150 mph)	4,000
Gulf Coast	Houston, Tex., to Birmingham, Ala. (719 miles)	Incremental (speed unknown)	To be determined

SOURCE: "Table 2.3: Scope, Approach, and Costs for 11 High-Speed Rail Corridors" in *Surface Infrastructure: High-Speed Rail Projects in the United States*, U.S. General Accounting Office, Washington, D.C., 1999"

CHAPTER 3
HIGHWAYS

The transportation system in the United States provides U.S. residents with one of the highest levels of personal mobility in the world. Americans use roads and highways more often than any other mode of transport. U.S. passenger and freight travel is dominated by the automobile, the truck, and the highway system, which accounts for more than 90 percent of all travel and more than 86 percent of the value of all goods and services shipped. The nation's productivity and international competitiveness depend on fast and reliable transportation, making the status of highways and bridges of paramount importance to the vitality of the U.S. economy.

EARLY ROADS

Before the arrival of Europeans, eastern America was crisscrossed by thousands of Indian trails that cut through forests, connecting villages and natural waterways. Colonial settlers were very dependent on these waterways. While they did expand some of the existing overland trails, most of their road-building was aimed at carrying goods to and from rivers and seaports. A few hard-surfaced roads were constructed near the larger cities.

As the colonies grew, Americans found they needed land, as well as water, routes. By the early 1700s, the government had established a land postal service between the main cities along the eastern seaboard. Foot carriers or horse-mounted riders delivered the mail, but they averaged only four miles an hour and did not work at night. Not surprisingly, a letter mailed in 1729 took four weeks to travel the 600 miles from Boston, Massachusetts, to Williamsburg, Virginia.

By 1750, enough roads were established that a regular stagecoach service was instituted between Philadelphia and New York City, and by the time of the American Revolution, a stagecoach could travel from Philadelphia to Paulus Hook Ferry (now Jersey City), New Jersey, in two days. At today's speeds, the trip would take less than two hours.

NEW ROADS FOR A NEW NATION

The first intercity highway constructed in the newly independent United States connected Philadelphia and Lancaster, Pennsylvania. Built in 1793–94 with private funds, it was surfaced with stone and gravel, and travelers were required to pay a toll to use it. In fact, almost all road-building during this period was done privately, with builders charging tolls for the use of their roads—a practice that would endure for the next 120 years.

The one major road financed with federal funds during this period was the famous Cumberland Road, or National Pike. Opened in 1818, it ran east-west, connecting Cumberland, Maryland, with Wheeling, West Virginia, and, later, Vandalia, Illinois. The road was heavily traveled by pioneers seeking to settle ever farther west, stimulating trade and linking the Midwest with the central government. Initially a free-access road, the Pike became subject to tolls as successive portions of it came under the control of the various states through which it passed.

Despite the construction of these new highways, most of the roads in the young nation were undeveloped, rutted, winding tracks, subject to damage by rain and snow. The new railroad industry and further development of local waterways and canals diverted attention away from road-building and maintenance. Slow, horse-drawn wagons and coaches, with their small capacity, could hardly compete economically with trains and barges.

A BOOST IN INTEREST

Ironically, the railroads were largely responsible for a renewed interest in road building. Because of their ability to haul large quantities of goods over long distances, the railroads were instrumental in opening up the territories west of the Mississippi River. Towns sprang up all along the western-bound tracks. Many settlers used the vast tracts of land for farming. While the railroads could haul produce from the rural town to the big city, they were of little comfort to the farmer whose wagon, loaded with agricultural produce, was stuck in a mud-filled, rutted road on the way to the station. Better roads were needed.

During this same period, roads gained an unlikely ally—the bicyclist. Bicycling rapidly became a popular national fad, and Americans joined riding clubs for exercise and pleasure. Frustrated with the limited mileage and poor conditions of existing roads, these "wheelmen" banded together to establish "good roads." In fact, what became known as the Good Roads Movement was a major force in the development of our present-day system of roads and highways.

In 1891, the Good Roads Association was formed in Missouri, and by 1901, over 100 cycling organizations were vigorously campaigning for road expansion and improvement. These groups lobbied local and federal governments for financial aid, and their spokesmen traveled throughout the country, promoting not only the need for better roads, but also the idea that road improvement and new road construction would inevitably require new taxes.

The success of the Mecklenburg Road Law demonstrated the value of government support for roads. In 1879, Mecklenburg County, North Carolina, levied a road tax on all property in the county in an effort to improve the roads—a venture that would aid the many farmers and rural residents of the area. Soon, Mecklenburg County had the best roads in the entire state.

While the federal government had been eager to offer incentives for railroad development, it did not immediately see the benefits of providing similar support for road-building. Nonetheless, the need for better roads could not be ignored forever. In response to the combined clamor of farmers and bicyclists, the U.S. Department of Agriculture created the Office of Road Inquiry in 1893. The role of the office was to investigate, educate, and distribute information on road-building.

THE CAR IS BORN

It would be hard to overestimate the impact of the car on the development of U.S. society as a whole, and on the field of transportation in particular (see Chapter 4). At the turn of the twentieth century, horses provided the main form of transportation. Then, in 1908, Henry Ford introduced the Model T. Although it was not the first automobile, it was the first to be mass-produced, and was relatively inexpensive. Automobile ownership was no longer limited to the wealthy, privileged few.

What had been a luxury quickly became a necessity. In 1910, 470,000 cars traveled the primitive American road system; by 1920, the number had swelled to over nine million. The existing roads were woefully inadequate for this amount of traffic.

In 1904, only 9 percent of the 2.4 million miles of road in the United States was surfaced. What little control existed over a road's location, size, and maintenance lay almost entirely in the hands of local authorities. A beautiful wide, paved road might end abruptly at a state line, simply because the neighboring state had different budgeting priorities. Largely owing to the efforts of the Good Roads Movement and other interested parties, however, the groundwork had already been laid for federal involvement, and local governments turned to Washington for financial assistance.

FEDERAL INVOLVEMENT AND FEDERAL AID

It was not until 1916 that federal funds for road development became uniformly available to all states. The Federal Aid Road Act of 1916 provided partial funding and technical assistance to the states to build a network of new highways. All building projects had to be approved by the Federal Bureau of Public Roads. The states' responsibilities included project initiation, supplying the balance of the funding, and the administration and maintenance of finished roads within state boundaries. The roles and duties of the states and federal government established in the 1916 act have remained basically the same in all later highway legislation.

In 1944, Congress passed the Federal Aid Highway Act (70 Stat. 838) to create the 40,000-mile National System of Interstate and Defense Highways, although major funding did not become available until the passage of the Federal Aid Highway Act of 1956 (70 Stat. 374). While these two laws would eventually produce one of the most complete interstate highway systems in the world, the original rationale for the development of a highway network was to permit the rapid movement of troops and equipment around the country in case of war. From an original commitment of 50 percent, the federal government eventually provided nearly 90 percent of construction and repair costs for roads in the Federal Aid System.

Revenue for this increased federal spending came from the Highway Trust Fund, which was established by the Highway Revenue Act of 1956 (70 Stat. 374, Title II). The fund was sourced by money from highway taxes, equipment taxes (such as manufacturers' and car-sales taxes), and gasoline taxes. In 1987, Congress passed the Surface Transportation and Uniform Relocation Assistance Act (PL 100-17), which allocated another $87.9 billion over a five-year period to establish or continue federal highway and mass-transit programs.

In 1991, the Intermodal Surface Transportation Efficiency Act (ISTEA; PL 102-240) became law. The act established the Bureau of Transportation Statistics (BTS), which collects data and studies freight activity and passenger travel throughout the country in order to improve the nation's highway system.

TABLE 3.1

Functional systems mileage

Functional System	Rural	%Change 1988-1998	Urban	%Change 1988-1998	Total	%Change 1988-1998	%of Total Mileage
Interstate	32,910	-1.4	13,424	17.3	46,334	3.4	1.2
Other Freeways/ Expressways	–	–	9,213	20.9	9,213	20.9	0.2
Other Principal Arterial	98,956	18.3	53,373	4.2	152,329	15.4	3.9
Minor Arterial	137,599	-6.8	90,006	19.5	227,605	2.1	5.8
Major Collector	433,205	-0.9	–	–	433,205	-0.9	11.0
Minor Collector	272,822	-7.4	–	–	272,822	-7.4	7.0
Collector	–	–	88,674	13.6	88,674	13.6	2.3
Local	2,096,779	-2.1	594,008	14.1	2,690,787	1.0	68.6
Total	**3,072,271**	**-2.0**	**848,698**	**14.0**	**3,920,969**	**1.0**	**100.0**

SOURCE: "Functional Systems Mileage" in *Our Nation's Highways, Selected Facts and Figures,* Federal Highway Administration, U.S. Department of Transportation, Washington, D.C., 1998

In June 1998, President Bill Clinton signed the largest public-works program in U.S. history—the Transportation Equity Act for the 21st Century (TEA-21; PL 105-178). TEA-21 reauthorized ISTEA, which expired in 1997. TEA-21 will increase transportation spending in every state. The act commits $218 billion over the six-year period from 1998 to 2003 for transportation programs. The funds will be spent on highway and bridge projects ($175 billion), mass transit ($41 billion), and safety programs ($2 billion). TEA-21 builds on the programs undertaken in ISTEA and improves upon them. Significant features of TEA-21 include:

- Assuring a guaranteed level of federal funds for surface transportation through 2003.

- Extending the Disadvantaged Business Enterprises program by providing minority and women-owned businesses nationwide with 10 percent participation in highway and transit contracting undertaken with federal funding.

- Strengthening safety programs to increase the use of safety belts and encouraging the passage and enforcement of 0.08 percent blood-alcohol-level standards for drunk driving in every state.

- Continuing the program structure established for highways and transit under ISTEA and adding new programs.

- Investing in research to maximize the performance of the transportation system and emphasizing the development of Intelligent Transportation Systems to help improve operations and management of transportation systems and vehicle safety.

The National Highway System

ISTEA (see above) changed the way the federal government classified roads, by introducing the National Highway System, or NHS. (The term "highway," as used here, refers not only to major highways, but also to rural roads and urban streets that lead to or connect major roads and that, collectively, make up the highway network or system.)

The National Highway System Designation Act of 1995 (PL 104-59) provided a framework for the NHS consisting of 157,000 miles of roads—or 4 percent of all public roads. The NHS defines five different types of highways:

1. Interstate highways, which crisscross the country (46,000 miles).

2. Key primary and urban arterials, which carry the major portion of traffic entering and leaving urban areas (89,000 miles).

3. The Strategic Highway Corridor Network, consisting of 15,000 miles of 21 "corridors" linking major military installations and defense facilities designated by the Department of Defense.

4. Major connectors (2,000 miles).

5. High-priority corridors (5,000 miles), which are highways that serve regional travel and connect with other modes of transportation, such as railway stations, harbors, and airports.

TODAY'S HIGHWAY SYSTEM

The nation's highway network consists of over 3.9 million miles of roads and streets, with most (78 percent) located in rural areas. (See Table 3.1.) This network accommodates more than 2.6 trillion vehicle miles of travel each year. (See Table 3.2.) Bridges are a critical link in the nation's infrastructure (the basic facilities on which the growth of a community or state depends). In 1998, there were about 582,976 bridges on the highway network. (See Table 3.3.) Nearly 78 percent of these bridges were in rural areas. (See Table 3.4.) Also included in the network are almost 4,500 miles of toll roads, bridges, and tunnels.

TABLE 3.2

Annual vehicle-miles of travel (millions)

Functional System	Rural	% Change 1988-1998	Urban	% Change 1988-1998	Total	% Change 1988-1998	% of Total Travel
Interstate	252,317	39.2	377,840	46.1	630,157	43.2	23.9
Other Freeways/ Expressways	–	–	167,357	43.1	167,357	43.1	6.3
Other Principal Arterial	238,193	48.6	390,830	22.4	629,023	31.2	23.8
Minor Arterial	166,633	9.8	310,126	33.8	476,759	24.3	18.0
Major Collector	204,623	11.5	–	–	204,623	11.5	7.7
Minor Collector	54,773	16.5	–	–	54,773	16.5	2.1
Collector	–	–	132,393	33.4	132,393	33.4	5.0
Local	120,985	29.2	225,821	23.8	346,806	25.6	13.1
Total	1,037,524	26.9	1,604,367	32.8	2,641,891	30.4	100.0

SOURCE: "Annual Vehicle-Miles of Travel (millions)" in *Our Nation's Highways, Selected Facts and Figures,* Federal Highway Administration, U.S. Department of Transportation, Washington, D.C., 1998

TABLE 3.3

Bridges by owner, 1996 and 1998

Owner	Number of bridges	
	1996	1998
Federal	6,171	7,448
State	273,198	273,897
Local	299,078	298,222
Private	2,378	2,278
Unknown/Unclassified	1,037	1,131
	581,862	582,976

SOURCE: "Exhibit 2-8. Bridges by owner, 1996 and 1998," in *1999 Status of the Nation's Surface Transportation: Conditions and Performance Report,* Department of Transportation, Federal Highway Administration, Washington, DC

Highway Classifications

The more than 3.9 million miles of roads in the United States are functionally classified as arterials, collectors, or local roads, depending on the type of service they provide. These categories are subdivided into rural and urban areas. (Table 3.1 shows highway mileage by function.)

Arterials, which are further classified as principal or minor, provide connections to other roads. They usually have higher design standards, with wider or multiple lanes. In rural areas, principal arterials are subdivided into interstate and other principal arterials (OPAs). In urban areas, principal arterials are subdivided into interstate, other freeways and expressways (OF&Es), and OPAs.

Collectors are usually two-lane roads that serve shorter trips. They collect and distribute traffic to and from the arterial systems. They often provide the fastest and most convenient way to reach a local destination. In rural areas, collectors are subdivided into major and minor collectors.

Most public road mileage is classified as local. Local roads provide the access between residential and commercial properties and the more heavily traveled highways.

TABLE 3.4

Bridges by functional system, 1996 and 1998

Functional system	Number of bridges	
	1996	1998
Rural bridge		
Interstate	28,638	27,530
Other arterial	72,970	73,324
Collector	144,246	143,140
Local	211,059	210,670
Subtotal rural	456,913	454,664
Urban bridge		
Interstate	26,596	27,480
Other arterial	59,064	60,901
Collector	14,848	14,962
Local	24,441	24,969
Subtotal urban	124,949	128,312
Bridge total	581,862	582,976

SOURCE: "Exhibit 2-9. Bridges by functional system, 1996 and 1998," in *1999 Status of the Nation's Surface Transportation: Conditions and Performance Report,* Department of Transportation, Federal Highway Administration, Washington, DC

Nationwide, states have jurisdictional responsibility for approximately 20 percent of the total public road and street mileage in the United States. The federal government owns and maintains only those roads on federal Indian reservations and in national parks—about 3 percent. Local governments control the remaining 77 percent (See Table 3.5). Of the nation's bridges, in 1998 the states owned and maintained 273,897, and the federal government owned 7,448. There were 298,222 bridges that were locally owned and maintained, while 2,278 were owned by private entities. (See Table 3.3.)

WHO PAYS WHAT?

Financing for roads and highways comes from both the public and private sectors. A variety of revenue sources finance the nation's highways, including direct user fees, such as license fees, tolls, and taxes on both gasoline and vehicles; and indirect fees, such as income taxes and local property assessments. Federal, state, and local governments funded more than $109.9 billion in 1998, up from $35.3 billion in 1978 (See Figure 3.1.)

The largest share of money used to finance highways comes from highway-user fees, including tolls ($69.2 billion). General funds account for $13.8 billion, while other taxes, investment income, and bond proceeds pay for the remaining $26.9 billion. (See Figure 3.2.)

Highway construction, maintenance, and operating costs have risen dramatically—primarily because of inflation. Figure 3.1 shows the costs of keeping the nation's highways in shape, and Figure 3.2 illustrates the way capital is spent. Most road construction is devoted to improving existing highways and streets, through such projects as resurfacing, widening pavement, and minimizing curves. Most new roads are built by local governments to serve residential users only.

PROBLEMS FACING THE HIGHWAY SYSTEM

Highway Conditions

Most experts agree that U.S. roads and bridges are below standard, although analysts differ on the degree of the problem. Table 3.6 illustrates the percentage of interstate highways that need improvement, according to the Federal Highway Administration (FHWA). The FHWA found that, in 1994, about 18.8 percent of the interstate highways in the nation were in poor or mediocre condition; in 1997, that figure was estimated to be 18.3 percent. In 1998, approximately 30 percent of the nation's bridges were structurally deficient or functionally obsolete. (See Table 3.7.) Structurally deficient bridges are those that need significant maintenance, rehabilitation, or replacement. Functionally obsolete bridges are those that do not have lane widths, shoulder widths, or vertical clearances adequate for traffic demand.

The FHWA reports that the percentage of roadways in good paved condition has risen over the past few years. In 1997, 57 percent of rural interstates were in good or very good condition, up from 43 percent in 1994. Likewise, 40.5 percent of urban interstates were in good or very good condition in 1997, up from 33 percent in 1994. (See Figure 3.3.) The number of interstate bridges classified as deficient decreased, as did the number of faulty bridges on arterial and collector roads. Naturally, because of traffic loads and environmental conditions, roadways will continue to deteriorate, requiring ongoing rehabilitation programs to maintain the pavement structure in acceptable condition.

Traffic Congestion

Highway congestion continues to be a major concern for both urban and suburban areas of the nation. Population and business activities are, by definition, concentrated in metropolitan areas. Since 1980, about 86 percent of

TABLE 3.5

Ownership of roads and streets

Jurisdiction	Rural Mileage	%	Urban Mileage	%	Total Mileage	%
State	662,805	21.6	111,359	13.1	774,164	19.7
Local	2,291,098	74.6	735,863	86.7	3,026,961	77.2
Federal	118,369	3.9	1,485	0.2	119,854	3.1
Total	3,072,272	100.0	848,707	100.0	3,920,979	100.0

SOURCE: "Ownership of U.S. Roads and Streets" in *Our Nation's Highways, Selected Facts and Figures,* Federal Highway Administration, U.S. Department of Transportation, Washington, D.C., 1998

FIGURE 3.1

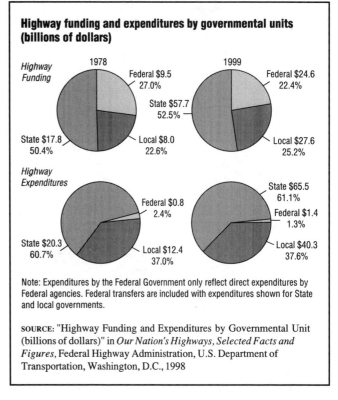

Highway funding and expenditures by governmental units (billions of dollars)

Note: Expenditures by the Federal Government only reflect direct expenditures by Federal agencies. Federal transfers are included with expenditures shown for State and local governments.

SOURCE: "Highway Funding and Expenditures by Governmental Unit (billions of dollars)" in *Our Nation's Highways, Selected Facts and Figures,* Federal Highway Administration, U.S. Department of Transportation, Washington, D.C., 1998

the country's population growth has been in metropolitan areas, with about 75 percent in the suburbs. This tremendous growth has greatly exceeded the nation's highway development. The Department of Transportation projects that this suburbanization will put an even greater demand on the already-strained urban highway system.

Most peak-hour congestion in the United States occurs in metropolitan areas with populations over one million. In 1998, the Federal Transit Administration (FTA) estimated that traffic congestion cost U.S. businesses $40 billion a year in economic losses, a figure that would have been some $20 billion higher had it not been for the increase in mass transit over the past decade.

Highway congestion is expressed as the ratio of traffic volume during rush hour to the capacity, or service flow, of the road (V/SF). The higher the value of the ratio,

FIGURE 3.2

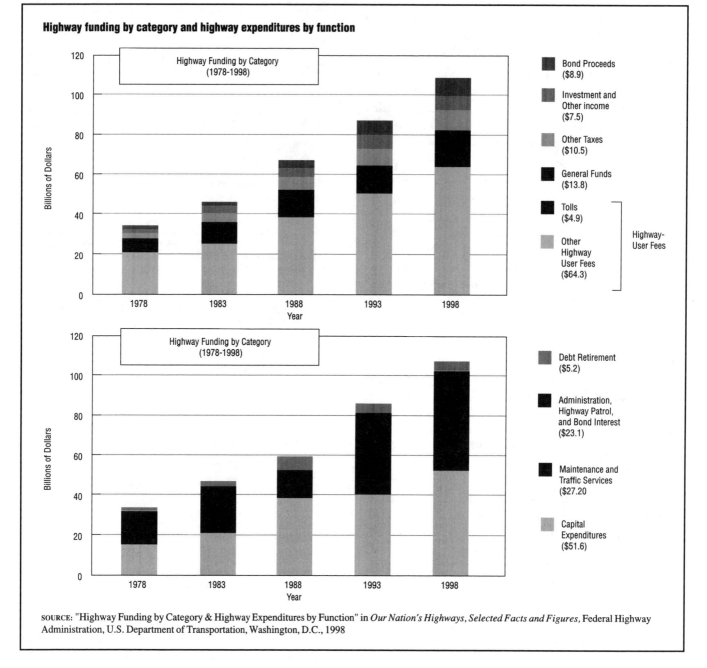

Highway funding by category and highway expenditures by function

Highway Funding by Category (1978-1998)

Bond Proceeds ($8.9)

Investment and Other income ($7.5)

Other Taxes ($10.5)

General Funds ($13.8)

Tolls ($4.9)

Other Highway User Fees ($64.3)

Highway-User Fees

Highway Funding by Category (1978-1998)

Debt Retirement ($5.2)

Administration, Highway Patrol, and Bond Interest ($23.1)

Maintenance and Traffic Services ($27.20

Capital Expenditures ($51.6)

SOURCE: "Highway Funding by Category & Highway Expenditures by Function" in *Our Nation's Highways, Selected Facts and Figures,* Federal Highway Administration, U.S. Department of Transportation, Washington, D.C., 1998

the more crowded the highway. For example, above 0.80, travelers on the road experience notable slowdowns. A ratio of more than 0.95 indicates serious congestion, and at 1.00 any incident will cause stop-and-go travel. Figure 3.4 shows that, in 1998, travel-congestion rates—the percentage of peak-period miles traveled under congested conditions—were about 56 percent on the urban Interstate System and 47 percent on urban National Highways—a slight rise over the previous several years.

Highway Safety

Highway safety is one of the nation's most important concerns. The federal government's primary involvement in highway safety is through the introduction of up-to-date highway designs and nationwide traffic-control devices. But national programs discouraging alcohol and drug abuse, promoting proper use of seatbelts, and supporting various vehicle-safety programs (such as defensive-driving courses) also contribute greatly to improved highway safety.

Highway fatality rates have declined significantly in both rural and urban areas over the past decade. This is partly due to changes in driving habits, such as the increased use of seat belts; the decline in drunk driving; and the improvement in both highway and vehicle design. Interstates are the safest type of highway, with the lowest fatality rates. Highway fatality rates have declined on both arterial and collector roads, especially in rural areas, but the rate of decline has been slower in urban areas.

TABLE 3.6

Urban and rural highway pavement conditions, 1994–1997

Highway functional class	Year	Poor	Mediocre	Fair	Good	Very good	Total miles reported	Poor or mediocre	Fair or better
Urban subtotal	1994	9.1%	15.4%	40.8%	18.9%	15.3%	232,504	24.4%	75.1%
	1995	8.9%	15.5%	39.4%	18.8%	17.0%	237,396	24.5%	75.2%
	1996	8.8%	15.1%	40.3%	19.9%	15.4%	242,148	23.9%	75.6%
	1997	9.3%	15.0%	40.5%	20.4%	14.9%	241,116	24.3%	75.8%
Rural subtotal	1994	5.4%	11.4%	40.7%	19.7%	16.0%	676,996	16.9%	76.3%
	1995	5.7%	10.4%	38.1%	20.1%	18.8%	643,749	16.1%	77.0%
	1996	5.0%	9.7%	38.8%	24.8%	14.8%	681,913	14.7%	78.4%
	1997	5.6%	10.4%	40.8%	28.1%	15.1%	636,248	16.0%	84.0%

NOTES: Numbers may not total due to rounding. Condition for rural and urban Interstates and other principal arterials, urban other freeways and expressways, and rural minor arterials based on International Roughness Index data from the Federal Highway Administration. Condition for urban minor arterials and collectors and rural major collectors based on Present Serviceability Rating data from the Federal Highway Administration.

KEY: **Poor** = needs immediate improvement. **Mediocre** = needs improvement in the near future to preserve usability. **Fair** = will likely need improvement in the near future, but depends on traffic use. **Good** = in good condition; will not require improvement in the near future. **Very good** = new or almost new pavement; will not require improvement for some time.

SOURCE: "Table 1-2: Highway Pavement Conditions: 1994-1997" in *Transportation Statistics Annual Report 1999*, Bureau of Transportation Statistics, U.S. Department of Transportation, Washington, D.C., 1999

TABLE 3.7

Bridge conditions (as of June 1998)

Conditions	NHS[1] No.	NHS[1] %	Other FA Highways[2] No.	Other FA Highways[2] %	Non-FA Highways[3] No.	Non-FA Highways[3] %	Total Highways No.	Total Highways %
Structurally Deficient	8,895	6.9	21,197	12.4	62,984	22.3	93,076	16.0
Functionally Obsolete	20,953	16.2	23,724	13.9	34,829	12.3	79,506	13.6
All Other Bridges	99,149	76.9	126,091	73.7	185,147	65.4	410,387	70.4
Total Bridges in Inventory	128,997	100.0	171,012	100.0	282,960	100.0	582,969	100.0

[1]Includes all Interstate and other principal arterials.
[2]Includes all other highways except minor collectors and local roads and streets.
[3]Includes rural minor collectors and local roads and streets.

SOURCE: "Bridge Conditions (as of June 1998)" in *Our Nation's Highways, Selected Facts and Figures*, Federal Highway Administration, U.S. Department of Transportation, Washington, D.C., 1998

The first motor vehicle death in the United States occurred in New York City on September 13, 1899. By 1955, a total of 3 million people had lost their lives in motor vehicle accidents; between 1966 and 1997, there were another 1.5 million fatalities. In 1979, 53,524 people died in motor vehicle accidents. The number dropped to 40,982 in 1992, but has risen since then, leveling off at about 43,000 in 1999. Looking at the statistics per miles traveled, there were 1.5 deaths per 100 million vehicle miles traveled (VMT) in 1999—the lowest rate on record. (See Figure 3.5.) Because total travel is growing, the number of persons killed and injured may increase, although the rate is declining. (See Figure 3.6.)

Preserving the System: Growth and Maintenance of Roads and Bridges

While travel on roads and highways has soared 1,000 percent since the mid-1940s, road mileage (the number of miles of roads) has grown only about 62.5 percent since the turn of the century. In 1960, there were 3.5 million miles of roads in the United States; in 1998, just under 4 million miles. (See Table 3.1 and Table 3.5.)

The increase in road travel naturally causes more wear and tear on the nation's road surfaces. Transportation experts agree that the nation's congested and decaying network of roads must be continually rebuilt and that the investment of billions of dollars would pay for itself by promoting economic growth and productivity.

To pay for this future need, the Federal Highway Administration (FHWA) has developed two investment-requirement estimates for maintenance and new construction. The Cost to Maintain Conditions and Performance plan calculates the funds needed to keep the system running at its current level; the Cost to Improve Conditions and Performance calculates funds needed to improve the system. The FHWA estimated the cost to maintain the

FIGURE 3.3

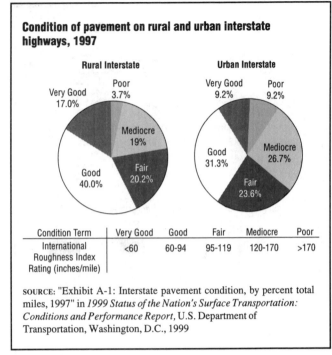

Condition of pavement on rural and urban interstate highways, 1997

Rural Interstate

Very Good 17.0%
Poor 3.7%
Mediocre 19%
Good 40.0%
Fair 20.2%

Urban Interstate

Very Good 9.2%
Poor 9.2%
Mediocre 26.7%
Good 31.3%
Fair 23.6%

Condition Term	Very Good	Good	Fair	Mediocre	Poor
International Roughness Index Rating (inches/mile)	<60	60-94	95-119	120-170	>170

SOURCE: "Exhibit A-1: Interstate pavement condition, by percent total miles, 1997" in *1999 Status of the Nation's Surface Transportation: Conditions and Performance Report,* U.S. Department of Transportation, Washington, D.C., 1999

1997 level of highway and bridge conditions for the period 1998–2007 at $117.5 billion, while the cost to improve the system was calculated to be $226.0 billion. (See Table 3.8.)

Both scenarios include the costs of repairing pavement and bridges in poor or fair shape, eliminating unsafe conditions, and adding capacity. Under the Cost to Maintain plan, some facilities will improve and some will worsen, but overall, the system will stay as is. The estimates for Cost to Maintain are the lowest reasonable level of investment. Under the Cost to Improve scenario, all existing deficiencies will be improved. These estimates reflect the highest reasonable level of investment.

INTELLIGENT TRANSPORTATION SYSTEMS

Intelligent transportation systems combine automotive technology, computers, communications, and electronics to ease travel by reducing congestion and improving safety—all while remaining cost-efficient. Some examples of intelligent transportation systems include in-vehicle mapping systems, electronic message signs that give motorists traffic information, and sophisticated traffic-control centers. Under TEA-21, the Department of Transportation will fund projects to develop systems that "talk and listen" to one another, allowing different technologies to work together.

Smart Roads—A Traffic Management System for the Future?

Not surprisingly, during peak traffic periods, two-thirds of the cars on interstate highways are moving at less than

35 miles an hour. In cities such as New York, Los Angeles, Chicago, and Houston, many are barely moving at all. Simply put, the National Highway System has reached its capacity. But because of limited space in and around cities, building more roads is not always an option. In seeking some solution to the congestion, government, academic, and industry leaders are experimenting with an automated highway and driver-information system, known as Intelligent Vehicle Highway Systems (IVHS), to route cars around bottlenecks, prevent tie-ups, and increase safety.

Other technological advances are also providing some possible solutions to the growing problem of highway congestion. A promising demonstration of some of these high-tech solutions—such as "smart cars," automated highways, and intelligent transportation systems—took place in 1997 at a short test track at Miramar College in California. An onboard computer with radar, video, and laser sensors led smart cars along radar-reflective tape, while other vehicles were guided by a series of magnets embedded every four feet along one lane.

Such advanced technology is still years away from being employed on a large scale, but some high-tech methods of traffic management are currently in use across the country. A Minneapolis system uses video cameras, electronic road signs, orchestrated traffic lights, and radio station updates to help coordinate traffic. This experiment has helped raise average speeds on a three-mile stretch of Interstate 394 by 35 percent, and reduced accidents by 27 percent.

In Seattle, an experimental system uses electronic surveillance of entrance ramps and synchronization of traffic lights to keep traffic moving steadily. It has reduced travel time from 22 to 11.5 minutes on a 6.9-mile section of highway.

Commuters on the Dallas Tollway and on toll roads in New Jersey and New York are now using an electronic toll-taking system, called E-Z Pass. The system uses radio waves to identify cars, and automatically deducts tolls from prepaid accounts. Motorists do not have to stop, but only slow down, as they go through tollbooths. Electronic toll-taking is also being used in many other states, including Illinois, Wisconsin, Indiana, Pennsylvania, and Missouri. This technology is not without its glitches, though: several systems have malfunctioned, resulting in motorists being sent unwarranted violation citations in the mail.

California has an electronic toll-taking system called FasTrack. It is now in use on all of the bridges in the San Francisco Bay area and on some toll roads in Southern California. Also in California, a private company has opened a toll road on a heavily congested section of State Route 91 that runs through Yorba Linda. Commuters can now cruise through this former trouble spot at 65 miles an hour for a fee of $2.50, which is collected electronically.

FIGURE 3.4

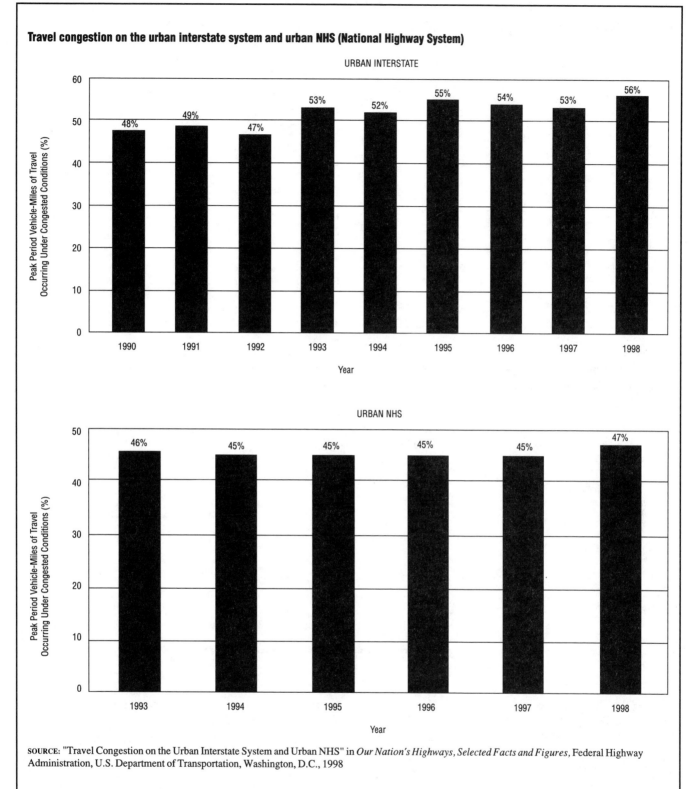

Travel congestion on the urban interstate system and urban NHS (National Highway System)

URBAN INTERSTATE

URBAN NHS

SOURCE: "Travel Congestion on the Urban Interstate System and Urban NHS" in *Our Nation's Highways, Selected Facts and Figures,* Federal Highway Administration, U.S. Department of Transportation, Washington, D.C., 1998

High-Occupancy Vehicle Lanes

High-occupancy vehicle (HOV) lanes are freeway lanes restricted during peak traffic hours to vehicles containing two or more passengers. They encourage carpooling and, therefore, relieve congestion, cut gasoline consumption, and reduce air pollution.

There are more than 40 HOV projects in use in North America. They are dispersed among 25 metropolitan areas and cover roughly 400 miles, varying by hours of operation (2–24 hours a day) and occupancy requirements (two passengers, three or more passengers, and bus-only lanes).

FIGURE 3.5

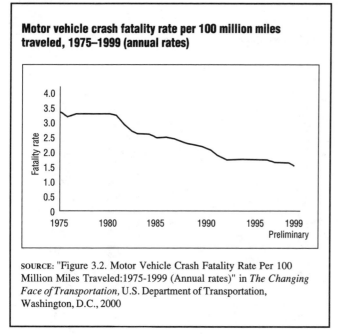

Motor vehicle crash fatality rate per 100 million miles traveled, 1975–1999 (annual rates)

SOURCE: "Figure 3.2. Motor Vehicle Crash Fatality Rate Per 100 Million Miles Traveled:1975-1999 (Annual rates)" in *The Changing Face of Transportation,* U.S. Department of Transportation, Washington, D.C., 2000

FIGURE 3.6

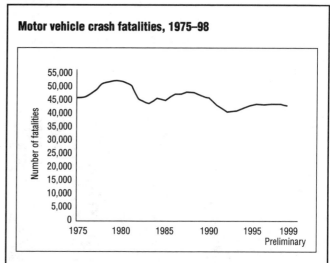

Motor vehicle crash fatalities, 1975–98

SOURCE: National Highway Traffic Safety Administration, *Traffic Safety Facts 1998,* cited as "Figure 3.3: Motor Vehicle Crash Fatalities: 1975–98," in *The Changing Face of Transportation,* U.S. Department of Transportation, Washington, D.C., 2000

TABLE 3.8

Expected costs to either maintain or improve the interstate highway system, 1998–2007

	10-Year Cost to Maintain (Billions of 1997 Dollars)			10-Year Cost to Improve (Billions of 1997 Dollars)		
	Rural	Urban	Total	Rural	Urban	Total
Highway/Bridge Preservation & Widening						
Work on Existing Highways						
Highway Preservation	19.1	29.9	49.1	25.0	37.3	62.2
Widening	1.7	15.1	16.8	11.8	50.5	62.3
Subtotal, Existing Highways	20.9	45.0	65.9	36.8	87.7	124.5
Bridge Work	4.4	19.3	23.7	9.9	37.9	47.8
Subtotal Work on Existing						
Highways & Bridges	25.2	64.4	89.6	46.7	125.6	172.3
New Construction	3.6	13.3	17.0	6.7	25.9	32.6
System Enhancements	2.9	8.0	10.9	5.4	15.6	21.0
Total Investment	**31.8**	**85.7**	**117.5**	**58.8**	**167.1**	**226.0**

SOURCE: "Exhibit A-16: 1998–2007 Cost to Maintain and Cost to Improve the Interstate System" in *1999 Status of the Nation's Surface Transportation: Conditions and Performance Report,* U.S. Department of Transportation, Washington, D.C., 1999

Critics feel that HOV lanes are underused, and point out that the nine-to-five lifestyle for which they were planned is no longer valid, since work hours for many commuters are frequently unpredictable. They complain that HOV lanes are fully used only a few hours a day. They also note that a number of cities have found their HOV programs ineffective and have returned their lanes to normal traffic flow.

San Diego County, California, has turned some of its HOV lanes into HOT (high-occupancy toll) lanes. Under this plan, a vehicle with only one occupant may travel the HOV lanes for a fee of $50 a month. However, in other areas where this is not an option, frustrated commuters sometimes violate the two-occupant limit

and travel in the HOV lane anyway. Others buy lifelike dummies and place them in the passenger seat, in order to make it appear that there are two people in the vehicle. These drivers are subject to large fines if they are caught: in California, violators must pay a minimum fine of $270.

A spokesperson for the Department of Transportation admits that it is difficult to get people to give up the convenience of their own vehicles, but as traffic continues to increase, he predicts, HOV lanes will become increasingly popular. Supporters of HOV lanes call attention to the fact that these lanes, like highways, are designed for the future as well as the present. They point out that when highways are built, they are planned not only for current traffic, but also for the traffic that is projected 20 to 25 years in the future. According to these supporters, HOV lanes will help ease today's rush-hour congestion and will still be suitable 10 to 15 years from now.

CHAPTER 4
AUTOMOBILES

REVOLUTION ON THE ROAD

It would have taken a vivid imagination to envision the future potential of the first self-propelled land vehicle, created by Nicholas Cugnot in 1769. Powered by a steam engine, it could reach a maximum speed of three miles an hour and travel 15 miles without refueling. Twenty years later, in 1789, Oliver Evans patented a 42,000-pound, steam-powered carriage that could run on land or in the water.

The invention of the internal-combustion engine was a major development in automobile building. Gottlieb Daimler introduced the gasoline-powered car in Germany in 1887. The first successful American model was built by Charles and Frank Duryea in 1892–93, and by the turn of the century, eight thousand "horseless buggies" traveled the rough, unpaved roads of America.

The first factory devoted exclusively to the manufacture of automobiles was built by Ransom E. Olds in Detroit, Michigan, in 1899. Nine years later, Henry Ford's mass-produced, relatively inexpensive Model T transformed the automobile from a luxury into an affordable necessity. Americans' love affair with the car had begun.

The automobile rapidly changed the nation's way of life. Workers no longer had to live near the factories where they worked, so they moved into the newly developing suburbs. Industry did not have to be built on waterways or railroad lines, because trucks could go anywhere there were roads. Shopping centers, fast-food restaurants, and motels are all the result of increased mobility brought about by the automobile. Drive-in franchise restaurants meant that a hamburger bought at a fast-food chain in Detroit would taste the same as one purchased at a drive-in from the same chain in Des Moines or Denver. From drive-in movies, popular in the 1950s and 1960s, to drive-through banks and cleaning establishments, Americans became accustomed to spending more time in their cars. For many people today, the car is a second home—a place where they can eat meals, listen to a CD, and talk on the phone as they drive.

As with many inventions, the automobile has been a mixed blessing. Along with giving people a previously unimagined degree of freedom, it has contributed to urban sprawl, air and noise pollution, and a general decline in public transportation, and has been responsible for millions of injuries and deaths. The car has also changed family life dramatically, since the younger generation can now come and go much more freely. For most teenagers, receiving a driver's license is an important rite of passage and a symbol of independence.

THE AUTO INDUSTRY TODAY

The transportation system in the United States provides U.S. residents with the highest level of personal mobility—in terms of trips made and miles traveled—in the world. The automobile dominates U.S. passenger travel.

In 1950, there were 23 major car manufacturers in the United States; today, there are only two: General Motors Corporation and the Ford Motor Company. (In 1998, the Chrysler Corporation, the third member of the former "Big Three," merged with Daimler-Benz of Germany and is now known as DaimlerChrysler AG.) However, a number of foreign companies, including Honda, Toyota, Volkswagen, and BMW, now make many of their cars in this country. The economic health of the former "Big Three" has generally reflected that of the nation as a whole. The automobile market was weak during the early 1990s, but recovery started in 1992 and continues into 2001.

PRODUCTION AND SALES

Between 1997 and 1998, the domestic production of automobiles and trucks dipped slightly, from 12.1 million units to 12.0 million units, but this was still up sharply from the 8.8 million units in 1991 and 9.7 million in 1992.

TABLE 4.1

U.S. car and truck production summary, 1998

	Cars	% Tot.	Trucks	% Tot.	Total
1998	5,554,373	46.3	6,448,290	53.7	12,002,663
1997	5,933,921	48.9	6,196,654	51.1	12,130,575
1996	6,082,835	51.4	5,747,322	48.6	11,830,157
1995	6,339,967	52.9	5,655,281	47.1	11,995,248
1994	6,601,220	53.9	5,638,068	46.1	12,239,288
1993	5,982,120	55.1	4,873,342	44.9	10.855,462
1992	5,666,891	58.4	4,041,384	41.6	9,708,275
1991	5,439,864	62.0	3,333,144	37.0	8,773,008
1990	6,077,903	62.2	3,689,536	37.8	9,767,439
1989	6,821,291	62.8	4,035,501	37.2	10,856,792
1988	7,137,433	63.6	4,084,575	36.4	11,222,008

SOURCE: "U.S. car and truck production summary" in *Ward's Automotive Yearbook, 1999,* Ward's Communications, Southfield, MI, 1999

TABLE 4.2

Top cars and trucks in the United States, 1998

Top 10 U.S. car sales

	Units	Market Share	Unit change from 1957
Toyota Camry	429,595	5.3%	+10.0%
Honda Accord	401,071	4.9%	+4.3%
Ford Taurus	371,074	4.6%	+3.9%
Honda Civic	334,562	4.1%	+6.0%
Ford Escort	291,936	3.6%	+2.5%
Chevy Cavalier	256,099	3.1%	-15.2%
Toyota Corolla	250,501	3.1%	+14.7%
Saturn	231,522	2.8%	-7.4%
Chevy Malibu	223,703	2.7%	+36.0%
Pontiac Grand Am	180,428	2.2%	-11.7%

Top-selling light trucks in 1998

Pickup		Sport/Utility		Van	
Ford F-series	787,552	Ford Explorer	431,488	Caravan	293,819
Chevy C/K	533,177	Jeep Grand Cherokee	229,135	Windstar	190,173
Ram Pickup	410,130	Ford Expedition	225,703	Econoline	169,899
Ford Ranger	328,136	Chevy Blazer	219,710	Villager	156,971

Top-selling cars by market segment in 1998

	Small	Middle	Large	Luxury
1st	Escort	Camry	LeSabre	DeVille
2nd	Cavalier	Accord	Grand Marquis	Town Car
3rd	Saturn	Taurus	Crown Victoria	Volvo 70

U.S. light vehicle market share (includes each company's total import and domestic volumes)

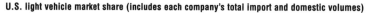

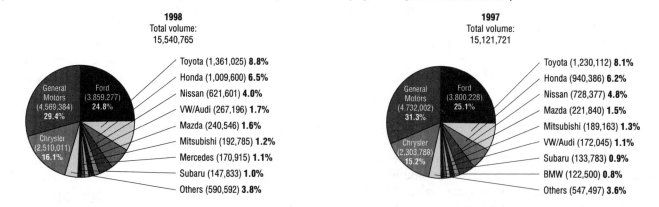

SOURCE: "Calendar 1998" in *Ward's Automotive Yearbook, 1999,* Ward's Communications, Southfield, MI, 1999

Trucks accounted for 53.7 percent of the total production in 1998; cars, for 46.3 percent. (See Table 4.1.) Production of sport utility vehicles (SUVs) accounted for a large part of the increase. SUVs, which are classified as light trucks, have become the fastest-growing sector of the motor-vehicle market. More than two million SUVs were pro-

FIGURE 4.1

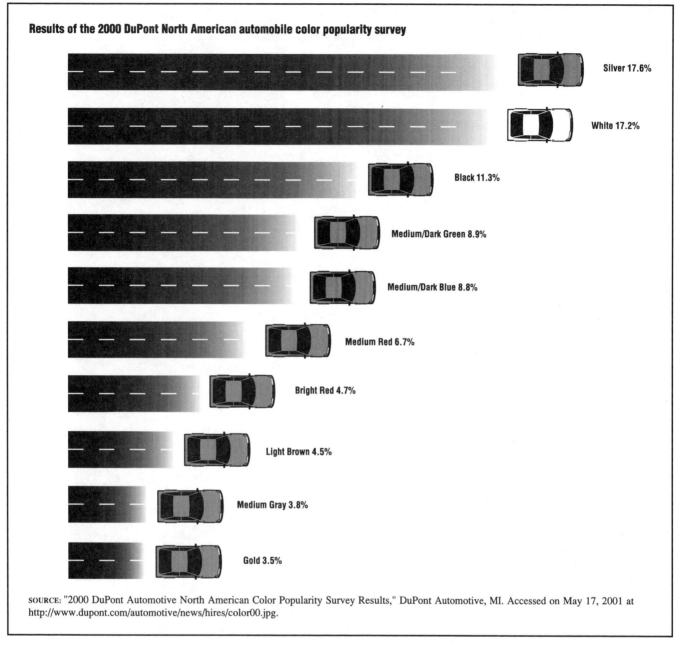

Results of the 2000 DuPont North American automobile color popularity survey

Silver 17.6%

White 17.2%

Black 11.3%

Medium/Dark Green 8.9%

Medium/Dark Blue 8.8%

Medium Red 6.7%

Bright Red 4.7%

Light Brown 4.5%

Medium Gray 3.8%

Gold 3.5%

SOURCE: "2000 DuPont Automotive North American Color Popularity Survey Results," DuPont Automotive, MI. Accessed on May 17, 2001 at http://www.dupont.com/automotive/news/hires/color00.jpg.

duced in 1997—an increase of 16 percent over 1996. That trend continued in 1998, with SUVs accounting for 18.9 percent of light-vehicle production in the United States.

In 1991, retail sales of new vehicles dropped to 12.5 million, the lowest level since 1983. Not surprisingly, both were recession years in the United States. To lure consumers back into dealer showrooms, the automobile industry launched massive advertising campaigns and offered rebates and discounts to buyers. In 1993, helped by a recovering economy, U.S. retail sales rose to 14.2 million vehicles. Sales rose again in 1994, to 15.4 million units, dipped slightly to 15.1 million in 1995, and rose to 15.5 million in 1998. In that year, the top-selling cars were the Toyota Camry, Honda Accord, and Ford Taurus. Most people who chose pickup trucks purchased the Ford

F-series, Chevrolet C/K, or Dodge Ram Pickup. The most popular SUVs were the Ford Explorer, Jeep Grand Cherokee, and Ford Expedition. In the van category, the Dodge Caravan, Ford Windstar, and Ford Econoline were the top sellers. (See Table 4.2.)

Car and truck sales have continued to show significant increases. According to the National Automobile Dealers Association (NADA), a record 17.4 million cars and trucks were sold in 2000. This topped a five-year average of over 15 million vehicles. Industry analysts expected a slight decline for 2001, but still forecast sales of more than 16 million cars and trucks.

Silver and white were the most popular colors among U.S. car and light-truck buyers in 2000. According to a

FIGURE 4.2

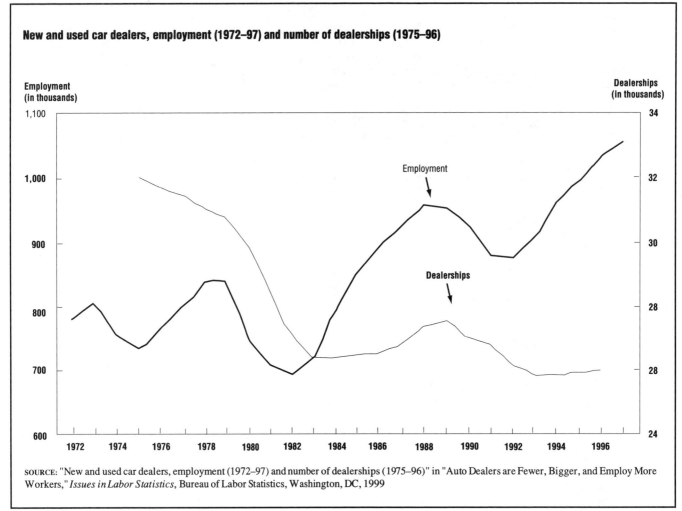

New and used car dealers, employment (1972–97) and number of dealerships (1975–96)

SOURCE: "New and used car dealers, employment (1972–97) and number of dealerships (1975–96)" in "Auto Dealers are Fewer, Bigger, and Employ More Workers," *Issues in Labor Statistics*, Bureau of Labor Statistics, Washington, DC, 1999

survey conducted by DuPont Automotive, silver was also the top choice in Europe and Asia. Medium brown and medium/dark green declined in popularity, as did former favorites like red and teal. (See Figure 4.1.) Color is important: research indicates that 40 percent of American consumers will switch vehicle brands if they cannot get their color of choice.

The number of new-car dealerships peaked at 51,000 in 1950. By 1996, there were only 26,000 car dealers, and by 2000, that figure had fallen to 22,250. Two factors responsible for this decline are the increasing popularity of new-car leasing and the arrival of the high-volume auto "superstore," which sells not only new cars but also high-quality used and previously leased vehicles. Another change in the industry is the increasing number of car sales on the Internet. With online car sales luring away more and more customers, many dealers have created their own, state-of-the-art Web sites to compete with these Internet sellers.

Although there are fewer new-car dealerships today, more people are employed by dealers than ever before. In 1950, there were fewer than 800,000 employees. By 1999,

that number had grown to more than 1.1 million. Figure 4.2 shows trends in the numbers of dealerships and numbers of employees for the years 1972–97.

According to NADA, in 1999, more used cars were sold (20.1 million) than new cars. There are three primary reasons for this growth in the used-car market. First, the average price of a new car in 1999 exceeded $24,000, up drastically from the 1987 average of $13,000. A used car cost an average of $13,200 in 1999. The second reason is that the increased popularity of leasing has expanded the supply of high-quality used cars, many of them fitted with options that the buyer cannot afford in a new vehicle. Finally, the overall quality of cars has improved to the point that, now, a used car offers excellent value for the money.

Even though the nation's economy is healthy, many potential new-car customers are choosing to either drive their old cars longer or head for the used-car lot. In 2000, the median age of cars on the road was 8.3 years, which was up significantly from the 1991 figure of 6.7 years. In 1997, the median age for trucks—including pickups, SUVs, and minivans—reached a record 7.8 years, but by 2000, that figure had declined to 6.9 years. Cars 14 years old and older accounted for more than 27 percent of all autos being driven in the late 1990s, compared with only 12 percent in 1980. In 1997, according to the Department of Transportation (DOT), 52.5 million cars on America's roads were at least 10 years old.

WORLD PRODUCTION

In 1998, 37.6 million cars and 14.7 million trucks and buses were manufactured worldwide. This was down slightly from 1997, when more than 38 million cars and 15 million trucks and buses were produced—the highest figure ever. (See Figure 4.3.) The United States' output in 1998 was 12 million units, besting even Japan (10 million)—at one time, the world's leader. Germany placed a distant third, with 5.7 million units. North America, Asia, and Western Europe each manufactured roughly one-third of the world's vehicles in 1998.

It is no longer an easy task defining the term "import"—particularly when it comes to cars. In the 1950s, U.S. companies, with few exceptions, made cars in the U.S., and foreign cars were made in other countries. Today, major foreign automakers, such as Honda, Toyota, and BMW, have manufacturing plants in the U.S., employing American workers and using many American-made parts. In addition, Chrysler, formerly one of the "Big Three" U.S. automakers, is now owned by DaimlerChrysler AG, of Germany, but Chrysler automobiles are still made in the U.S. To add to the complexity, Ford Motor Company, a U.S. company, has purchased controlling interests in Volvo, Mazda, Jaguar, Aston Martin, and Land Rover. Although owned by Ford, these companies still manufacture vehicles in their home countries. General Motors has also been active in overseas acquisitions, purchasing all or part of Isuzu, Suzuki, Subaru, Fiat, Saab, and Opel.

Japanese Imports Remain Strong

Because many Japanese do not own private vehicles—preferring, instead, to use public transportation to get to and from work—most vehicles made in Japan are sent abroad, especially to the United States. According to the Polk Company, in 1998 three of the five top-selling personal vehicles in the United States were Japanese: the Toyota Camry (first place), Honda Accord (second place), and Honda Civic (fourth place). (See Table 4.2.) Since 1996, domestic manufacturers have produced more trucks per year than cars, with the trend towards more trucks increasing. Between 1994 and 1998, trucks went from 47.1 percent of automobiles manufactured in America to 56.8 percent. Asian and European manufacturers are also producing more trucks per year than in the past, with increases of 5.9 and 5.2 percent respectively between 1994 and 1998. They still make many more cars than trucks however, with trucks making up only 29.2 percent of automobiles manufactured by Asian companies, and 8.9 percent of European companies' automobiles.

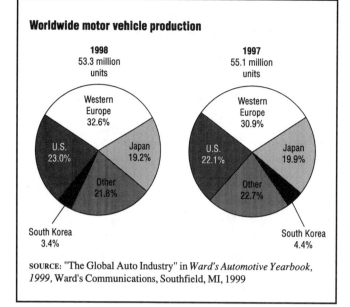

FIGURE 4.3

Worldwide motor vehicle production

1998
53.3 million units

Western Europe 32.6%
U.S. 23.0%
Japan 19.2%
Other 21.8%
South Korea 3.4%

1997
55.1 million units

Western Europe 30.9%
U.S. 22.1%
Japan 19.9%
Other 22.7%
South Korea 4.4%

SOURCE: "The Global Auto Industry" in *Ward's Automotive Yearbook, 1999,* Ward's Communications, Southfield, MI, 1999

American Car Sales in Japan

While Japanese imports account for a large segment of the U.S. vehicle fleet, relatively few American cars have been sold in Japan in the past. U.S. car manufacturers long expressed frustration over their inability to make inroads into Japan's auto market. These manufacturers felt that the Japanese market was essentially closed to them, because of the high import duties levied on many American cars and because of the difficulty of establishing dealerships in Japan.

The Japanese countered that the success of German auto manufacturers, such as Mercedes-Benz, BMW, and Volkswagen, in Japan was clear evidence that the American car manufacturers were not trying hard enough. According to a spokesperson for Nissan, Detroit was failing in its attempts to design cars specifically for the Japanese market: for instance, placing the steering wheel on the right instead of the left. In addition, none of the American companies built vehicles in Japan using Japanese workers.

In the early 1990s, American automakers pressed the U.S. government to negotiate more favorable trade agreements with Japan. Talks between representatives of the Japanese and U.S. governments continued from 1993 to 1995. The two sides failed to work out a bilateral trade agreement, and the talks finally broke down. On May 16, 1995, U.S. Trade Representative Mickey Kantor announced proposed tariffs of 100% on 13 models of Japanese cars imported into the U.S. Trade talks resumed to avoid these tariffs, which could have hurt trade on both sides. On June 28, 1995, the proposed tariffs were avoided when the U.S. and Japan signed the Automotive Trade Agreement, which made it much easier for American-made cars to be sold in Japan. U.S. carmakers have responded by starting

TABLE 4.3

Fuel economy standards for passenger cars and light trucks, model years 1978–2001 in miles per gallon (mpg)

Model Year	Passenger Cars	Light Trucks[1] Two-wheel Drive	Light Trucks[1] Four-wheel Drive	Combined[2, 3]
1978	18.0[4]	...	...	...
1979	19.0[4]	17.2	15.8	...
1980	20.0[4]	16.0	14.0	...[5]
1981	22.0	16.7[6]	15.0	...[5]
1982	24.0	18.0	16.0	17.5
1983	26.0	19.5	17.5	19.0
1984	27.0	20.3	18.5	20.0
1985	27.5[4]	19.7[7]	18.9[7]	19.5[7]
1986	26.0[8]	20.5	19.5	20.0
1987	26.0[9]	21.0	19.5	20.5
1988	26.0[9]	21.0	19.5	20.5
1989	26.5[10]	21.5	19.0	20.5
1990	27.5[4]	20.5	19.0	20.0
1991	27.5[4]	20.7	19.1	20.2
1992	27.5[4]	...	...	20.2
1993	27.5[4]	...	...	20.4
1994	27.5[4]	...	...	20.5
1995	27.5[4]	...	...	20.6
1996	27.5[4]	...	...	20.7
1997	27.5[4]	...	...	20.7
1998	27.5[4]	...	...	20.7
1999	27.5[4]	...	...	20.7
2000	27.5[4]	...	...	20.7
2001	27.5[4]	...	...	20.7

[1] Standards for model year 1979 light trucks were established for vehicles with a gross vehicle weight rating (GVWR) of 6,000 pounds or less. Standards for model year 1980 and beyond are for light trucks with a GVWR of 8,500 pounds or less.

[2] For model year 1979, light truck manufacturers could comply separately with standards forfour-wheel drive, general utility vehicles and all other light trucks, or combine their trucks into a single fleet and comply with the standard of 17.2 mpg.

[3] For model years 1982-1991, manufacturers could comply with the two-wheel and four-wheel drive standards or could combine all light trucks and comply with the combined standard.

[4] Established by Congress in Title V of the Motor Vehicle Information and Cost Savings Act.

[5] A manufacturer whose light truck fleet was powered exclusively by basic engines which were not also used in passenger cars could meet standards of 14 mpg and 14.5 mpg in model years 1980 and 1981, respectively

[6] Revised in June 1979 from 18.0 mpg.

[7] Revised in October 1984 from 21.6 mpg for two-wheel drive, 19.0 mpg for four-wheel drive, and 21.0 mpg for combined.

[8] Revised in October 1985 from 27.5 mpg.

[9] Revised in October 1986 from 27.5 mpg.

[10] Revised in September 1988 from 27.5 mpg.

SOURCE: "Table 1-1: Fuel Economy Standards for Passenger Cars and Light Trucks Model Years 1978 through 2001 (in MPG)" in *Twenty-Fourth Annual Report to Congress, 1999,* National Highway Traffic Safety Administration, Department of Transportation, Washington, D.C., 1999

to design cars tailored specifically to the needs of the Japanese market.

THE COST OF OWNING AND MAINTAINING A VEHICLE

Driving Is Not Cheap

The average new car cost more than $24,000 in 1999. This figure included optional equipment, such as air conditioning and automatic transmission, as well as state taxes and title costs. In addition to the purchase price, the owner of a new car has considerable operating costs, including gas and oil, tires, and maintenance. The cost of driving a car varies by the size of the car. In 1999, a small-car owner paid 9.2 cents in operating costs per mile; a midsize-car owner, 10.7 cents; a large-car owner, 12 cents; an SUV owner, 11.6 cents; and a van owner, 10.4 cents. In 2000 and 2001, the cost of gasoline rose sharply, adding significantly to American drivers' operating costs.

Car-ownership costs include insurance; license, registration, and taxes; depreciation; and finance charges. In 1999, a small-car owner paid $4,661 in ownership costs; a midsize-car owner, $5,275; a large-car owner, $6,445; an SUV owner, $6,332; and a van owner, $5,722. The total annual cost for a small car driven 20,000 miles was $7,256; for a midsize car, $8,219; a large car, $9,685; an SUV, $9,297; and a van, $8,628.

In 1927, Massachusetts became the first state to require drivers to carry auto liability insurance. Today, all states require drivers to show some proof of financial ability to pay in case of an accident, and most require drivers to show proof of liability insurance before they can register a vehicle or renew a vehicle registration. Not surprisingly, car insurance is big business. According to Dianna Gordon ("The High Price of Auto Insurance," *State Legislatures,* Denver, CO, March 1998) Americans paid an estimated $142 billion for auto insurance in 1997.

Insuring a car today is an expensive proposition. A survey by the National Association of Insurance Commissioners revealed that, in 1997, drivers in New Jersey paid the most for car insurance—an average of $1,125.89 a year. Washington, D.C. residents had the second-highest rates, at $1,039.34, followed by New York, at $952.82. At the other end of the scale, Iowa drivers paid the least for car insurance ($456.02), followed by South Dakota, ($476.26), and Wyoming ($477.48). The national average for 1997 was $705.87.

THE BEST ACCORDING TO DRIVERS AND EXPERTS

According to a 2000 J.D. Power and Associates survey of new-car owners, Saturn owners are the happiest with their vehicles. Cadillac and Lexus tied for second place, followed by Infiniti and, in a four-way tie, Buick, Land Rover, Mercedes-Benz, and Volvo.

In 2001, *Consumer Reports* magazine selected the Volkswagen Passat as its top choice in the family-sedan and station-wagon categories. The Honda Civic EX was chosen best small car, while the hybrid Toyota Prius, with an average fuel economy of 41 mpg, was selected best "green" (environmentally friendly) car. The Honda S2000 roadster ranked as the most fun to drive. Among SUVs, the Lexus RX300 was chosen as best midzise SUV, while the Toyota RAV4 was picked as best small SUV. The Toyota Tundra ranked as best pickup truck, and the Honda Odyssey as best minivan. The Mercedes-Benz E320 4Matic Wagon was selected best car overall.

TABLE 4.4

Domestic and import passenger car and light truck fuel economy averages for model years 1978–1999 in miles per gallon (MPG)

| Model Year | Domestic | | | Import | | | All Cars | All Light Trucks | Total Fleet | Light Truck Share of Fleet (%) |
	Car	Light Truck	Combined	Car	Light Truck*	Combined				
1978	18.7	...	...	27.3	...	...	19.9	...	...	...
1979	19.3	17.7	19.1	26.1	20.8	25.5	20.3	18.2	20.1	9.8
1980	22.6	16.8	21.4	29.6	24.3	28.6	24.3	18.5	23.1	16.7
1981	24.2	18.3	22.9	31.5	27.4	30.7	25.9	20.1	24.6	17.6
1982	25.0	19.2	23.5	31.1	27.0	30.4	26.6	20.5	25.1	20.1
1983	24.4	19.6	23.0	32.4	27.1	31.5	26.4	20.7	24.8	22.5
1984	25.5	19.3	23.6	32.0	26.7	30.6	26.9	20.6	25.0	24.4
1985	26.3	19.6	24.0	31.5	26.5	30.3	27.6	20.7	25.4	25.9
1986	26.9	20.0	24.4	31.6	25.9	29.8	28.2	21.5	25.9	28.6
1987	27.0	20.5	24.6	31.2	25.2	29.6	28.5	21.7	26.2	28.1
1988	27.4	20.6	24.5	31.5	24.6	30.0	28.8	21.3	26.0	30.1
1989	27.2	20.4	24.2	30.8	23.5	29.2	28.4	21.0	25.6	30.8
1990	26.9	20.3	23.9	29.9	23.0	28.5	28.0	20.8	25.4	30.1
1991	27.3	20.9	24.4	30.1	23.0	28.4	28.4	21.3	25.6	32.2
1992	27.0	20.5	23.8	29.2	22.7	27.9	27.9	20.8	25.1	32.9
1993	27.8	20.7	24.2	29.6	22.8	28.1	28.4	21.0	25.2	37.4
1994	27.5	20.5	23.5	29.7	22.0	27.8	28.3	20.8	24.7	40.2
1995	27.7	20.3	23.8	30.3	21.5	27.9	28.6	20.5	24.9	37.4
1996	28.1	20.5	24.1	29.6	22.2	27.7	28.5	20.8	24.9	39.4
1997	27.8	20.2	23.3	30.1	22.1	27.5	28.7	20.6	24.6	41.6
1998	28.1	20.5	23.3	30.0	22.9	27.6	28.7	20.9	24.6	44.5
1999	28.2	20.4	23.7	28.4	22.5	26.9	28.3	20.7	24.5	43.5

*Light trucks from foreign-based manufacturers.

NOTE: Beginning with model year 1999, the agency ceased categorizing the total light truck fleet by either domestic or import fleets.

SOURCE: "Table II-2: Domestic and Import Passenger Car and Light Truck Fuel Economy Averages for Model Years 1978-1999 (in MPG)" in *Twenty-Fourth Annual Report to Congress, 1999*, National Highway Traffic Safety Administration, Department of Transportation, Washington, D.C., 1999

GOVERNMENT REGULATION

The Corporate Average Fuel Efficiency (CAFE) Standards

In 1973, the Organization of Petroleum Exporting Countries (OPEC) imposed an oil embargo that provided a painful reminder to America of how dependent it had become on foreign sources of fuel. In 1972, the year before the embargo, the United States consumed 31 percent of the world's oil, and depended on foreign sources—particularly the Middle East—for 28 percent of that oil. As a result of the embargo, and in an effort to make the United States less dependent on foreign oil, Congress passed the 1975 Automobile Fuel Efficiency Act (PL 96-426), which set the initial Corporate Average Fuel Efficiency (CAFE) standards.

The CAFE standards required each domestic automaker—at the time, Ford, General Motors, Chrysler (now DaimlerChrysler AG), and American Motors (which merged with Chrysler)—to increase the average fuel economy of its new cars each year, until achieving 27.5 mpg by 1985. Under the CAFE rules, car manufacturers could still sell bigger, less efficient cars, but they also had to sell smaller, more efficient cars to meet the *average* fuel efficiency rates. Automakers that failed to meet each year's CAFE standards were required to pay fines. Those that managed to surpass the standards

earned credits that they could use in years when they fell below the CAFE requirements.

Faced with the CAFE standards, American car companies became much more inventive, using innovations such as electronic fuel injection and front-wheel drive to make their cars—particularly their large, luxury models—more fuel-efficient. Ford's prestigious Lincoln Town Car achieved better mileage in 1985 than its tiny Pinto did in 1974.

The Persian Gulf War in the early 1990s was another strong reminder to the United States of its continuing heavy dependence on foreign oil. In the war's aftermath, some members of Congress proposed raising the CAFE standards by as much as 40 percent, to 45 mpg for cars and 35 mpg for light trucks. Those in favor of raising the standards claimed that it would save about 2.8 million barrels of oil a day. They also noted that if cars became even more fuel-efficient, emissions of carbon dioxide—a "greenhouse" gas that has been identified as a primary contributor to global warming—would be significantly reduced. Moreover, the nation's millions of drivers would save money in gas costs. Despite some serious debate, these proposals gained little support.

Table 4.3 shows CAFE standards for 1978–2001, while Table 4.4 gives CAFE averages for 1978–99. In recent years, passenger cars have been losing market

TABLE 4.5

Alternative transportation fuels

Gasoline
A motor vehicle fuel that is a complex blend of hydrocarbons and additives, produced primarily from the products of petroleum and natural gas. Typical octane (R+M/2) level is 89.

Methanol
Commonly known as wood alcohol, CH_3OH, a light volatile flammable alcohol commonly made from natural gas. Energy content about half that of gasoline (implies range for the same fuel volume is about half that for gasoline, unless higher efficiency is obtained). Octane level of 101.5, allowing use in a high compression engine. Much lower vapor pressure than gasoline (low evaporative emissions, but poor starting at low temperatures).

Natural gas
A gas formed naturally from buried organic material, composed of a mixture of hydrocarbons, with methane (CH_4) being the dominant component. Octane level of 120 to 130. Energy content at 3,000 psi about one-quarter that of gasoline.

Liquid petroleum gas, LPG
A fuel consisting mostly of propane, derived from the liquid components of natural gas stripped out before the gas enters the pipeline, and the lightest hydrocarbons produced during petroleum refining.

Ethanol
Grain alcohol, C_2H_5OH, generally produced by fermenting starch and sugar crops. Energy content about two thirds of gasoline. Octane level of 101.5. Much lower vapor pressure than gasoline.

Hydrogen
H_2, the lightest gas. Very low energy content even as a cryogenic liquid, less than that of compressed natural gas. Combustion will produce no pollution except NO_x. Can be used in a fuel cell, as well as in an internal combustion engine.

Electricity
Would be used to run electric motors, with batteries as a storage medium. Available batteries do not attain high energy density, creating range problems. Fuel cells are an alternative to batteries. Fuel cells run on hydrogen, obtained either directly from hydrogen gas or from hydrogen "carriers" (methanol, natural gas) from which the hydrogen can be stripped.

Reformulated gasoline
Gasoline that has been reblended specifically to reduce exhaust and evaporative emissions and/or to reduce the photochemical reactivity of these emissions (to avoid smog formation). Lower vapor pressure than standard gasoline (which reduces evaporative emissions), obtained by reducing quantities of the more volatile hydrocarbon components of gasoline. Addition of oxygenates to reduce carbon monoxide levels.

SOURCE: "Table 4.7. Alternative Transportation Fuels" in *Replacing Gasoline: Alternative Fuels for Light-Duty Vehicles,* Office of Technology Assessment, Congress of the United States, Washington, D.C., 1990

share to SUVs. Because SUVs are classified as light trucks, they are subject to a less stringent fuel economy standard of 20.7 mpg.

ALTERNATIVE FUELS

The use of alternative, non-petroleum-based fuels is becoming an increasingly popular way to reduce vehicle emissions and overall energy use. Table 4.5 shows the variety of fuels that have been under consideration as alternative fuel sources for vehicles. According to the Department of Energy, there are about 456,000 alternative-fuel vehicles on American roads in 2001.

Ethanol

To help reduce the nation's dependence on imported oil, Congress in 1991 enacted the National Defense Authorization Act (PL 101-510). The law includes a provision directing federal agencies to purchase gasohol (gasoline containing 10 percent ethanol, a combustible liquid made from corn or other grains) when it is available at prices equal to or lower than those of gasoline. Federal agencies have taken a number of steps to encourage the use of gasohol. In 1991, Executive Order 12759 required federal agencies that operate more than 300 vehicles to reduce their gas consumption by 10 percent—an obvious incentive to use gasohol. Despite these measures, however, use of gasohol has increased only slightly, mainly because gasohol costs more than gasoline and is sometimes unavailable due to the high cost of transporting and storing it. Most support for gasohol seems to come from farm states, where the main ingredients for ethanol are grown.

Fueling stations for gasohol and ethanol are hard to find. The National Ethanol Vehicle Coalition in Jefferson City, Missouri now promotes the use of E85—which consists of 85 percent ethanol and 15 percent gasoline—but stations that sell ethanol are few and far between, and are concentrated in the Midwest. Nonetheless, Ford, General Motors, and DaimlerChrysler all produce flexible-fuel vehicles that can run on ethanol, gasoline, or a mixture of the two. These flex-fuel systems are available on several regular-production models, such as the Ford Taurus, Ford Explorer, Dodge Caravan, Chrysler Voyager, and Chrysler Town and Country.

Natural Gas and Propane

Drivers who choose to use propane and natural gas as fuel for their vehicles face the same dilemma as ethanol users: where to find a pump? Experts believe that any fueling system needs a large customer base, and no one will buy cars that run on alternative fuel until a fueling system has been set up. Natural gas requires less refinery work than gas, and is already distributed around the continental United States; it also burns more cleanly than gasoline. However, as Amoco, which has the largest natural gas reserves of any major gas company, found out, the public has been slow to embrace it.

In the mid-1990s, Amoco built 37 natural gas fueling stations (basically compressors that would fill a tank to the necessary pressure) for $250,000–$300,000 each. The company has closed all but four of the stations, and will close the rest as the contracts expire. Each pump sold only about the equivalent of 20 gallons a day. None of the pumps made enough money to pay for the installation costs, and only one pump—located in Atlanta, Georgia—came close to covering its maintenance costs. That pump was built for the 1996 Olympics, when natural gas-powered vehicles were brought in for display.

In 1997, Chrysler began producing a natural gas version of its Dodge Ram pickup truck. Ford now produces several natural gas vehicles, including a Crown Victoria and the Ford F-150 light truck. Chevrolet offers a natural gas version of the Chevy Cavalier. Some of these vehicles are designed as "bi-fuel users," which means that they can switch from natural gas to gasoline when needed. Existing automobiles and trucks can also be converted to natural gas systems. A number of cities—including New York; Las Vegas; and Long Beach, California—have taxicab fleets that use natural gas, and some large cities have even begun using natural gas in their bus fleets.

Gradually, compressed natural gas (CNG) fueling stations have been built across the county, but they are not yet commonplace. In 1999, there were only about 1,300 natural gas refueling stations in the country, compared with more than 200,000 gasoline stations. In some cases, local natural gas companies build the CNG stations; large companies that have their own fleet of natural gas vehicles build others. Still, it is difficult to sell CNG technology with few fueling stations, and even more difficult to establish a network of fueling stations without a mass market for the fuel. Nonetheless, according to the Department of Energy, the number of vehicles running on natural gas has grown from 69,000 in 1997 to more than 111,000 in 2001.

Propane, also called liquefied petroleum gas (LPG), has been the most successful alternative fuel to date, but its growth has not been as dramatic as that of natural gas. According to the Department of Energy, in 1997, about 71 percent of the approximately 368,000 alternative-fuel vehicles in the country used propane. In 2001, propane fuels about 59 percent of the 456,000 alternative-fuel vehicles.

Hydrogen

For decades, advocates of hydrogen have promoted it as the fuel of the future—abundant, clean, and cheap. Hydrogen researchers from universities, laboratories, and private companies claim their industry has already produced vehicles that could be ready to market if problems of fuel supply and distribution could be solved. Other experts contend that economics and safety concerns may limit hydrogen's wider use for decades.

Electric Vehicles

In the early days of the automobile, electric cars outnumbered internal-combustion vehicles. With the introduction of technology for producing low-cost gasoline, however, electric vehicles fell out of favor. But as cities became choked with air pollution—much of it attributed to heavy urban traffic—the idea of an efficient electric car once again emerged. In order to make it acceptable to the public, however, several considerations had to be addressed: How many miles could an electric car be driven before needing to be recharged? How light would the vehicle need to be? And could the car keep up with the speed and driving conditions of busy freeways and highways?

In 1993, tax breaks became available for people who buy cars that run on alternative energy sources; these breaks are especially generous for purchasers of electric cars. The breaks are intended to compensate for the price difference between electric cars and the average gas-powered car, and to jump-start production of these vehicles. By 2003, 10 percent of all new cars offered for sale in California must be zero-emission vehicles. New York, Massachusetts, Maine, and Vermont each have similar laws—all set to take effect in 2003.

Electric vehicles (EVs) come in three types: battery-powered; fuel cell; and hybrids, which are powered by both an electric motor and a small conventional engine.

BATTERY-POWERED VEHICLES. With a push from government mandates for cleaner cars, U.S. companies like General Motors and Ford began serious research into what could be the next generation of electric vehicles. In 1997, General Motors was the first to get an electric vehicle into production.

EV1, a two-seater by General Motors, was the first commercially available electric car. In 1999, GM introduced its second-generation EV1, the Gen II. It uses a lead-acid battery pack and has a driving range of approximately 95 miles. The Gen II is also offered with an optional nickel-metal hydride battery pack, which increases its range to 130 miles. EV drivers have a charger installed at their home, allowing them to recharge the car overnight. There are also some public places where rechargers are available. (See Figure 4.4.)

Ford is currently producing a Ford Ranger in an EV model, and also manufactures electric trucks for the U.S. Postal Service.

FUEL-CELL VEHICLES. A fuel cell uses an electrochemical process that converts a fuel's energy into usable electricity. Some experts think that, in the future, vehicles driven by fuel cells could replace vehicles with combustion engines. Fuel cells produce very little sulfur and nitrogen dioxide, and generate less than half the carbon dioxide of internal-combustion engines. Rather than needing to be recharged, they are simply refueled. Hydrogen,

FIGURE 4.4

The General Motors EV1 was the first modern electric car made available for the public to lease, in 1997. *(AP/Wide World Photos: Reproduced by permission.)*

natural gas, methanol, and gasoline can all be used with a fuel cell. A New York-based firm, Plug Power, L.L.C., together with Arthur D. Little and the Department of Energy, has successfully tested fuel-cell cars.

DaimlerChrysler's Mercedes-Benz division has produced the first prototype fuel-cell car. The NECAR4, which has zero-emissions and runs on liquid hydrogen. Unfortunately, the hydrogen must be kept cold at all times, which makes the design impractical for widespread use. However, they will soon have another model, which runs on methanol and should be more practical. The NECAR4 travels 280 miles on a full 11-gallon tank. The prototype was introduced in 1999, and consumers may be able to purchase a production version as early as 2004.

Ecostar—an alliance between Ford, DaimlerChrysler, and Ballard Power Systems—is working on developing new fuel cells to power vehicles. Other automakers have experimented with fuel-cell prototype cars as well, but these vehicles are not yet commercially available. They are expected to be on the roads by 2004.

HYBRIDS. Hybrid cars have both an electric motor and a small internal-combustion engine. A sophisticated computer system automatically shifts from using the electric motor to the gas engine, as needed, for optimum driving. The electric motor is recharged while the car is driving and braking. Because the gasoline engine does only part of the work, the car gets very good fuel economy. The engine is also designed for ultra-low emissions.

As of 2001, there are two hybrids on the market in the United States: the Toyota Prius, a comfortable sedan with front and back seating; and the two-passenger Honda Insight. Both cars were sold in Japan for several years before being introduced to the U.S. market. Ford has created a hybrid SUV, the Ford Escape, which will be available in 2003.

SAFETY ON THE ROAD

According to the National Safety Council, there were 41,300 motor-vehicle fatalities in 1999. These figures dropped 1 percent from 1997, and were down a significant 14.5 percent from the 48,290 fatalities in 1987. In 1999, approximately 2.2 million persons suffered nonfatal injuries in motor-vehicle accidents. Motor-vehicle fatalities were concentrated most heavily among the youngest people who can legally drive, and among the oldest segment of

FIGURE 4.5

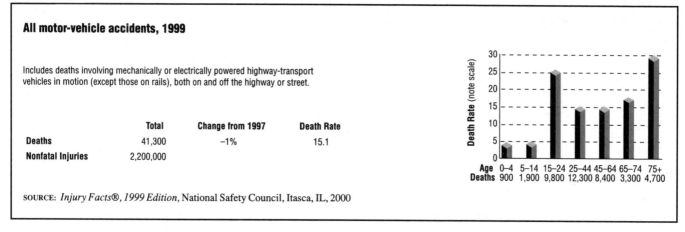

All motor-vehicle accidents, 1999

Includes deaths involving mechanically or electrically powered highway-transport vehicles in motion (except those on rails), both on and off the highway or street.

	Total	Change from 1997	Death Rate
Deaths	41,300	−1%	15.1
Nonfatal Injuries	2,200,000		

Age	0–4	5–14	15–24	25–44	45–64	65–74	75+
Deaths	900	1,900	9,800	12,300	8,400	3,300	4,700

SOURCE: *Injury Facts®, 1999 Edition*, National Safety Council, Itasca, IL, 2000

the population. Roughly 9,800 fatalities were from the 15 to 24 age group, representing 24 percent of all motor-vehicle deaths. While only 4,700 people over the age of 75 died in motor vehicle accidents, 11 percent of all fatalities, this was a very high number relative to their percentage of the population. (See Figure 4.5.) According to the National Highway Traffic Safety Administration (NHTSA), there were 41,611 auto-related fatalities in 2000.

What Makes a Safe Car?

As in the past, today's consumers are advised, for reasons of safety, to buy the largest car they can afford, with as many airbags and other safety features as they can afford. Experts advise buyers to look for features such as height-adjustable seat belts, antilock brakes, traction control, all- or four-wheel drive, and daytime running lamps. Car buyers are also advised to test-drive the car to make sure they can sit comfortably and use the gas and brake pedals with ease. It is also important, after buying the car, to read the owner's manual to learn how to use the various safety features.

Car manufacturers have sought to improve safety through a wide range of technological advances. Today's cars are designed not only to help prevent an accident, but to protect passengers if an accident should happen. Safety and car quality are foremost in the minds of many new-car buyers. The Insurance Institute for Highway Safety, which represents large national insurance firms and tests motor vehicles for safety, reports that 68 percent of car buyers claim safety as their most important criterion when shopping for a car.

Because of their inherent design, light trucks and SUVs often exhibit handling and balance inferior to that of a standard car. They often have a high profile and narrow base, making rollovers all too easy. Until recently, safety in the light-truck segment of the automobile market received less attention than safety in cars. However, as carmakers have come to recognize that "safety sells," and federal agencies have responded to citizen input, most new light

trucks must now meet the same standards as cars. Some of the safety features already in use on SUVs and light trucks include air bags, side-impact protection, rollover protection, head restraints, and antilock brake systems.

Despite the stricter safety requirements, light trucks still pose serious safety issues. In 1998, the NHTSA reported that SUVs are twice as likely to roll over as passenger cars—a fact that is reflected in the average rate of 98 rollover fatalities per million registered vehicles for SUVs, compared with 47 fatalities per million for cars.

Other government studies have shown that these vehicles' design and weight pose dangers to cars. DOT research shows that, when an SUV strikes a passenger car head-on, the occupants of the car are five times as likely to die as the occupants of the SUV. In side-impact collisions, car occupants are 30 times more likely to die. In a recent government test, a Chevrolet Lumina midsize sedan, a Ford Explorer SUV, a Chevrolet S-10 pickup truck, and a Dodge Caravan minivan were each crashed at 35 mph into the front, driver-side corner of a Honda Accord sedan traveling in the opposite direction at the same speed. The Explorer did the most damage; the Lumina, the least. After analyzing the crash-test dummies in the Accord, it was determined that the Explorer caused more than three times as much head injury, and twice as much chest and neck injury, as the Lumina. (The crash dummies were wearing seat belts, and the air bags deployed properly.)

SEAT BELTS. Seat belts have been standard equipment in cars for years. In 1984, New York became the first state to enact laws mandating their use. The old lap belt and shoulder restraints, however, have given way to newer, more effective devices. The "inertial reel" design, favored by safety experts and most European carmakers, allows a passenger to move around, but the reel pulls tight when the passenger sits upright.

As of 2001, 49 states and the District of Columbia have mandatory laws for the use of seat belts—New Hampshire is the lone exception—and all 50 states and

TABLE 4.6

Restraint use rates for passenger car occupants in fatal crashes, 1988 and 1998

Type of Occupant	Restraint Use Rate (Percent)	
	1988	1998
Drivers	40	61
Passengers		
Front Seat	37	60
Rear Seat	25	45
5 Years Old and Over	30	52
4 Years Old and Under	49	71
All Passengers	32	53
All Occupants	**36**	**58**

SOURCE: "Restraint use rates for passenger car occupants in fatal crashes, 1988 and 1998" in *Traffic Safety Facts 1998: Overview,* National Highway Traffic Safety Administration, U.S. Department of Transportation, Washington, D.C., 1999

the District of Columbia have laws mandating the use of child restraints. The NHTSA estimates that more than 15,000 lives could be saved annually if car occupants wore seat belts. Mandatory seat-belt laws help encourage people to buckle up. If caught driving without a seat belt, the driver can be ticketed. The highest fine, $50, is imposed in three states: New Mexico, New York, and Texas. Table 4.6 compares restraint use in 1988 and 1998.

In 1998 President Clinton signed the Transportation Equity Act for the Twenty-first Century (TEA-21; PL 105-178), reauthorizing the Intermodal Surface Transportation Efficiency Act (ISTEA; PL 102-240), which had expired in 1997. Under TEA-21, states are given incentives, such as grants, to improve transportation safety. One part of the incentive program allows the transportation secretary to make grants to states that adopt "primary" safety-belt laws (which allow a law-enforcement officer to pull a driver over for not wearing a seat belt). There are also grants for states that offer education courses in child protection.

CHILD SAFETY SEATS. Despite recent increases in the use of child safety seats, motor-vehicle accidents remain the leading cause of death among U.S. children ages one to four, according to the U.S. Department of Transportation. Researchers at the University of California, Irvine, found that adult drivers who fail to wear safety belts are one-third as likely to use car restraints for their young children as drivers who use safety belts themselves. About 60 percent of children killed in car crashes are not buckled in, although there are often child safety seats in the cars.

In 1997, 604 children under age five were killed in motor-vehicles crashes—more than half of those children were totally unrestrained. DOT estimates that, in 1998, 173 children's lives might have been saved if they had been buckled into child safety seats. The National Transportation Safety Board also points out that many parents

do not install child safety seats correctly and often do not realize it until after a crash. An estimated 80 percent of child seats in cars are not properly installed. The lack of correctly installed child car seats contributed to the deaths of about 50 preschool children in 1995. The NTSB supports a nationwide network of installation sites for child seats, where parents and other caregivers can go to learn how to install the seats correctly.

ERGONOMICS. "Ergonomics," as it relates to cars, is the science of design to promote easy visibility and driving. In the past, there was a trend toward unnecessary lights and controls on the dashboard. People spent too much time searching dashboard dials to find the gas gauge or the button to turn on the radio. In a car traveling 65 miles an hour, such distractions can cause major problems, including fatal accidents. To address this problem, manufacturers are trying to simplify driving; controls and displays are now generally well placed and easy to see and access, thus reducing the need for drivers to take their eyes off the road.

AIR BAGS. Frontal collisions are the cause of almost half of all vehicle fatalities. The NHTSA believes that air bags may be the most important safety breakthrough in decades. As of 1995, every new car, domestic and imported, had to offer air bags as an option. Beginning with model year 1998, all new passenger cars were required to have driver and passenger air bags along with safety belts. These laws applied to light trucks beginning in model year 1999.

Air bags are designed to inflate when a car is involved in a collision when traveling more than 14 miles an hour. The device inflates in one-thirtieth of a second, about the same length of time as it takes to blink. Some companies are now introducing air bags in side panels, which would protect drivers and passengers from side-impact collisions. Federal regulators, however, point out that some of the side air bags on cars' rear seats could injure children riding too close to a door. The NHTSA has urged manufacturers to test side air bags thoroughly to protect children from injury. The NHTSA has concluded that air bags, together with lap/shoulder belts, offer the most effective safety protection available for passenger-vehicle occupants.

This lifesaving technology does have a drawback. The air bags inflate quickly, to create a buffer between the upper body and the steering wheel, dashboard, and windshield. Ideally, the air bag is completely expanded before it comes in contact with the passenger. However, if the air bag is still inflating when it makes contact, injury and even death can occur. Passenger air bags have killed children and small adults by hitting them in the face. The force of the expanding air bag, which inflates at about 200 miles an hour, causes the neck to break. For this reason, the NHTSA warns that children and infants should always be placed in the back seat of the vehicle. If a small adult or child must sit in the front seat of the car, experts advise that the seat should be adjusted as far back as possible. Air bags are useless in rear-impact crashes or rollovers.

In 1999, Ford Motor Company announced that it had found a way to make air bags inflate more safely. The new system is based on a computer that senses the car's speed, the weight and positions of the people inside, and the severity of the collision. Some parts of the new system were installed in the 2000 Taurus. Within three years, the complete system should be on all new Fords sold in the United States. There will be no extra cost for the improved system. Although Ford was first to introduce the system, other automakers have similar systems in production.

The system will use a two-stage air bag that will expand at full force in higher-speed collisions and more slowly in lower-speed crashes. The bags will not inflate in minor, fender-bender accidents. The bag will inflate more slowly if the driver or passenger is sitting closer to it, and will also adjust to the weight of the rider, inflating with full force for a normal-size person and with less force for a smaller person.

ANTILOCK BRAKE SYSTEMS. Next to seat belts and air bags, antilock braking systems (ABS) are probably the most important recent innovation in auto technology. Skids are caused when one or more tires lose grip on the road and "lock up" (stop spinning). Antilock brakes help to prevent wheel lockup and help maintain steering control during sudden stops, evasive maneuvers, and on slippery surfaces. As with air bags, ABS is now a standard feature on most new cars—even on many inexpensive, entry-level models.

A December 1996 study by the Insurance Institute for Highway Safety found that cars with ABS are more likely than cars without ABS to be in fatal crashes, many of which involve only a single vehicle. Experts find this puzzling, but suggest that drivers may be taking more risks with antilock brakes, or not using them properly. Antilock brakes need hard, continuous pressure to engage, rather than the pumping action that many drivers learned when they first started driving.

FRONT-WHEEL, REAR-WHEEL, AND FOUR-WHEEL DRIVE. In a car, not every wheel is created equal. Most cars are equipped to send power from the engine to either the wheels in the front (front-wheel drive) or to the ones in the back (rear-wheel drive). Some deliver power to all four wheels at once (four-wheel or all-wheel drive). All have different advantages.

Front-wheel drive vehicles have the weight of the engine pushing down on the tires, thus improving traction on slippery roads. Large-car owners prefer rear-wheel drive. If a car is towing a boat or trailer, rear-wheel drive puts extra force on the rear axle, which creates extra traction. Also, rear-wheel drive is called the "driver-friendly" option. When the driver pushes down on the gas pedal, the weight is transferred to the rear wheels, allowing faster starts, which makes this option popular with sports-car owners and other high-performance drivers. Spreading the power to all four wheels (four-wheel drive) provides a better grip on the road, an important safety feature for driving on snow, ice, or unpaved roads.

A new alternative is the so-called Traction Control System (TCS), a variant of ABS. When a wheel begins to spin while accelerating, TCS gently brakes only the spinning wheel, thus slowing it down until it regains traction. The technology of TCS is simpler than that of four-wheel drive, and uses less fuel. In the future, TCS will possibly become a popular, and cheaper, option for new-car buyers.

SPACE-AGE TECHNOLOGY—SMART CARS. With the help of a new technology known as Intelligent Vehicle Highway Systems (IVHS), the cars of the future will largely be mobile computers and will provide safety features that not only reduce accidents, but also provide even more driver comfort. (See Figure 4.6.) Ford is working on an infrared vision system that can "see" through the heaviest fog, and has planned a new head-up display (HUD) that projects an image of what is ahead onto the windshield, so the driver can see it while still looking straight-ahead. The windshield display (similar to the displays used in advanced military fighter aircraft) provides a much better view of the road, showing lanes, cars, and obstacles, all without diverting the driver's attention from the conditions ahead.

U.S. safety officials are currently testing an electronic black box that automatically calls 911 for help after an auto accident. When the vehicle crashes, an electronic box beneath the back seat transmits the exact location to a satellite through the car's cellular telephone.

DaimlerChrysler is developing several crash-avoidance systems, including the Protector—a braking system that, using radar, senses when a vehicle is approaching an obstacle and brakes the car. They are also working on Lane Assistant and Lane Departure Warning systems, which use video-camera imaging to alert a driver whose attention may have strayed. General Motors also has HUDs in some of its vehicles, and the current Cadillac De Ville features a night-vision infrared system that can "see" beyond the range of the headlights and projects a virtual image near the front edge of the hood.

The NHTSA, in cooperation with industry and academia, is working to further develop these and other crash-avoidance systems. These include:

- Cruise-control systems that will automatically maintain a safe distance from the vehicle ahead

FIGURE 4.6

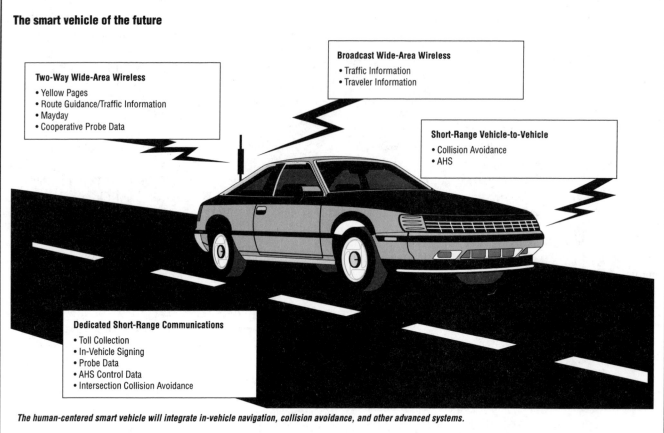

The smart vehicle of the future

Two-Way Wide-Area Wireless
• Yellow Pages
• Route Guidance/Traffic Information
• Mayday
• Cooperative Probe Data

Broadcast Wide-Area Wireless
• Traffic Information
• Traveler Information

Short-Range Vehicle-to-Vehicle
• Collision Avoidance
• AHS

Dedicated Short-Range Communications
• Toll Collection
• In-Vehicle Signing
• Probe Data
• AHS Control Data
• Intersection Collision Avoidance

The human-centered smart vehicle will integrate in-vehicle navigation, collision avoidance, and other advanced systems.

SOURCE: "Figure 4.7. The Smart Vehicle of the Future" in *National Intelligent Transportation Systems Program,* Federal Highway Administration, Washington, D.C., 1996

• Lane-tracking systems that will help alert and prevent a driver from drifting into the next lane or off the highway

• A cooperative intersection that will communicate data on traffic signals and oncoming vehicles, reducing the risk of intersection collisions

• Automated collision-notification systems that will guide emergency service personnel to the scene of an accident

High-tech equipment is available in many luxury cars today. Some of these "extras" include onboard navigational systems to guide drivers around traffic jams and bad weather; systems that automatically call for help if an air bag deploys; tires that can run for 50 miles after they've gone flat; and sensors that automatically turn on the wipers when they detect rain on the windshield.

Engineers in the United States, Europe, and Japan are developing "smart cars" capable of driving themselves. These cars enable a driver to enter a freeway, turn the driving responsibilities over to the car, and read the morning paper on the way to the office. In 1997, a combination of "smart cars," automated highways, and "intelligent" trans-portation systems was demonstrated in California. Cars followed along highway lanes, automatically slowing down and speeding up in response to traffic flow. The vehicles were directed by a combination of radar, video, and laser sensors commanded by an onboard computer. The National Automated Highway System Consortium sponsored the demonstration.

At many car-rental agencies across the United States, drivers can rent "smart cars" equipped with microcomputers, multiple antennas, a cellular phone, and a transponder that communicates with global-positioning satellites, providing the driver with information about traffic trouble spots and sightseeing attractions. In California, New Jersey, Texas, and other states, drivers on certain toll roads do not have to stop and pay tolls. A scanner, which "reads" a barcode sticker on the windshield, identifies the car and automatically debits the driver's account. Oklahoma has electronic collections systems on each of its 10 toll roads. Similar systems are also used overseas.

What Makes an Unsafe Driver?

According to the NHTSA, approximately three-quarters of the more than six million motor-vehicle collisions that occur annually on U.S. highways are caused because the drivers' attention is diverted in the moments before the collision. Although auto manufacturers continue to build safer and safer cars, it is primarily the driver who ultimately determines whether or not a car or truck will be involved in an accident. Many factors play a part in traffic fatalities, including the amount of alcohol consumed before getting behind the wheel, the age of the driver, and the speed of the vehicle. When other factors are controlled, driver characteristics far outweigh vehicle factors in predicting a crash.

ALCOHOL IMPAIRMENT. The use of alcohol as a contributing factor in fatal traffic accidents has been steadily decreasing since 1982—most likely because of tougher enforcement of liquor and DWI ("driving while intoxicated") laws in most states and the elevation of the drinking age to 21. In 1982, about 57 percent of all traffic fatalities involved an intoxicated driver (including motorcyclists). In 1998, the NHTSA reported that 38 percent of all traffic deaths involved a driver who was legally intoxicated (blood alcohol content, or BAC, of 0.10 or higher). This amounts to nearly 16,000 alcohol-related fatalities.

The highest rates of intoxication were for drivers in their early twenties. In 1999, about 36 percent of all drivers aged 21–24 involved in a fatal accident were legally drunk. The rate of intoxication decreased steadily with age, and only about 5 percent of all drivers over the age of 75 involved in fatal accidents were drunk.

TEA-21 (1998 Transportation Equity Act for the Twenty-First Century) provides incentive grants from a $500 million fund to states that have enacted, and are enforcing, laws that lower the legal-intoxication limit from 0.10 to 0.08 BAC. As further incentive, in October 2000, Congress passed the Transportation Appropriations Bill, which contains a mandate for 0.08 BAC as the national standard for impaired driving. According to the bill, states that do not enact 0.08 BAC laws by 2004 will have 2 percent of certain highway-construction funds withheld, with the penalty increasing to 8 percent by 2007. Currently, 24 states have adapted 0.08 BAC laws.

TELEPHONES. In 1999, more than 60 million people in the United States subscribed to wireless telephone services, and 85 percent of them used their cellular telephones while driving. Experts warn that the distraction caused by using a telephone while driving quadruples the risk of a crash—about the same degree of danger posed by driving while intoxicated. Research has indicated that it is driver lack of attention, not the act of dialing, that causes most of the accidents. The fact that the accident rate was the same whether the driver used a handheld phone or a hands-free unit seems to bear this out. In 2001, New York became the first state to pass a law prohibiting the use of handheld cell phones while driving. Other states are expected to follow.

Although the NHTSA agrees that cellular telephone use increases the risk of a collision, it points out that there are benefits of having a cell phone available in motor vehicles. It reported that, in 1996, cell phone users placed 2.8 million calls for emergency assistance, and that, in many instances, cellular phones reduced response time to automobile accidents, thus saving lives.

YOUNG DRIVERS AND ACCIDENTS. The youngest drivers, those under age 20, are the most likely to be involved in motor-vehicle accidents. After age 20, accident rates decrease—a notable exception being drivers over the age of 69 who are involved in traffic fatalities. (See Figure 4.7.) Drivers between the ages of 16 and 24, particularly male, are disproportionately high contributors to traffic accidents and highway deaths. Young drivers also pose the greatest loss for insurers. According to the American Automobile Association (AAA) Foundation for Traffic Safety, about 75 percent of all citations issued to young drivers are for speeding.

Young males consistently have the costliest insurance claims. Because of this, many insurance companies are referring young drivers to "high-risk" insurers, thus reducing the number of young policyholders they have to carry.

Many young people object to being penalized with high insurance rates, and are proposing "age-free" insurance policy programs. Under such policies, young drivers would be required to pass rigorous driver-education courses and sign a contract agreeing to abide by safety-belt laws, drinking-and-driving laws, and other safety regulations. In return, they would pay higher premiums for a specified time and then be eligible for refunds if they lived up to the terms of the contract.

Citing inadequate driver training as a primary contributor to poor driving skill among teenagers, several organizations, such as the NHTSA, the Insurance Institute for Highway Safety, and the National Association of Independent Insurers, have proposed a "graduated licensing" program. Under such a program, teens would not go directly from learner's permit to adult license. Rather, there would be an intermediate stage, involving more restrictions and greater supervision, during a teen's most dangerous driving years: 16–18.

OLDER DRIVERS AND ACCIDENTS. As the U.S. population matures, an increasing number of elderly drivers will be on the road. Given the number of miles they drive, elderly persons are disproportionately involved in collisions—particularly two-vehicle collisions. The National Safety Council has found that there are definite crash patterns among older drivers. They often fail to yield the right-of-way and sometimes do not pay attention to, or do not see signs and signals.

FIGURE 4.7

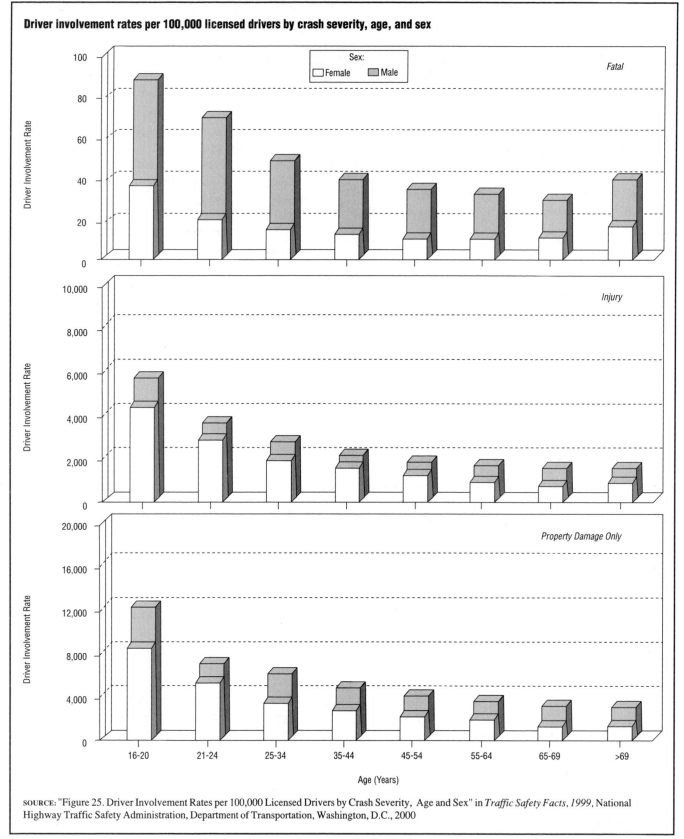

Driver involvement rates per 100,000 licensed drivers by crash severity, age, and sex

SOURCE: "Figure 25. Driver Involvement Rates per 100,000 Licensed Drivers by Crash Severity, Age and Sex" in *Traffic Safety Facts, 1999,* National Highway Traffic Safety Administration, Department of Transportation, Washington, D.C., 2000

Senior citizens' driving skills may diminish in other ways, including functional losses in vision, reaction time, and information processing. They often have more diffi-culty with backing and parking maneuvers. Older drivers also have the most accidents making left turns across traf-fic. The American Automobile Association's Foundation for Traffic Safety notes, however, that it is not chronologi-cal age, but the driver's overall functional ability that pre-

TABLE 4.7

Improper driving as a factor in accidents, 1999

Kind of improper driving	Fatal accidents 1999	Injury accidents 1999	All accidents 1999
Improper driving	72.6%	67.2%	62.2%
Speed too fast or unsafe	23.0	13.0	10.6
Right of way	20.1	25.8	22.9
Failed to yield	10.8	19.2	13.8
Passed stop sign	4.6	1.7	3.2
Disregarded signal	4.7	4.9	5.9
Drove left of center	9.6	1.7	1.3
Improper overtaking	1.1	0.9	1.2
Made improper turn	1.2	2.4	3.0
Followed too closely	0.5	3.4	6.3
Other improper driving	17.1	20.3	16.9
No improper driving stated	27.4	32.8	37.8
Total	100.0%	100.0%	100.0%

Note: Based on reports from 7 state traffic authorities.

SOURCE: *Injury Facts®, 1999 Edition*, National Safety Council, Itasca, Illinois, 2000

dicts difficulties. This means that one cannot assume that a driver who is 60 is necessarily more able to drive than one who is 75.

Older people enjoy the freedom and independence of driving their own cars as much as anyone else. Looking toward the future, when many more senior citizens will be on the road, the AAA has sponsored a study to develop guidelines for a "grade" licensing program—a license that carries some restrictions. Several states are already experimenting with this type of program, which attempts to balance the risks and safety needs of older drivers and others. The ultimate goal, however, is to help elderly drivers maintain their mobility for as long as they can safely do so.

ACCIDENTS AND DRIVER ERROR. Most accidents on the road result from the interaction of three factors: driver, vehicle, and road conditions. While motorists have little or no control over highway conditions, and usually cannot predict whether their vehicles will perform correctly, they can control the way they drive. Table 4.7 lists the various types of improper driving that resulted in injuries or fatal accidents in 1999.

Right-of-way mistakes and speeding caused the most accidents and fatal injuries. The National Safety Council estimated that, in 1999, driver error (improper driving) contributed to 62.2 percent of all accidents. (See Table 4.7.) Of collisions between motor vehicles, angle collisions (collisions that are not head-on, rear-end, rear-to-rear, or side-swipe) caused the most deaths, while rear-end collisions caused the most nonfatal injuries and injury accidents.

ROAD RAGE AND AGGRESSIVE DRIVING. "Aggressive" driving is erratic and dangerous driving characterized by speeding, tailgating, failing to yield, weaving in and out of traffic, passing on the right, making improper lane changes, and running stop signs and lights. Sometimes,

aggressive driving escalates into road rage, when a driver becomes enraged at another driver for tailgating, cutting them off, or some other real or imagined offense. The raging driver may make hand and facial gestures, scream, honk, flash headlights, or even try to intercept and confront the other driver. There have been many documented cases of enraged drivers running other cars off the road, shooting at vehicles, or even getting out of their cars to beat up or kill another driver.

Reported incidents of aggressive driving have soared in the past decade. According to the American Automobile Association, almost 13,000 people have been injured or killed since 1990 by aggressive driving. The AAA studied 10,037 aggressive-driving incidents between 1990 and 1997 and found that the majority of aggressive drivers are men between the ages of 18 and 26. However, the AAA also found that there were hundreds of cases involving older men and women who just "snapped." The NHTSA estimates that about one-third of all highway crashes, and about two-thirds of highway fatalities, can be blamed on aggressive driving.

An AAA member survey showed that most motorists named aggressive drivers as their top concern on the roads. More drivers feared the aggressive driver (44 percent) than the drunk driver (31 percent). Growing concern about these drivers and the problems they cause on the roads has led the NHTSA to develop a number of programs to combat aggressive driving, including an education-and-awareness program and a demonstration project to study effective enforcement.

Recently, Arizona passed a law that makes aggressive driving a misdemeanor offense. It is defined as an event in which a driver speeds and commits two or more listed traffic offenses. Such offenses include failing to obey a traffic control device, driving recklessly, passing a vehicle on the right by traveling off the pavement, changing lanes erratically, following too closely, and failing to yield the right-of-way. The offender may receive a fine of up to $2,500, six months in jail, and have his driver's license suspended for 30 days. In addition, the driver must attend driver-training classes. Arizona is the first state to make aggressive driving a legal offense, although eight other states have introduced similar bills in their legislatures.

While few would dispute that there are aggressive drivers on the road, some people believe that there is no such thing as road rage, and that it is a product of media hype. They point out that traffic injury and fatality rates are decreasing nationwide. According to Howard Fienberg, a research analyst at the Statistical Assessment Service in Washington, D.C., "If you give people the term road rage, which is not defined anywhere, they react to it and associate it with just about anything."

AUTO CRIME

Thefts

Car theft increased by nearly two-thirds between the early 1980s and early 1990s, peaking at 1.66 million incidents in 1991. Since then, car theft has been decreasing, with approximately 1.3 million vehicles stolen in 1998. Thanks to theft-prevention devices in many cars, there are fewer casual thieves, although there are still many professionals. When a professional auto thief steals a car, it is either quickly stripped for parts or shipped out of the country. In recent years, vehicle-recovery rates have fallen from about 70 percent to 50 percent.

The National Insurance Crime Bureau, an Illinois-based nonprofit organization that studies vehicle theft and insurance fraud, estimates that, each year, about 200,000 stolen vehicles—nearly half the number of stolen vehicles that are never recovered—are shipped out of the country. Many of these vehicles are hidden in big steel containers and loaded onto trucks, flatbed railcars, or cargo ships. Luxury SUVs, such as the Mercedes M-class and Lexus RX-300, are currently in the greatest demand overseas.

In 2000, the three most frequently stolen automobiles were the Honda Accord, Toyota Camry, and Oldsmobile Cutlass. The Accord and Camry have long been popular with car thieves, mainly because they're plentiful and many of their parts are interchangeable across different model years. But cars are not the only targets. According to an NICB study, in 1999, nearly one-third of the top 50 most frequently stolen vehicles were SUVs, pickup trucks, and minivans. The most popular of these were the full-size Chevrolet pickup, Jeep Cherokee and Grand Cherokee, Ford F-150, and Dodge Caravan.

A stolen vehicle's parts are often worth much more than the vehicle itself. According to the Texas Automobile Theft Prevention Authority, the estimated resale value of a 1993 GM Sierra is $7,000, while the estimated total value of stolen parts from that same vehicle is $21,000. Following is a breakdown of the black-market value of some of the major nonmechanical parts: camper top, $1,000; bumper assembly, $450; grille assembly, $865; hood, $410; radiator housing, $1,475; fenders, $490; horn, $65; wheels, $1,395; passenger-compartment items (panels, air outlets, glove compartment), $2,200; doors and hinges, $3,410; bed (tailgates, fuel-tank shield, bumper steps), $2,870; and trailer hitch, $275.

Air-Bag Theft

Officials estimate that more than 50,000 air bags are stolen each year nationwide. As air bags have become more common in cars and light trucks, they have also become more popular with thieves. Police estimate that half of all recovered stolen vehicles are missing at least one air bag. According to the National Insurance Crime Bureau, air bags—particularly those on the driver side—are easy to steal because they are held in place with only a few nuts and bolts. Stolen air bags can be sold for $100–$200, or, if passed off as new, for as much as $1,000.

Carjacking

Carjacking is the theft of a motor vehicle by force or threat of force. According to a 1996 survey, most carjackings occur at night, and 60 percent take place in open, public locations such as parking lots and at traffic lights.

According to the Bureau of Justice Statistics (*Carjackings in the United States, 1992–1996,* U.S. Department of Justice, Washington, D.C., March 1999), there were 48,787 attempted carjackings annually between 1992 and 1996, nearly half of which were completed. About 9 in 10 (92 percent) completed carjackings involved a weapon, compared with 75 percent of all attempted carjackings. About one-fourth (23 percent) of all completed carjackings involved injury to the victim, compared with 10 percent of all attempted carjackings. While all completed carjackings were reported to the police, only 57 percent of attempted carjackings were reported.

In many carjackings, the criminal is a young male who is after the vehicle or its expensive, flashy accessories. The carjacker may accost the person sitting in the vehicle, eject the victim, and then take off with the car. Some police officials believe that, because of the effectiveness of newer anti-theft devices, many thieves actually find it easier to steal cars at gunpoint.

GOVERNMENT ACTION AGAINST CARJACKING. In October 1996, President Bill Clinton signed the Carjacking Correction Act of 1996 (PL 104-217), which made carjacking a federal offense. The law stipulates that, if bodily injury is inflicted on the victim, the maximum sentence can be increased from 15 to 25 years. When Clinton signed the act, he said he hoped that it would increase the security of all Americans—particularly women.

In August 1997, Louisiana passed a state law called the "Shoot the Carjacker" law, giving motorists in that state the authority to use deadly force against their assailants. Although there are laws throughout the United States that permit self-defense, this is the first law that specifically focuses on self-defense against carjacking.

CHAPTER 5
BICYCLES, MOTORCYCLES, AND RECREATIONAL VEHICLES

BICYCLES

Bicycles played an important role in the development of roads in America. In the early 1900s, the bicycle was a form of transportation as well as recreation. However, the growing number of cars (and the increasing hazards for cyclists) led to a decline in the use of bicycles as a serious mode of transportation. More recently, bicycling has regained popularity as a form of exercise and sport. In 1998, the Bicycle Market Research Institute reported that the bicycle industry was a $5 billion-per-year industry, up from $4.3 billion in 1993 and $3.6 billion in 1990.

Who Rides Bikes?

According to the National Sporting Goods Association (NSGA) *Sports Participation in 2000* report, there was a slight increase in bicycle riders, from 42.4 million in 1999 to 42.5 million Americans in 2000, a growth of 0.3 percent. That was after a 2.6 percent decline from 43.5 million in 1998. Bicycling ranked as the fifth most popular recreational activity in the United States in 1999, which is down from a third place ranking in 1998. Industry figures show that 94.5 percent of those who ride bikes ride primarily for recreation and fitness, .3 percent participate in racing, and 5.2 percent ride bicycles mainly for transportation.

According to Richard Killingsworth, a health scientist for the Centers for Disease Control and Prevention (CDC) in Atlanta, Georgia, less than one percent of children between the ages of 7 and 15 rides a bike to school, and only 2.5 percent of youngsters who live within two miles of school ride their bikes there. These figures indicate a 60 to 70 percent decline from the 1970s. Analysts blame this drop on parental fears of crime and traffic, tight scheduling of organized play, fewer sidewalks, and more time spent watching television and playing computer games. Most of today's bicycle sales are to adult riders.

According to bicycle industry analysts, somewhat more men (53 percent) than women (47 percent) ride

bikes. Twenty-four million people ride mountain and hybrid (combination) bikes, and 1.7 million tour on their bicycles. According to Kevin Condit, marketing director for Adventure Cycling, a non-profit organization that offers tours and helps cyclists plan their own trips, interest in bicycle tours grew at about 10 percent per year through the 1990s.

COMMUTERS. Most bicycle commuters live on the West Coast, where 1 out of every 100 bicyclists travels to school or to the workplace by bike. Most bicycle commuters (80 percent) are male, and 70 percent of those are between the ages of 15 and 34. These bicycle riders are, on average, less educated and earn less than other commuters. (Cyclists in this age group earn approximately $24,000 per year, while the median income for noncyclists in the 15- to 34-year age group is about $29,000 annually.) On the other hand, middle-aged bike travelers, 45 to 54 years old, earn slightly more ($36,000) than other commuters of the same age group ($35,000).

Long Beach, California, has installed bikestations. Commuters who wish to bike to work ride to the bikestation, where a valet parks the cycle for the day. Bikestations also offer repairs, bike rentals, changing rooms, and outdoor cafés. They are part of a variety of new federally funded programs developed to encourage Americans to ride their bicycles.

MOUNTAIN BIKERS. Mountain biking officially took off as a sport in 1971, and became an Olympic event in 1996. The mountain bike has upright seating, 26-inch wheels, and larger tires that are more shock-absorbent than traditional road bike tires, making the ride more comfortable. Its range of gears allows for more versatility. According to the Bicycle Federation of America, mountain bikes made up 43 percent of bicycles sold by dealers and specialty retailers in 1998, down from 63 percent in 1995. Mountain bikes are now considered to be a

TABLE 5.1

Bicycles sold, 1973–2000

Year	Bicycles Sold (Millions), 20" and up wheel sizes	Bicycles Sold (Millions), all wheel sizes
2000	11.9*	18.1*
1999	11.6*	17.5*
1998	11.1*	15.8*
1997	11.0*	15.2*
1996	10.9	15.4
1995	12.0	16.1
1994	12.5	16.7
1993	13.0	16.8
1992	11.6	15.3
1991	11.6	
1990	10.8	
1989	10.7	
1988	9.9	
1987	12.6	
1986	12.3	
1985	11.4	
1984	10.1	
1983	9.0	
1982	6.8	
1981	8.9	
...1973	15.2 (record high)	

*Indicates projection from The Bicycle Council based on a compilation from numerous sources. The Bicycle Manufacturers Association no longer exists.

SOURCE: "A Look at the Bicycle Industry's Vital Statistics," in *2000 STATPAK,* National Bicycle Dealer's Association, Costa Mesa, CA, 2000

TABLE 5.2

Nonoccupant traffic fatalities, 1988–98

Year	Pedestrian	Pedalcyclist	Other	Total
1988	6,870	911	136	7,917
1989	6,556	832	107	7,495
1990	6,482	859	124	7,465
1991	5,801	843	124	6,768
1992	5,549	723	98	6,370
1993	5,649	816	111	6,576
1994	5,489	802	107	6,398
1995	5,584	833	109	6,526
1996	5,449	765	154	6,368
1997	5,321	814	153	6,288
1998	5,220	761	131	6,112

SOURCE: "Table 5: Nonoccupant Traffic Fatalities, 1988–1998," in *Traffic Safety Facts 1998: Overview,* National Highway Traffic Safety Administration, Washington, D.C., 1998

maturing segment of the industry. The declining sales of mountain bikes may be in part a reflection of an emerging market for what are being called "comfort" bicycles, which look very much like mountain bikes, but have soft saddles, a more upright seating position, and easier gearing.

A Positive Outlook for the Industry

Bicycle sales have experienced a series of ups and downs in the past several decades. A dramatic increase in gasoline prices in the 1970s and a growing concern over health and fitness combined to produce record overall sales of about 15.2 million bicycles in 1973. Sales then tumbled to 6.8 million in 1982, rose to 12.6 million in 1987, fell sharply to 9.9 million the following year, and reached 13 million in 1993. In 2000, an estimated 11.9 million bicycles were sold. (See Table 5.1.)

Bicycle sales are generally linked to two factors: market saturation and changing demographics. To continue the growth that bicycle sales enjoyed at their peak, owners would have to replace their bikes every three years. Currently, however, the average bike is replaced only once every seven years.

More companies are making a wider variety of cycles. Constant improvements are being made in design and materials, including aerodynamic handlebars and disc wheels. Indoor fitness equipment has also become an important part of the bicycle industry. Exercise bicycles and associated accessories have provided another path through which the bicycle industry can sell to people committed to physical fitness. Since cycling does not subject people to the pounding of some other sports, it can be a lifetime activity. About half the bicycle stores in the United States sell some indoor exercise equipment.

The Imports

In 1979, American manufacturers heavily dominated the U.S. bicycle market: 9 million domestic bikes were sold in the United States that year, compared to only 1.8 million manufactured overseas. By the late 1980s, the situation had changed, with 5.4 million bicycles imported, primarily from Taiwan and Korea, and only 4.5 million domestic bikes being sold.

In 1995, imports accounted for 42 percent of American bicycle sales. Among these, 52 percent came from the People's Republic of China (Mainland) and 42 percent from the Republic of China (Taiwan). In 1998, the statistics remained about the same, with nearly 60 percent of mass market bicycles produced in the United States and the rest coming from East Asia, primarily China. On the other hand, approximately 80 percent of specialty bicycles purchased in America are imported.

Bikes and Accidents

Bicycle riding can be a hazardous activity. Every year more than one million bicycle injuries are serious enough to require medical treatment. The National Highway Traffic Safety Administration (NHTSA) reported that 761 pedalcyclists were killed in 1998, down from 814 in 1997—about 2 percent of all traffic fatalities. (See Table 5.2.)

Fifty years ago, most bicyclists were children age 14 and under, and 48 percent of all deaths resulting from bicycle accidents came from this age group. In 1940, only 13 percent of those killed biking were age 25 and older, probably because riding a bike was then considered a

TABLE 5.3

Pedalcyclists killed, by related factors, 1999

Factors	Number	Percent
Riding, playing, working, etc., in roadway	178	23.7
Failure to yield right of way	137	18.3
Improper crossing of roadway or intersection	121	16.1
Failure to obey (e.g., signs, control devices, officers)	47	6.3
Not visible	40	5.3
Operating without required equipment	32	4.3
Failure to keep in proper lane or running off road	30	4.0
Darting into road	27	3.6
Inattentive (talking, eating, etc.)	27	3.6
Making improper turn	27	3.6
Erratic, reckless, careless, or negligent operation	20	2.7
Failing to have lights on when required	18	2.4
Improper lane changing	16	2.1
Riding on wrong side of road	16	2.1
Improper entry to or exit from trafficway	6	0.8
Other	61	8.1
None Reported	192	25.6
Unknown	19	2.5
Total Pedalcyclists	750	100.0

Note: The sum of the numbers and percentages is greater than total pedalcyclists killed as more than one factor may be present for the same pedalcyclist.

SOURCE: "Table 103: Pedalcyclists Killed, by Related Factors," in *Traffic Safety Facts 1999,* National Highway Traffic Safety Administration, Washington, D.C., 2000

TABLE 5.4

Teens and helmets

How often do you wear a helmet when riding a bicycle, motorcycle, or moped?

	All Teens (503)
All of the time	12%
Most of the time	13
Some of the time	11
Rarely	13
Never	37
Not applicable/don't ride these	14

SOURCE: "Teens and Helmets," in "Many Teens Have Cars Using Air Bags: Fewer Use Bike Helmets," *YOUTHviews,* vol. 6, no. 7, March 1999

child's activity. By 1998, however, the situation was far different, with persons ages 25 to 64 accounting for 46 percent of all deaths from bicycle accidents. Although one-third of pedalcyclists killed in traffic crashes in 1998 were between 5 and 15 years of age, the average bicycle fatality in 1998 was 25 years old.

Males (53 percent) make up a little more than half of all bike riders, but they are much more likely to be involved in bicycle accidents. In 1998, males accounted for more than 82 percent of the bike deaths. Not surprisingly, most of these fatal injuries (about 90 percent) involved collisions with motor vehicles. For 65 percent of the pedalcyclists killed, police reported one or more errors related to the cyclists' behavior. Table 5.3 shows that riding, playing, and working in the roadway (23.7 percent) and failure to yield the right-of-way (18.3 percent) accounted for most of the deaths, with improper crossing of roadway or intersection (16.1 percent) close behind.

Two factors affect cycling and safety. First, unlike the car driver, bicyclists are not surrounded by two or three tons of metal to help protect them in a crash or a fall. Second, most bicyclists do not wear protective helmets while riding.

BIKE HELMETS MAKE SENSE. Head injuries are the most common cause of death and serious disability in bicycling accidents. Riders who wear helmets reduce their risk of suffering brain damage in a biking accident by 85 percent. As of July 2001, there were bicycle helmet laws of some kind in 29 states, plus the District of Columbia.

According to the Bicycle Helmet Safety Institute, there are currently 19 state laws and 84 laws governing localities, with the majority being age-specific. For example, in California, all riders under age 18 and passengers under age 5 must wear a bicycle helmet. In 1998, Gallup International asked teens how often they wear a helmet when riding a bicycle, motorcycle, or moped (*YOUTHviews,* vol. 6, no. 7, March 1999). Gallup found that 37 percent of teenagers claimed they never wore a helmet when riding and 13 percent use their helmets "rarely." Another 12 percent wore their helmets all of the time, 13 percent wore one most of the time, and 11 percent claimed to wear a helmet some of the time. (See Table 5.4.) The NHTSA estimates that if all children ages 4 to 15 would wear helmets, 39,000 to 45,000 head injuries and 18,000 to 55,000 scalp and facial injuries would be prevented every year.

One of the biggest myths about bicycle riding is that lower speeds mean lower risk of injury. "Head injuries generally occur not because of the vehicle's speed, but because of vertical distance—how far your head travels to hit the pavement," observes Harry Hurt, director of the University of Southern California's Head Protection Research Laboratory and principal investigator in research involving motorcycle and bicycle accidents. Most non-fatal bicyclist injuries do not involve a collision with a car; according to the NHTSA, more than 50 percent involve hitting the roadway surface. According to Hurt, the average height of a person on a bicycle seat is 5.3 feet. At that distance, simply falling off the bike can cause the head to hit the pavement at 12.6 miles an hour, which can lead to death or irreversible injury to the brain. Other studies by Hurt show that a fall from slightly less than 4 feet, at 11 miles per hour, can cause fatal brain damage.

Governmental Support for Bicycles

In the 1990s the federal government took several steps to encourage bicycle use. Provisions of the 1990 Clean Air Act Amendments (PL 101–549), the 1991 Intermodal Surface Transportation Efficiency Act (ISTEA; PL 102–240), and the 1998 Transportation Equity Act for the

Twenty-first Century (TEA-21; PL 105–178) encourage local communities to build bicycling into their transit plans. The Clean Air Act sets standards for air quality and requires some metropolitan areas to develop methods to reach compliance. These include taking steps to make bicycling a more viable transportation alternative. The ISTEA gives an even greater boost to bicycling by requiring states and communities to develop transportation facilities and plans that include nonmotorized travel. TEA-21 is intended to reduce air pollution from cars and cut back on traffic congestion by encouraging greater use of carpools, mass transit, and bicycles. TEA-21 also continues to support transportation enhancements like bicycle and pedestrian trails and scenic highways.

Under ISTEA and TEA-21, individual cities and counties may decide how to spend their funds. Seattle installed bike racks on the front of all its city buses, and Massachusetts is building 50 miles of paved bike paths north and west of Boston.

RAILS-TO-TRAILS. Rails-to-Trails is part of a government program, started in 1986, designed to make use of the hundreds of miles of unused, scenic railway corridors. The Department of Transportation's Surface Transportation Board approves the abandonment of a line after service has been discontinued. Then a voluntary agreement, called railbanking, may be entered into between the railroad company and a park agency, allowing the rail corridor to be used as a trail until the railroad company might need the corridor for service again. In 1997, at least 52 trails were included in the railbanking program. A former 321-mile-long Nebraska railroad track is being converted to a biking, hiking, and horseback riding trail, which, when completed, will account for 11 percent of a coast-to-coast trail of interconnected pathways.

By 2001, Rails-to-Trails had turned more than 11,000 miles of tracks in all states into public recreation trails for bikers, hikers, and horseback riders. The organization hopes an additional 20,000 miles will be built by 2005. Much of the funding for Rails-to-Trails conversions was provided by ISTEA. The preservation and conversion of abandoned railway corridors was one of 10 specific non-highway projects for which ISTEA set aside $3.3 billion. TEA-21 continued to dedicate funds to improving bicycle access through more Rails-to-Trails. The Department of Transportation also contributes money ($30 million annually) through its Recreation Trails Trust Fund.

International Bicycle Use

In countries with high automobile ownership, the extent of bicycle use has varied depending upon public policy and popular attitudes. During the past two decades, railway passengers in Japan and Europe have increasingly relied on bicycles as a convenient, affordable way to reach train stations. On a typical workday, nearly three million bicycles are parked at rail stations throughout Japan. In Denmark, 25 to 30 percent of commuter rail passengers set off from home on bikes.

CHINA. Before 1979, the Chinese government rationed bicycles, and only one person in four or five had a bicycle. Following government reforms of 1979, rationing ended, and one-third of the road space was set aside for cyclists. By 1990, in Shanghai, there was one bicycle for every 2.2 residents—one of the highest densities in the world. By 1998, there were 9 million bicycles in Beijing, and one street, East Xisi (pronounced shee-suh), was used by up to 6,000 cycles per hour during peak periods. In October 1998, in order to ease traffic jams, East Xisi Street was turned into a bicycle-free zone, with its bicycle lanes turned into car lanes. The government has not indicated whether other bike-free streets are planned.

GREAT BRITAIN. The Millennium Commission in Great Britain created a project called Sustrans, sustainable transport. A major part of this was a National Cycle Network, which, in June 2000, opened a network of 5,000 miles of continuous traffic-free and traffic-calmed routes for cyclists and for walkers. The goal is to expand this network to 10,000 miles in urban and rural areas all over Great Britain. The project is funded by the national lottery, local authorities, and donations, and aims to reduce the emissions that contribute to global warming.

FINLAND. In 1993, the city of Helsinki, Finland instituted a policy aimed at doubling the number of trips residents make on bicycles by the year 2005, in order to benefit both city traffic and public health. The goal was to increase cycling to 12 percent of all trips made in the city, from 6 percent in 1995. They also set a goal to reduce the number of cycling accidents by one-third. City planners created bike lanes, bike parking, and bike-and-ride transit opportunities to facilitate the use of pedal transportation, along with marketing efforts to educate the public on the benefits of cycling. Officials expect millions of dollars in savings on road surfacing and infrastructure, parking spaces, reduction of noise, congestion, and emissions. They also expect a reduction in healthcare costs, due to increased fitness.

Finnish cycling interests continue to work to obtain more government funding to support the program and encourage local efforts to increase bicycle use. Another example of this is a private and public-sector partnership, the Helsinki City Bikes program, which was launched in June 2000. Riders deposit a 10 FIM (Finnish Markka) coin for the use of a specially designed City Bike. Upon arriving at their destination, they return the bike to one of 25 bike stands and get their deposit back. The bicycles are only for use in central Helsinki and are easy for law enforcement officers to spot if riders take them out of the City Bikes zone, because of their bright green color.

New Kinds of Cycles

Bicycle innovators are working on new developments for the industry. In the United States, several models of electric-powered bicycle are on the market. One, called the EV Warrior is currently being used by some police departments. It is similar to a moped, but with an electric motor which emits no pollution. Built from molded plastics, the cycle is outfitted like a recreational bike, but has two 24-volt, 900-watt electric motors mounted on the rear wheel. The vehicle can reportedly run for 20 miles before it needs a charge.

Electric bike manufacturers are targeting commuters, environmentalists, college students, messengers, and older riders, or anyone who enjoys riding a bike but would like a little help on the hills. The electric bicycle models cost from around $1,000 to $1,900. Manufacturers are also making kits that can be installed on any bicycle, to turn it into an electric bike for half the cost of a ready-made model.

MOTORCYCLES

Motorcycling is both a popular recreational activity and a source of transportation. According to the Motorcycle Industry Council, Inc., a non-profit, national trade association that represents the motorcycle industry, an estimated 27 million people rode motorcycles, scooters, or ATVs (all-terrain vehicles) in 1997. Industry and government agencies also use motorcycles in such varied activities as law enforcement, agriculture, and land resource management.

The Federal Motor Vehicle Safety Standards (FMVSS) define three categories or model types of motorcycles:

- On-highway—motorcycles designated for use on public roads. These machines must meet FMVSS standards. Generally, these vehicles have relatively large engines. Two-thirds (66 percent) of on-highway motorcycles have an engine displacement over 749 cubic centimeters (cc)

- Off-highway—motorcycles and all-terrain vehicles (ATVs) not meeting FMVSS standards. As a rule, these cycles have small engines. Nearly all (89 percent) off-highway cycles in use have an engine displacement less than 350cc

- Dual Purpose—motorcycles designed with the capability for use on public roads and off-highway recreational use. They must also be certified by the manufacturer as being in compliance with FMVSS. Over half (56 percent) have an engine displacement of less than 350cc

While the Federal Motor Vehicle Safety Standards regulate motorcycle manufacturing standards, the 50 states govern their operation, registration, and licensing.

Two-thirds (67 percent) of American motorcyclists ride on-highway bikes. About one of five (21 percent) ride

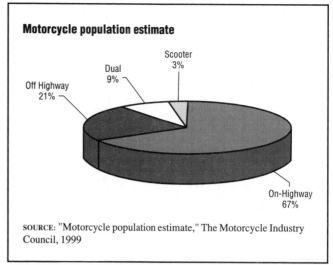

FIGURE 5.1

Motorcycle population estimate

SOURCE: "Motorcycle population estimate," The Motorcycle Industry Council, 1999

off-highway motorcycles (this percentage does not includes ATVs, only motorcycles); 9 percent ride dual-purpose cycles, and 3 percent own scooters. (See Figure 5.1.)

Numbers

In 1998, there were 5.16 million motorcycle owners in the United States. Regionally, California has traditionally led the nation in motorcycle population. In 1997, the estimated motorcycle population in California totaled 913,400 bikes; Texas was a distant second with 372,100. In 1997, 40,140 new units were sold in California and 20,030 were sold in Florida. The South had the highest motorcycle population in 1997, with 28 percent of all motorcycles in use. One-third (35 percent) of the nation's motorcycles, scooters, and ATVs were bought in the five states of California, Texas, New York, Florida, and Ohio. (See Table 5.5.)

Motorcycle sales peaked in 1970, when more than 1.1 million new units were sold. In 1980, 1 million were sold, and the number declined throughout the decade. The industry, however, recovered strongly during the 1990s, with sales growing 66 percent from 1992 to 1998. In 1997, 356,000 new motorcycles, domestic and imported, were sold, up from 309,000 in 1995 and 330,000 in 1996. Meanwhile, retail sales of new motorcycles reached $2.9 billion in 1997, more than double the retail sales of $1.3 billion in 1990. (See Table 5.5.)

A Global Industry

Just like the automobile industry, the motorcycle industry is a global enterprise. In countries as far flung as Thailand, Italy, Indonesia, Germany, and China, the motorcycle is a method of transportation and a form of fun and sport. In 1997, in the United States, six major brands of motorcycles accounted for 96 percent of the nation's new registrations. Japanese brands accounted for 67.5 percent of the market, with Honda selling 27.9 percent of the motorcycles, followed by Yamaha (13.6

TABLE 5.5

Value of the retail marketplace, 1997

State	Est. economic value of the retail marketplace ($000's)	Estimated retail sales of new motorcycles Units	($000's)
Alabama	$ 135,540	4,710	$ 33,750
Alaska	41,430	1,350	9,570
Arizona	190,700	6,320	49,010
Arkansas	82,250	2,890	19,000
California	1,129,850	40,140	319,780
Colorado	209,820	8,810	70,290
Connecticut	174,980	5,120	44,970
Delaware	34,330	960	7,930
Dist. of Columbia	13,330	470	3,080
Florida	569,820	20,030	161,260
Georgia	207,130	9,410	69,390
Hawaii	N/A	N/A	N/A
Idaho	77,920	2,950	18,000
Illinois	488,220	15,780	142,560
Indiana	288,420	9,880	76,720
Iowa	150,200	4,290	37,400
Kansas	99,040	2,950	24,660
Kentucky	117,750	4,220	29,320
Louisiana	155,900	4,820	38,820
Maine	69,300	1,870	16,010
Maryland	186,420	5,760	47,910
Massachusetts	201,970	7,540	67,660
Michigan	421,130	15,550	122,970
Minnesota	193,490	7,330	64,820
Mississippi	70,520	2,330	16,290
Missouri	177,120	5,740	45,520
Montana	53,200	1,640	12,290
Nebraska	60,650	1,590	14,010
Nevada	104,420	3,570	26,000
New Hampshire	133,780	3,650	33,310
New Jersey	268,270	10,060	86,650
New Mexico	86,790	2,670	21,610
New York	493,220	16,510	144,020
North Carolina	307,240	12,360	99,240
North Dakota	34,500	900	7,970
Ohio	487,120	16,710	142,240
Oklahoma	136,950	4,380	34,100
Oregon	169,070	6,040	43,450
Pennsylvania	500,720	17,340	146,210
Rhode Island	37,230	950	8,600
South Carolina	161,280	5,660	41,450
South Dakota	48,610	1,230	11,230
Tennessee	191,170	6,340	49,130
Texas	535,190	18,510	151,490
Utah	107,910	3,930	26,870
Vermont	32,990	920	7,620
Virginia	200,120	8,040	67,040
Washington	188,120	8,700	63,020
West Virginia	77,320	2,430	17,860
Wisconsin	283,530	9,580	91,580
Wyoming	36,020	1,070	8,320
U.S. Total	$10,222,000	356,000	$2,892,000

SOURCE: "Value of the retail marketplace, 1997," The Motorcycle Industry Council, 1999

FIGURE 5.2

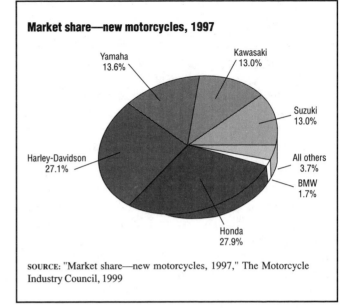

Market share—new motorcycles, 1997

Yamaha 13.6%
Kawasaki 13.0%
Suzuki 13.0%
All others 3.7%
BMW 1.7%
Harley-Davidson 27.1%
Honda 27.9%

SOURCE: "Market share—new motorcycles, 1997," The Motorcycle Industry Council, 1999

and a median household income of $44,100. Of the motorcycle owners employed in 1998, nearly one-half (46 percent) held professional/technical or mechanic/craftsmen positions. Table 5.6 shows the motorcycle owner profiles for 1980, 1985, 1990, and 1998. In 1998, one-third (33 percent) of motorcycle enthusiasts had median household incomes of $50,000 or more, up significantly from 2.4 percent in 1980, 6.1 percent in 1985, and 19.9 percent in 1990.

Although the largest percentage of motorcycle riders were high school graduates in the four years profiled, each of the years showed an increasing proportion of cyclists having attended college. The proportions of college graduates and those who had a post-graduate education have also steadily increased since 1980, while those who completed only grade school or some high school have declined. (See Table 5.6.) Motorcycle ownership has become attractive to growing numbers of middle-aged, often economically successful individuals, seeking the perceived freedom of driving a motorcycle.

In 1998, according to the Motorcycle Industry Council, the greatest percentage of motorcycle owners were male (92 percent), but the percentage of female owners grew to 8 percent in 1998, up from 6 percent in 1990 and 1 percent in 1960. Women riders spent more (an average of $317) than men ($255) on riding apparel in 1998. Female riders had more education than male riders; 57 percent of women had attended college, compared to 44 percent of men. Women (37 percent) were more likely than men (32 percent) to hold white-collar positions.

In 1998, about three-fourths (76 percent) of motorcycle owners paid cash for their bikes. Eighty-two percent of

percent), and Kawasaki and Suzuki with 13 percent each. Harley-Davidson was the second most popular motorcycle with 27.1 percent market share, while BMW ranked sixth with 1.7 percent. (See Figure 5.2.)

The Motorcycle Owner—A Profile

In 1998, the average motorcycle owner was 38 years old and married, with a high school diploma or more,

TABLE 5.6

TABLE 5.7

Motorcycle ownership profile by age, marital status, education, occupation and income: 1980, 1985, 1990 and 1998

Motorcyclist fatalities and injuries, 1989–99

	Percent of Total Owners			
	1998	**1990**	**1985**	**1980**
Age				
Under 19	3.9%	8.3%	14.9%	24.6%
18–24	10.6%	15.5%	20.7%	24.3%
25–29	10.3%	17.1%	18.7%	14.2%
30–34	11.7%	16.4%	13.8%	10.2%
35–39	15.9%	14.3%	8.7%	8.8%
40–49	26.2%	16.3%	13.2%	9.4%
50 and Over	18.4%	10.1%	8.1%	5.7%
Not Stated	3.0%	2.0%	1.9%	2.8%
Median Age	38.0 yrs.	32.0 yrs.	27.1 yrs.	24.0 yrs.
Mean Age	38.4 yrs.	33.1 yrs.	28.5 yrs.	26.9 yrs.
Household income for prior year				
Under $10,000	2.5%	3.4%	10.9%	9.1%
$10,000–$14,999	2.3%	4.4%	9.3%	13.0%
$15,000–$19,999	4.6%	7.8%	11.6%	13.9%
$20,000–$24,999	6.1%	10.8%	8.4%	12.9%
$25,000–$34,999	13.3%	21.4%	18.3%	12.5%
$35,000–$49,999	19.9%	19.6%	14.4%	5.9%
$50,000 and Over	33.0%	19.9%	6.1%	2.4%
Don't Know	18.3%	12.7%	21.0%	30.3%
Median	$44,100	$33,100	$25,600	$17,500
Martial status				
Single	39.8%	41.1%	47.6%	51.7%
Married	59.2%	56.6%	50.3%	44.3%
Not Stated	1.0%	2.3%	2.1%	4.0%
Highest level of education				
Grade School	2.7%	5.9%	7.5%	13.5%
Some High School	8.7%	9.5%	15.3%	18.9%
High School Graduate	36.6%	39.4%	36.5%	34.6%
Some College	28.3%	25.2%	21.6%	17.6%
College Graduate	15.9%	12.4%	12.2%	9.2%
Post Graduate	6.2%	5.2%	5.2%	3.1%
Not Stated	1.6%	2.4%	1.7%	3.1%
Occupation of owner				
Professional/Technical	29.4%	20.3%	19.0%	18.8%
Mechanic/Craftsman	16.4%	13.1%	15.1%	23.3%
Laborer/Semi-Skilled	12.3%	24.1%	23.2%	20.7%
Manager/Proprietor	7.6%	9.3%	8.9%	8.6%
Service Worker	7.3%	6.6%	6.4%	7.1%
Clerical/Sales	3.9%	6.8%	7.8%	9.3%
Farmer/Farm Laborer	2.8%	2.1%	5.1%	4.6%
Military	2.5%	1.5%	1.6%	1.9%
Other	14.7%	13.1%	4.6%	0.0%
Not Stated	3.1%	3.1%	8.3%	5.7%

Note: Percentages based on owners employed.

SOURCE: "Motorcycle ownership profile by age, marital status, education, occupation and income: 1980, 1985, 1990 and 1998," The Motorcycle Industry Council, 1999

Year	Fatalities	Registered Vehicles	Fatality Rate*	Vehicle Miles Traveled (millions)	Injury Rate**
1989	3,141	4,420,420	7.1	10,371	30.3
1990	3,244	4,259,462	7.6	9,557	33.9
1991	2,806	4,177,365	6.7	9,178	30.6
1992	2,395	4,065,118	5.9	9,557	25.1
1993	2,449	3,977,856	6.2	9,906	24.7
1994	2,320	3,756,555	6.2	10,240	22.7
1995	2,227	3,897,191	5.7	9,797	22.7
1996	2,161	3,871,599	5.6	9,920	21.8
1997	2,116	3,826,373	5.5	10,081	21.0
1998	2,294	3,879,450	5.9	10,260	22.4
1999	2,472	—	—	—	—

Year	Injuries	Registered Vehicles	Injury Rate*	Vehicle Miles Traveled (millions)	Injury Rate**
1989	83,000	4,420,420	189	10,371	805
1990	84,000	4,259,462	198	9,557	882
1991	80,000	4,177,365	193	9,178	876
1992	65,000	4,065,118	160	9,557	681
1993	59,000	3,977,856	149	9,906	600
1994	57,000	3,756,555	153	10,240	561
1995	57,000	3,897,191	147	9,797	587
1996	55,000	3,871,599	143	9,920	557
1997	53,000	3,826,373	137	10,081	526
1998	49,000	3,879,450	126	10,260	477
1999	50,000	—	—	—	—

* Rate per 10,000 registered vehicles.
** Rate per 100 million vehicle miles traveled.
— = not available.

SOURCE: "Table 1: Motorcyclist Fatalities and Injuries and Fatality and Injury Rates, 1989–1999," in *Traffic Safety Facts 1999: Motorcycles*, National Highway Traffic Safety Administration, Washington, D.C., 2000

from 30.3 (1989) to 22.4 deaths (1998) per 100 million miles. (See Table 5.7.)

The number of injuries also fell, from 83,000 in 1989 to 50,000 in 1999. Meanwhile, the injury rate tumbled from 805 injuries per 100 million miles traveled in 1989 to 477 in 1998. (See Table 5.7.)

The Motorcycle Industry Council attributes part of the decline in fatalities and injuries to increased participation in *RiderCourse* education and training programs developed by the Motorcycle Safety Foundation. These programs, designed for both beginning and experienced riders, are generally supported by state funding and administered by state agencies. Attendance at these programs rose from less than 80,000 in 1988 to almost 130,000 in 1997. (See Figure 5.3.) Safety helmet laws and a greater recognition of the dangers of drinking and driving have also contributed to the decline.

Nevertheless, when a motorcycle is involved in an accident, the rider's chances of being seriously hurt or killed are much higher than if he or she were riding in a vehicle that afforded more protection (car, truck, bus, etc.). In 1998, the mortality rate per registered vehicle for

on-highway motorcyclists stated that they rode for pleasure, and three-fourths (77 percent) rode in suburban or rural areas.

An Improving Safety Record

Over just one decade, the safety record for motorcycles has improved dramatically. In 1989, 3,141 people were killed on motorcycles. By 1999, this number had dropped to 2,472. While the number of miles traveled by motorcyclists hovered around 10 billion per year between 1989 and 1998, the fatality rate dropped during this period

FIGURE 5.3

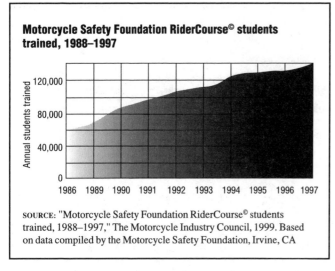

Motorcycle Safety Foundation RiderCourse© students trained, 1988–1997

SOURCE: "Motorcycle Safety Foundation RiderCourse© students trained, 1988–1997," The Motorcycle Industry Council, 1999. Based on data compiled by the Motorcycle Safety Foundation, Irvine, CA

FIGURE 5.4

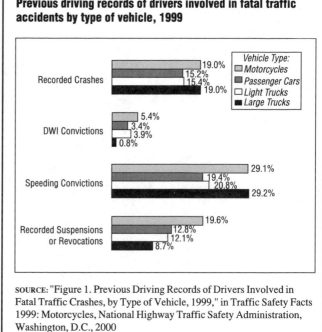

Previous driving records of drivers involved in fatal traffic accidents by type of vehicle, 1999

SOURCE: "Figure 1. Previous Driving Records of Drivers Involved in Fatal Traffic Crashes, by Type of Vehicle, 1999," in Traffic Safety Facts 1999: Motorcycles, National Highway Traffic Safety Administration, Washington, D.C., 2000

motorcyclists was 3.5 times higher than the fatality rate for automobile occupants. The injury rate was 1.4 times higher than for auto riders. Motorcycles make up 2 percent of all registered vehicles in the United States and account for only 0.4 percent of all vehicle miles traveled. But in 1998, motorcycle riders were 16 times as likely to die in a crash as occupants of a car. In 1999, motorcycles accounted for 6 percent of total traffic fatalities, 7 percent of all occupant fatalities, and 2 percent of all occupant injuries.

Most cyclists involved in fatal accidents have little or no professional instruction or training, and many do not have valid operating licenses. Nearly one of five motorcycle operators involved in fatal crashes in 1999 had previously been in an accident, and 5.4 percent had at least one previous driving while intoxicated (DWI) conviction. Nearly one-fifth (19.6 percent) had previous license suspensions, and 29.1 percent had prior speeding convictions. (See Figure 5.4.)

Severity of injury is directly related to speed, motorcycle size, and the amount of alcohol involved. Fatal motorcycle crashes in 1999 involved a higher percentage of intoxicated drivers (blood alcohol levels of 0.10 grams per deciliter or greater) than any other type of fatal vehicle crashes—28 percent for motorcycles, 20 percent for light trucks, 18 percent for passenger cars, and 1 percent for large trucks. Almost half (42 percent) of the 1,045 motorcycle operators who were killed in single-vehicle motorcycle crashes in 1999 were intoxicated, and three-fifths (61 percent) of those killed in single-vehicle crashes on weekend nights were intoxicated. (See Figure 5.5.)

The Helmet Issue

One of the things that makes motorcycling attractive to some people is the freedom of riding in the open air, although this can have its drawbacks, such as bad weather, insects flying into the driver's face, and debris flying up

from the road. As a result, motorcycle gear was invented to offer riders comfort and protection.

The most important piece of equipment for a motorcyclist is a helmet. Helmets protect the head in two ways. The outer shell resists penetration and abrasion, while the inner portion absorbs the shock by slowly collapsing on impact. Both the outer shell and the inner liner spread the force of an impact throughout the entire helmet. When a rider collides with the pavement while wearing a protective helmet, it should be not unlike landing head first on a thick cushion.

In addition, a motorcycle helmet reduces wind noise and windblast and deflects insects and pebbles that fly into the rider's face. (See Figure 5.6.) The helmet with an ANSI or Snell sticker means that it conforms to the standards of the American National Standards Institute or the Snell Memorial Foundation.

As of 1999, 21 states, the District of Columbia, and Puerto Rico require helmet usage by all motorcycle operators and passengers. In 26 states, only minors (drivers under 18 or 21) are required to wear helmets. Three states (Colorado, Illinois, and Iowa) have no laws requiring helmet use. (See Table 5.8.) In 1997, Arkansas and Texas amended their helmet laws, which had mandated universal use of helmets, to then require only that motorcycle drivers under 21 had to wear helmets. In the following year, helmet use decreased dramatically in those states. In 1998, motorcyclist fatalities increased by 21 percent in Arkansas and by 31 percent in Texas.

FIGURE 5.5

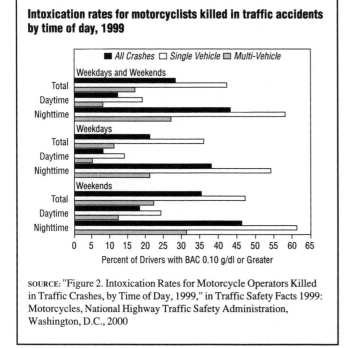

Intoxication rates for motorcyclists killed in traffic accidents by time of day, 1999

Percent of Drivers with BAC 0.10 g/dl or Greater

SOURCE: "Figure 2. Intoxication Rates for Motorcycle Operators Killed in Traffic Crashes, by Time of Day, 1999," in Traffic Safety Facts 1999: Motorcycles, National Highway Traffic Safety Administration, Washington, D.C., 2000

FIGURE 5.6

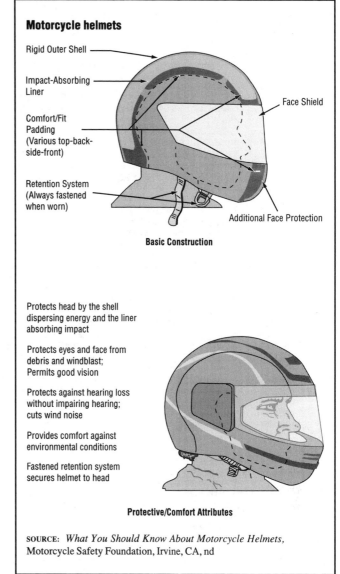

Motorcycle helmets

Rigid Outer Shell

Impact-Absorbing Liner

Comfort/Fit Padding (Various top-back-side-front)

Retention System (Always fastened when worn)

Face Shield

Additional Face Protection

Basic Construction

Protects head by the shell dispersing energy and the liner absorbing impact

Protects eyes and face from debris and windblast; Permits good vision

Protects against hearing loss without impairing hearing; cuts wind noise

Provides comfort against environmental conditions

Fastened retention system secures helmet to head

Protective/Comfort Attributes

SOURCE: *What You Should Know About Motorcycle Helmets,* Motorcycle Safety Foundation, Irvine, CA, nd

According to the National Highway Traffic Safety Administration (NHTSA), an unhelmeted motorcyclist involved in a crash is 40 percent more likely to incur a fatal head injury and 15 percent more likely to incur a non-fatal head injury than a helmeted motorcyclist. A Crash Outcome Data Evaluation System (CODES) study found that motorcycle helmets are 67 percent effective in preventing brain injuries and that unhelmeted motorcyclists involved in crashes were more than three times more likely to suffer brain injury than those using helmets.

Industry experts estimate that helmets are 29 percent effective in preventing fatal injuries to motorcyclists. The NHTSA estimated that helmets saved the lives of 551 in 1999. If all motorcyclists had worn helmets, 326 more lives could have been saved that year.

RECREATIONAL VEHICLES

Recreational vehicles (RVs) come in a variety of shapes and sizes, suited to the various needs of those who want to take the comforts of home with them when they travel. The Recreation Vehicle Industry Association (RVIA) recognizes five basic types of RVs: motor homes, travel trailers, folding camping trailers, truck campers, and van conversions. Motor homes and vans are motorized, while the rest must be towed or mounted to other vehicles.

Many RVs have comfortable beds, modern kitchens and bathrooms, and dining and living rooms. Many offer homelike luxuries, such as televisions, air conditioning, and microwave ovens. In 1998, some of the most popular electronic extra features included in RVs were surround-sound stereos, CD players, TVs, VCRs, and video game systems. New high-tech options include bedrooms that convert into offices, featuring a dedicated spot for computer and internet jacks, and moving walls that expand the interior living space for added comfort once the RV is parked. Known as a slideout, this feature allows the owner to electronically push a portion of the RV's exterior wall outward up to three and one-half feet to enlarge the living, dining, sleeping, or kitchen area. The only limitation on such amenities is cost. Costs for standard RVs range from an average of $5,600 for a folding camping trailer to $94,000 for a large motor home. (See Figure 5.7.)

Special luxury RVs, including buses designed for people to live in them for extended periods, can be very expensive. "Liberty Lady," a luxury model RV, sells in the $900,000 range and features brass fixtures, etched glass, and paneling. There are two TVs (one in the front and another in the back), four "environment zones" for

TABLE 5.8

State motorcycle helmet use requirements

State	Original Law	Subsequent Action, Date(s) and Current Status
AL	11/06/67	Helmet use required for all riders.
AK	01/01/71	Repealed effective 7-1-76 except for persons under 18 years of age, and all passengers.
AZ	01/01/69	Repealed effective 5-27-76 except for persons under 18 years of age.
AR	07/10/67	Helmet use required for all riders. Repealed effective 8/1/97 except for certain riders.
CA	01/01/85	Helmet use required by riders under 15 1/2 years of age. Effective 1-1-92 helmet use required for all riders.
CO	07/01/69	Repealed effective 5-20-77.
CT	10/01/67	Not enforced until 2-1-74. Repealed effective 6-1-76. Effective 1-1-90 adopted requirement for helmet use by persons under 18.
DE	10/01/68	Repealed effective 6-10-78 except for persons under 19 years of age. Also requires that a helmet be carried on the motorcycle for persons 19 and older.
DC	10/12/70	Helmet use required for all riders.
FL	09/05/67	Helmet use required for all riders.
GA	08/31/66	Helmet use required for all riders.
HI	05/01/68	Repealed effective 6-7-77 except for persons under 18 years of age.
ID	01/01/68	Repealed effective 3-29-78 except for persons under 18 years of age.
IL	01/01/68	Repealed effective 6-17-69 after being declared unconstitutional by the State Supreme Court on 5-28-69.
IN	07/01/67	Repealed effective 9-1-77. Effective 6-1-85 adopted requirement for helmet use by persons under 18.
IA	09/01/75	Repealed effective 7-1-76.
KS	07/01/67	7-1-67 to 3-17-70 for all cyclists. 3-17-70 to 7-1-72 only for cyclists under 21 years of age. 7-1-72 to 7-1-76 for all cyclists. 7-1-76 to 7-1-82 applied only to persons under 16 years of age. After 7-1-82 applies only to persons under 18 years of age. to 7-1-82 applied only to persons under 16 years of age. After 7-1-82 applies only to persons under 18 years of age.
KY	07/01/68	Helmet use required for riders under 21 years of age, riders operating with instruction permits, riders with less than 1 year of riding experience, and/or riders who do not provide proof of health insurance to county.
LA	07/31/68	Repealed effective 10-1-76 except for persons under 18 years of age. Readopted for all cyclists effective 1-1-82. Repealed effective 8-15-99 except for riders under age 18 and those who do not have a health insurance policy with medical benefits of at least $10,000.
ME	10/07/67	Repealed effective 10-24-77. Amended effective 7-3-80 to require use by cyclists under 15 years of age.
MD	09/01/68	Repealed effective 5-29-79 except for persons under 18 years of age. Effective 10-1-92 helmet use required for all riders.
MA	02/27/67	Helmet use required for all riders.
MI	03/10/67	Repealed effective 6-12-68. New law adopted effective 9-1-69. Helmet use required for all riders.
MN	05/01/68	Repealed effective 4-6-77 except for persons under 18 years of age.
MS	03/28/74	Helmet use required for all riders.
MO	10/13/67	Helmet use required for all riders.
MT	07/01/73	Repealed effective 7-1-77 except for persons under 18 years of age.
NE	05/29/67	Never enforced. Declared unconstitutional by State Supreme Court and repealed effective 9-1-77. Effective 1-1-89 helmet use required for all riders. required for all riders.
NV	01/01/72	Helmet use required for all riders.
NH	09/03/67	Repealed effective 8-7-77 except for persons under 18 years of age.
NJ	01/01/68	Helmet use required for all riders.
NM	05/01/67	Initial law applied only to cyclists under 18 years of age and to all passengers. Law requiring helmet use by all cyclists adopted effective 7-1-73. Repealed effective 6-17-77 except for persons under 18 years of age. effective 7-1-73. Repealed effective 6-17-77 except for persons under 18 years of age.
NY	01/01/67	Helmet use required for all riders.
NC	01/01/68	Helmet use required for all riders.
ND	07/01/67	Repealed effective 7-1-77 except for persons under 18 years of age.
OH	04/02/68	Repealed effective 7-1-78 except for persons under 18 years and first year novices.
OK	04/27/67	4-27-67 to 4-7-69 helmet use required for all motorcyclists. From 4-7-69 to 5-3-76 for cyclists under 21 years of age. 5-3-76 for cyclists under 18 years of age. cyclists under 18 years of age.
OR	01/01/68	Repealed effective 10-4-77, except for persons under 18 years of age. Effective 6-16-89 helmet use required for all riders. PA09/13/68 Helmet use required for all riders.
RI	06/30/67	Repealed effective 5-21-76 except for passengers on motorcycles. Effective 7-01-92 helmet use required for operators under 21 years of age, all passengers, and first year novices. years of age, all passengers, and first year novices.
SC	07/01/67	Repealed for ages 21 and over effective 6-16-80.
SD	07/01/67	Repealed effective 7-1-77 except for persons under 18 years of age.
TN	06/05/67	Helmet use required for all riders.
TX	01/01/68	Repealed effective 9-1-77 except for persons under 18 years of age. Effective 9-1-89 helmet use required for all riders. Effective 9-1-97 helmets required for riders under 21, those who have not completed a rider training course, and those without $10,000 medical insurance. 9-1-97 helmets required for riders under 21, those who have not completed a rider training course, and those without $10,000 medical insurance.
UT	05/13/69	Helmets required only on roads with speed limits of 35 mph or higher. Effective 5-8-77 law changed to require helmet use only by persons under 18 years of age. by persons under 18 years of age.
VT	07/01/68	Helmet use required for all riders.
VA	01/01/71	Helmet use required for all riders.
WA	07/01/67	Repealed effective 7-1-77. 7-1-87 helmet use required for riders under 18. Effective 6-8-90 helmet use required for all riders.
WV	05/21/68	Helmet use required for all riders.
WI	07/01/68	Repealed effective 3-19-78 except for persons under 18 years of age, and for all holders of learner's permits.
WY	05/25/73	Repealed effective 5-27-83 except for persons under 18 years of age.
PR	07/20/60	Helmet use required for all riders.

• 21 states plus the District of Columbia and Puerto Rico require helmet use for all riders.
• 26 states require helmet use for certain riders.
• 3 states do not require helmet use for riders.

SOURCE: "Table 124: Status of State Motorcycle Helmet Use Requirements," *Traffic Safety Facts, 1999,* Department of Transportation, National Highway Traffic Safety Administration, Washington, DC, 2000

FIGURE 5.7

RV types and terms

Recreation vehicle/RV (AR'-Vee)n.— A recreation vehicle, or RV, is a motorized ot towable vehicle that combines transportation and temporary living quarters for travel, recreation and camping. RVs do not include mobile homes, off-road vehicles or snowmobiles. Following are descriptions of specific types of RVs and their average retail price.

TOWABLES
An RV designed to be towed by a motorized vehicle (auto, van, or pickup truck) and of such size and weight as not to require a special highway movement permit. It is designed to provide temporary living quarters for recreational, camping or travel use and does not require permanent on-site hook-up.

$14,200
Conventional travel trailer
Ranges typically from 12 feet to 35 feet in length, and is towed by means of a bumper or frame hitch attached to the towing vehicle.

$22,600
Fifth-wheel travel trailer
This unit can be equipped the same as the conventional travel trailer but is constructed with a raised forward section that allows a bi-level floor plan. This style is designed to be towed by a vehicle equipped with a device known as a fifth-wheel hitch.

$5,000
Folding camping trailer
A recreational camping unit designed for temporary living quarters which is mounted on wheels and connected with collapsible sidewalls that fold for towing by a motorized vehicle.

$11,000
Truck camper
A recreational camping unit designed to be loaded onto or affixed to the bed chassis of a truck, constructed to provide temporary living quarters for recreational camping or travel use.

MOTORIZED
A recreational camping and travel vehicle built on or an integral part of a self-propelled motor vehicle chassis, It may provide kitchen, sleeping, and bathroom facilities and be equipped with the ability to store and carry fresh water and sewage.

$75,000
Motor home (Type A)
The living unit has been entirely constructed on a bare, specially designed motor vehicle chassis.

$43,000
Van camper (Type B)
A panel type truck to which the RV manufacturer adds any of the two following conveniences: sleeping, kitchen and toilet facilities. Also 110/120-volt hook-up, fresh water storage, city water hook-up and a top extension to provide more head room.

$47,000
Motor home (Type C)
This unit is built on an automotive manufactured van frame with an attached cab section. The RV manufacturer completes the body containing the living area and attaches it to the cab section.

$27,000
Conversion vehicles
Vans, trucks and sport utility vehicles manufactured by an automaker then modified for transportation and recreation use by a company specializing in customized vehicles. These changes may include windows, carpeting, paneling, seats, sofas, and accessories.

SOURCE: Recreational Vehicle Industry Association. Available at: http://www.rvia.org/consumers/recreationvehicles/types.htm

heating and air conditioning, a VCR and sound system, and a satellite dish. This RV also boasts a combination washer-dryer, full-size refrigerator, microwave and two-burner stove, closet with motorized carousel, and an outdoor entertainment center that includes another TV and stereo system. Other, more expensive models (up to $1.3 million) feature a 51-inch projection screen TV, global positioning equipment, air-operated pocket doors (similar to those seen on Star Trek), and a monitor that permits the owner to see who is at the front door.

Recreational Vehicles Sales

Deliveries of new RVs, including conversion vehicles (CVs), peaked in 1972 at just over 583,000 units. A sharp increase in fuel prices due to the 1973 Mideast oil embargo cut deliveries almost in half by 1974, but an expanding economy produced a rally during most of the remainder of the 1970s. Table 5.9 shows that, in 1980, a general recession dragged combined deliveries of recreation and conversion vehicles down to 178,500 units. Thereafter, deliveries climbed until 1989, when they dropped again.

The economic downturn of the early 1990s reversed the growth trend, and sales slipped 30 percent between 1988 and 1991, to only 293,700 RVs and CVs purchased. By almost every measure, 1994 marked an exceptional year for the RV industry. Total RV deliveries grew to 518,800, the highest since 1978. Retail value of those shipments was $12.2 billion, the largest sales volume ever to

TABLE 5.9

Recreational/Conversion vehicles shipments data, 1978–2000

| Year | Recreation Vehicles | | | Conversion Vehicles | | |
	RV Unit Shipments (In 000)	% Change From Prior Year	RV Retail Value (In Billions)	CV Unit Shipments (In 000)	%Change From Prior Year	CV Retail Value (In Billions)
1978	389.9	- 5.8	4.077	136.4	+ 13.6	$1.606
1979*	199.2	- 48.9	2.123	108.5	- 20.5	1.458
1980*	107.2	- 46.2	1.168	71.3	- 34.3	.783
1981	133.6	+ 24.6	1.253	99.8	+ 4.0	1.448
1982	140.6	+ 5.2	1.879	111.3	+ 11.5	1.539
1983	196.6	+ 39.8	3.485	104.2	- 6.4	2.837
1984	215.7	+ 9.7	4.393	175.3	+ 68.2	3.340
1985	186.9	- 13.4	3.936	164.8	- 6.0	3.093
1986	189.8	+ 1.6	4.031	181.9	+ 10.4	3.533
1987	211.7	+ 11.5	4.660	181.9	0.0	3.740
1988	215.8	+ 1.9	4.955	204.2	+ 12.3	4.233
1989	187.9	- 12.9	4.589	200.4	- 1.9	4.438
1990	173.1	- 7.9	4.113	174.2	- 13.1	4.110
1991	163.3	- 5.7	3.614	130.4	- 25.1	3.124
1992	203.4	+ 24.6	4.411	179.3	+ 37.5	4.492
1993	227.8	+ 12.0	4.713	192.4	+ 7.3	4.805
1994**	259.2	+ 13.8	5.691	259.6	+ 35.0	6.505
1995	247.0	- 4.7	5.894	228.2	- 12.1	6.210
1996	247.5	+ 0.2	6.328	219.3	- 3.9	6.038
1997	254.5	+ 2.8	6.904	184.3	- 16.0	5.024
1998	292.7	+15.0	8.364	148.6	-19.4	4.393
1999	321.2	+9.7	10.413	152.6	+2.7	4.964
2000	300.1	-6.6	9.529	118.2	-22.5	4.133

* Gas & Credit Crunch
** Beginning in 1994, CV shipment figures include truck and sport-utility vehicle conversions.

SOURCE: "RV Shipments Data," Recreation Vehicle Industry Association, Reston, Va., 2001

that date. In 1995, 475,200 RVs were delivered. Although shipments of RVs have climbed since 1995, shipments of CVs have generally dropped off, except for a rise in 1999. In 2000, 418,300 RVs and CVs, with a record high retail value of $13.7 billion, were shipped. (See Table 5.9.)

Who Owns RVs?

The Recreation Vehicle Industry Association (RVIA) reports that in 1998 an RV could be found in nearly 10 percent of all vehicle-owning households in the United States—representing ownership of 9.3 million RVs. Almost half (45 percent) of RV owners are between 35 and 54 years old. About 40 percent are over age 55. In 1998, the typical RV owner was 48 years old, married, and had an income of $47,000.

In 1998, RV owners reported having possessed their current vehicle for 5.7 years, and said they intended to remain owners for another 10.6 years. RV owners reported that they used their RVs an average one to three weeks in the previous year. Forty percent of former RV owners plan to buy another recreational vehicle in the future. Among households that have never owned an RV, 50 percent reported an interest in purchasing an RV sometime in the future. Many of these potential buyers are 30 to 49 years old, indicating a strong sales potential for the industry. In addition to RV owners, many American rent RVs for a single vacation or trip.

A growing number of single people, especially women, are taking to the road alone in their RVs. Although most RV travelers are married, more single, divorced, and widowed women are becoming interested in RV travel. RVing Women, a club based in Arizona, has a membership of 4,000 in the United States and Canada.

Wooing the "Mature" Consumer

The number of Americans age 55 and older is expected to increase by 27 percent from 2000 to 2010, as the early baby boomers reach their "mature" years. This age group will represent about 26 percent of all Americans—74.8 million citizens—by 2010.

The RVIA hopes to capitalize on this increase in the number of older Americans, who traditionally have larger net worth and higher disposable incomes. Many in this older age group will enjoy early retirement and a more flexible schedule, which permits more leisure activity. Studies indicate that, since 1980, RV ownership has increased 50 percent among householders over the age of 55. Americans over 55 owned 40 percent of the 9.3 million RVs on the road in 1998.

CHAPTER 6
THE TRUCKING INDUSTRY

Unlike boats, which must travel through water, and railroads, which must follow steel tracks, trucks can go anywhere there is a road. While they may not be able to carry as much freight as barges or railway cars, trucks can reach almost any destination, connecting coast to coast and border to border.

In 1998, trucks transported 86.5 percent of the general freight business (in terms of revenues) in the United States, up from 81 percent in the previous year. This accounted for nearly 5 percent of the country's gross domestic product, or $486.1 billion, compared to $371.9 billion in 1997. Trucks hauled 63.3 percent (7.7 billion tons) of the nation's intercity freight in 1998. Trucks transported 79 percent of all goods traded in North America in 1998, up from 72 percent in 1995. Increased trade between the U.S., Canada, and Mexico, as a result of the North American Free Trade Agreement (NAFTA), is responsible for a large portion of the new demand, since trucks dominate cross-border freight movement. In 1998, trucks carried nearly 75 percent of the goods traveling between the U.S. and Canada, and 83 percent of the goods between the U.S. and Mexico. That year, industry analysts predicted that trucking demand would continue to grow through the next decade.

TYPES OF CARRIERS

The American Trucking Association (ATA) identifies three broad categories of motor carriers: 1) Class I, II, and III intercity carriers, 2) owner-operators, and 3) private motor carriers. Intercity carriers are trucking companies that maintain fleets of trucks and employ people to drive them. Owner-operator carriers are independent truckers who own their trucks and operate for hire. These operators enter and exit the market at will, making it difficult to obtain data on their operations. Private carriers are owned and operated by companies for the purpose of hauling only their own materials and products. Class I carriers are those with annual gross operating revenues of $5 million or more; Class IIs have revenues between $1 million and $5 million; and Class IIIs, which make up the majority of carriers, have revenues of less than $1 million.

TYPES OF TRUCKS

The trucking industry includes all trucks hired to transport goods from one point to another. A truck can be one of hundreds or thousands owned and operated by a major freight-hauling company, or it may be the single tractor-trailer of an independent operator. These include straight trucks; 3-, 4-, and 5-axle semitrailers; flatbed trailers; Rocky Mountain doubles; and mammoth turnpike doubles. (See Figure 6.1 for typical types and dimensions.)

Every truck, trucker, and trucking company plays a vital role in the nation's economy and lifestyle. Trucks connect raw materials to factories, factories to stores, and stores to homes. Oklahomans eat California lettuce, Nebraskans dine on Gulf shrimp, and Texans consume Florida corn. Works of art are enjoyed by millions of people as exhibits travel by truck from city to city. Cars manufactured in Detroit are brought by truck to the dealer's lot in Maine.

Big Rigs: Blessing or Curse

The largest trucks on the highways are often called "truck trains" or "monster trucks." They are triple trailers, measuring just under 100 feet, and turnpike doubles, which are twin 45- to 48- foot trailers. The larger trucks are also called longer combination vehicles (LCVs), or extra-long vehicles (ELVs). (See Figure 6.1.)

These trucks are much bigger, longer, and heavier than the standard, five-axle 18-wheeler that motorists have become accustomed to. A triple-trailer rig stretches about one-third the length of a football field. Each type of

FIGURE 6.1

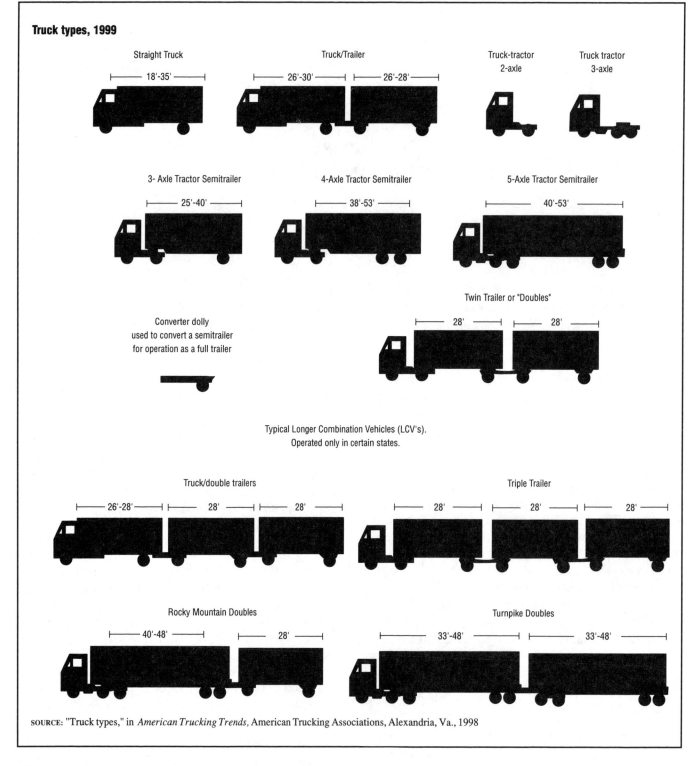

Truck types, 1999

Straight Truck
18'-35'

Truck/Trailer
26'-30'   26'-28'

Truck-tractor 2-axle

Truck tractor 3-axle

3- Axle Tractor Semitrailer
25'-40'

4-Axle Tractor Semitrailer
38'-53'

5-Axle Tractor Semitrailer
40'-53'

Twin Trailer or "Doubles"
28'   28'

Converter dolly used to convert a semitrailer for operation as a full trailer

Typical Longer Combination Vehicles (LCV's). Operated only in certain states.

Truck/double trailers
26'-28'   28'   28'

Triple Trailer
28'   28'   28'

Rocky Mountain Doubles
40'-48'   28'

Turnpike Doubles
33'-48'   33'-48'

SOURCE: "Truck types," in *American Trucking Trends,* American Trucking Associations, Alexandria, Va., 1998

large truck weighs about 125,000 pounds. By comparison, the average family sedan is about 16 feet long and weighs 3,500 pounds.

PROPONENTS OF BIG RIGS. Those who favor the use of these large freight haulers claim that big trucks provide a more efficient way to move goods, and cut fuel consumption and pollution, because there are fewer trucks on the road. The trucking industry believes that

the bigger rigs make sense—not only for their companies, but also for their customers, and are the only way to meet demand.

Truckers claim that the more even distribution of extra weight over more length means little added wear and tear to the highways. The Federal Highway Administration (FHWA), however, reports that the lifetime of bridges and overpasses will be cut from 50 years to 29 years if additional axles are not added to these longer and heavier vehicles.

Trucking company officials also claim that they take very strict measures to ensure that the trucks are operated safely, that only the most qualified drivers are allowed to operate the LCVs, and that the drivers must submit to regular drug and alcohol tests. In addition, drivers are not allowed to drive more than 10 hours a day. In bad weather, they must park the rigs.

OPPONENTS OF LCVS. Many people have reservations about the safety of the massive trucks on the highways. Organizations opposing LCVs are concerned about the danger they represent to other drivers. A brochure prepared by Citizens for Reliable and Safe Highways (CRASH) included a photo of a school bus crushed like a soda can by an LCV. Although the accident rate for LCVs is lower than that of other freight carriers, an accident involving a monster truck is often worse because of the size and weight of the vehicle. The railroads oppose LCVs because they consider these trucks to pose serious competition to their market niche. The Association of American Railroads has released printed and television material opposing LCVs. If more shippers begin depending on double and triple trucks, it could cost the railroad industry up to $2 billion a year.

Laws Regulating Size and Weight

The federal government began regulating the size and weight of trucks in 1956, to preserve the nation's investment in the then-new interstate highway system, but states that already had higher weight limits were "grandfathered"—allowed to keep their previous levels. With the Surface Transportation Assistance Act (STAA) of 1982 (PL 97-424), Congress required states to adopt the federal weight limits on interstate highways. In 1991, the Intermodal Surface Transportation Efficiency Act (ISTEA; PL 102-240), prohibited states from allowing any expansion of LCV carriers. ISTEA expired on September 30, 1997, and a new bill reauthorizing ISTEA for six more years was passed in May 1998. The Transportation Equity Act for the Twenty-first Century (TEA-21; PL 105-178) continued the same provisions of ISTEA, but required the Transportation Research Board to conduct a broad study of the impacts of federal size and weight laws for trucks.

Supporters of the bigger trucks still want to raise the limits on truck size and are pushing for more triple-trailer trucks (three linked 26- to 29-foot trailers). These "triples," as they are called, currently make up less than one-tenth of 1 percent of the U.S. commercial fleet. At present, they may operate on only 17,923 miles of state and federal highways, or 1.6 percent of the nation's roads.

Proponents of larger trucks are also urging that the federal limit of 80,000 pounds gross weight on large trucks be increased to 97,000 pounds gross weight. They argue that a truck carrying heavy cargo, like automobile tires or steel products, is traveling partially empty at that weight limit, which is inefficient and nonproductive. Furthermore, if the trucks were permitted to carry 97,000 gross pounds, backers say, four trucks could carry the weight now being carried by five trucks, lessening highway congestion.

Opponents argue that reconfiguring the trucks, rather than enlarging them or allowing them to carry more weight, makes more sense. They cite the dangers of increased accidents when more trucks with heavier loads are traveling at high speeds.

In August 2000, the Department of Transportation (DOT) submitted to Congress the Comprehensive Truck Size and Weight Study, which examined several scenarios for truck size and weight restrictions in an effort to determine potential damage to the highways system and danger to the public. Although it was noted that heavier trucks effectively shorten the life of a highway, no definitive figures were given for damages. Similarly, no statistics were given for accidents related to large trucks; however, the study did show that some larger, heavier trucks are more prone to rollover and less able to avoid sudden obstacles at highway speeds than smaller, lighter trucks. In September 2000, the Federal Highway Administration issued notice of proposed rulemaking related to truck size and weight, inviting comments from the public.

PAYING THEIR SHARE

Trucks cause considerable damage to road surfaces because they are very heavy and travel a great number of miles. Truck owners are taxed to help pay their share of road repair and maintenance. In 1998, according to the American Trucking Association, trucks paid $28.7 billion in federal and state highway-user taxes, of which $13.1 billion went to the federal government and $15.6 billion to the states. The average annual state user-fee on a typical five-axle tractor-trailer was $4,945 as of January 2000. In 1997, a Department of Transportation Highway Cost Allocation Study showed that combination trucks paid for 90 percent of highway costs attributed to truck damage. That figure dropped to 80 percent with a new user-fee structure that went into effect in 2001.

TRUCK SALES

The 1990–1991 recession led to a temporary drop in the sale of large trucks. In 1991, total truck sales were 3,842,100. Sales then increased with the improving economy, and by 1998, this figure had nearly doubled, to 7,179,800. In 1999, 7,951,700 trucks were purchased. (See Table 6.1.) There were over 79 million registered trucks on American roads in 1998.

TABLE 6.1

Retail large truck sales, 1990–99

Year	Class 1	Class 2	Class 3	Class 4	Class 5	Class 6	Class 7	Class 8	Total
1990	2,865.7	1,097.0	20.9	27.5	5.1	38.2	85.3	121.3	4,261.0
1991	2,723.6	876.3	21.3	23.8	3.3	22.4	72.6	98.7	3,842.1
1992	3,217.0	1,021.1	25.5	25.6	3.6	27.7	73.2	119.1	4,512.8
1993	3,787.6	1,200.6	26.9	33.3	4.3	26.6	80.8	157.9	5,318.1
1994	4,132.1	1,505.9	35.3	44.5	4.1	20.3	98.2	185.7	6,026.0
1995	4,031.4	1,631.3	39.9	52.6	4.3	23.3	106.7	201.3	6,090.8
1996	4,403.9	1,689.7	51.8	58.7	7.3	19.4	103.5	170.1	6,504.4
1997	4,516.1	1,709.7	52.8	56.5	9.2	18.1	110.7	178.6	6,651.5
1998	4,615.2	2,037.7	102.5	43.4	25.2	31.6	114.7	209.5	7,179.8
1999	4,944.1	2,364.0	122.4	49.4	30.4	48.1	131.0	262.3	7,951.7

SOURCE: "Retail Truck Sales," Ward's Communications, Southfield, MI, 1999

TABLE 6.2

Number of truck drivers, 1990–99

In thousands

Year	Total Drivers	Women	Minority
1990	2,607	3.9%	21.9%
1991	2,666	4.1%	22.8%
1992	2,694	4.6%	22.1%
1993	2,786	4.5%	21.1%
1994	2,815	4.5%	23.1%
1995	2,861	4.5%	23.0%
1996	3,019	5.3%	22.7%
1997	3,075	5.7%	24.5%
1998	3,097	5.3%	26.9%
1999	3,116	4.9%	26.8%

SOURCE: "Number of truck drivers," in *American Trucking Trends*, American Trucking Associations, Alexandria, VA, 2000

TRUCKING EMPLOYMENT

Although the drivers of heavy-duty trucks are the most visible to the public, they made up only 3.1 million of the 9.7 million persons employed in the trucking industry in 1998. Other employees included mechanics and administrative personnel. Women were only 4.9 percent of the drivers in 1999, down from a high of 5.7 percent in 1997. Minorities made up 26.8 percent of the total number of heavy-duty drivers in 1999, up from 21.9 percent in 1990. (See Table 6.2.)

Truck Driver Testing and Training

No federal or state laws require truck drivers to receive specific, formal training. They are, however, required to have a commercial license. Disturbed by the studies that cited driver error as a major cause of truck accidents, Congress passed the Commercial Motor Vehicle Safety Act of 1986 (PL 99-570). The act's goals were to improve driving ability, remove problem truck drivers from the road, and establish a uniform, standardized licensing system. In 1988, the Federal Highway Administration (FHWA) issued a final ruling establishing minimum federal standards for states to implement in testing commercial dri-

vers, including all truck drivers. Since 1992, all truck drivers have had to pass both written exams and driving tests that meet federal standards. The test is considered much more difficult than the standard exam for an automobile license. The federal manual to help prepare truck drivers for the required test is 120 pages in length.

Most truck drivers learn to drive their large rigs either through formal training in truck driver training schools or community colleges, through their companies, or informally from friends and relatives. In the mid-1980s, the trucking industry created the Professional Truck Drivers Institute (PTDI) to improve truck-driver training by developing a training school certification program, and in 1989, the program certified the first eight training schools. As of 2000, 71 truck driving schools across the country had been certified. PTDI strongly urges prospective drivers to train at one of the certified schools to ensure that they are being trained properly and to increase their chances of being hired by a trucking company, but there is no legal requirement that they do so. Some trucking companies have their own specific driver training requirements.

Truck Drivers, Drugs, and Accidents

In 1988, the U.S. Department of Transportation (DOT) issued regulations on drug-testing policies for safety-sensitive airline, railroad, motor carrier (trucking), and shipping employees. Since 1989, tests have been given before employment, after accidents, periodically, when there is reasonable suspicion, and randomly. Employers must conduct unannounced drug tests on 50 percent of their employees each year. Approximately three million workers in the trucking industry are covered by the regulations. The random-testing rule initially caused considerable controversy, mainly over the irregular testing schedule of independent truckers, which is difficult to enforce and expensive for the industry.

FHWA also issued regulations under the 1986 Commercial Motor Vehicle Safety Act (see above) that prohibit truck drivers from driving under the influence of alcohol

FIGURE 6.2

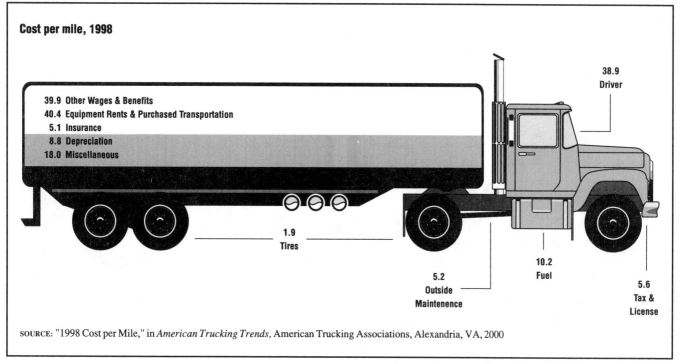

Cost per mile, 1998

39.9 Other Wages & Benefits
40.4 Equipment Rents & Purchased Transportation
5.1 Insurance
8.8 Depreciation
18.0 Miscellaneous

38.9
Driver

1.9
Tires

5.2
Outside
Maintenence

10.2
Fuel

5.6
Tax &
License

SOURCE: "1998 Cost per Mile," in *American Trucking Trends,* American Trucking Associations, Alexandria, VA, 2000

or any illegal drug. The first violation results in a one-year suspension from driving a commercial motor vehicle; the second infraction is justification for permanent disqualification as a driver. Truck drivers are also required to undergo a medical checkup every two years, to evaluate both mental and physical fitness.

TRUCKING INDUSTRY COSTS

The average tractor-semitrailer is very expensive to operate. The typical "big rig" gets only 5 to 8 miles per gallon and travels 80,000 to 100,000 miles per year. According to the American Trucking Association, operating a truck cost the typical trucking company about $1.90 per mile in 1998. The major expenditures were wages and employee benefits (not including the driver), 39.9 cents per mile; purchasing or renting the trucks, 40.4 cents; and driver's salary, 38.9 cents. (See Figure 6.2.)

THE EFFECTS OF DEREGULATION

Following years of government controls, Congress passed the Airline Deregulation Act of 1978 (PL 95-504), the Staggers Act of 1980 (railroads; PL 96-448), and the Motor Carrier Act of 1980 (PL 96-296), which lifted many restrictions on market entry and exit, pricing, scheduling, and routing in the transportation industry.

The arguments for and against deregulation followed a similar pattern in all areas of transportation. Supporters argued that deregulation would benefit both the industry and the consumer by stimulating competition. Competition would, in turn, result in lower rates and better service

for the consumer, eliminate poorly managed companies, and increase industry profits.

Opponents of deregulation were concerned that a lack of controls would allow the major players with the most resources to gain the bulk of the consumer market, forcing even well-managed smaller companies out of business. Another fear was that the small or out-of-the-way consumer might be left out as companies concentrated on high-volume, highly profitable market segments.

Number of Carriers Entering the Market

After the trucking industry was deregulated, thousands of new companies sprang up, hoping to take advantage of the new ease of entry into the market and the ability to set their own prices. In addition, many existing companies quickly expanded and entered new markets.

The number of motor carriers peaked in 1986, and in subsequent years, truck company failures substantially outpaced those in other industries. The American Trucking Associations reported that 2,708 trucking companies failed in 1997, more than double the 1,345 carriers that went out of business in 1987. Competition is so tough that truckers often find it hard to make a living without being constantly on the road.

As of March 2000, 501,744 interstate motor carriers were on file with the Office of Motor Carriers. This was up 9.3 percent from December 1998. Most of these carriers (80.3 percent) ran 20 or fewer trucks. Companies operating 6 or fewer trucks amounted to 72 percent of the total. Figure 6.3 shows the distribution of motor carriers across the country.

FIGURE 6.3

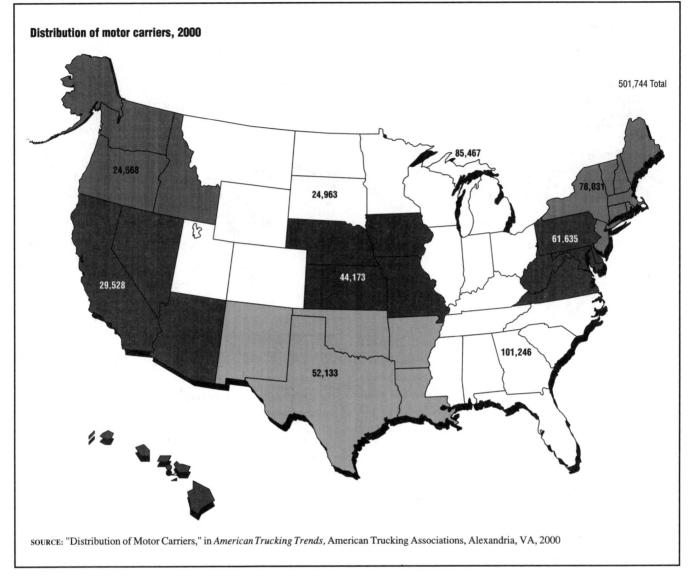

Distribution of motor carriers, 2000

501,744 Total

24,568

24,963

85,467

78,031

61,635

29,528

44,173

101,246

52,133

SOURCE: "Distribution of Motor Carriers," in *American Trucking Trends,* American Trucking Associations, Alexandria, VA, 2000

The most successful companies in the new world of deregulation have been the four trucking "giants"—United Parcel Service (UPS), Consolidated Freightways, Roadway Express, and Yellow Freight Systems, Inc. When other companies went out of business, the larger corporations were able to buy terminals and equipment at bargain prices. They also hired the best of their bankrupt competitors' drivers and acquired the failed enterprises' customers. This helped consolidate their dominance in the industry. Most transportation analysts believe that the giants of the industry will likely become stronger as new companies find it more difficult to acquire the capital they need to grow, and the major companies take advantage of the cost savings that size can provide.

SAFETY OF TRUCKS

The Federal Motor Carrier Safety Administration reported that, in 1999, 5,362 people died in crashes involving large trucks in the United States, amounting to 13 percent of all motor vehicle fatalities for that year. Truck tractors pulling semi-trailers made up 65 percent of trucks involved in fatal crashes and more than 50 percent of trucks involved in nonfatal crashes. Doubles accounted for only 2 percent of trucks involved in crashes, and triples for less than 0.5 percent. (See Figure 6.1 for illustrations of doubles and triples.)

In 1999, a total of 5,374 people died in crashes involving heavy trucks (greater than 26,000 pounds). One of eight traffic deaths on the highway resulted from a collision involving a large truck. Between 1989 to 1999, the vehicle involvement rate per 100 million miles traveled declined significantly from 3.5 to 2.5, a reduction of 29 percent. Of truck-related fatalities, 78 percent of persons killed were occupants of another vehicle, 8 percent were not occupants of any vehicle, and 14 percent were occupants of a large truck (Table 6.3). Table 6.4 shows the numbers of people killed and injured in crashes involving at least one large truck for each year between 1994 and

1999. (Differences in tracking methods account for the variations between Table 6.3 and Table 6.4.) Large trucks were much more likely to be involved in a fatal multi-vehicle crash than were passenger cars. Most of the collisions involving large trucks occurred during the daytime (74 percent), and on weekdays (85 percent).

The National Center for Statistics and Analysis, part of the National Highway Traffic Safety Administration, reported that in half of the two-vehicle fatal crashes involving a large truck and another type of vehicle, both vehicles were proceeding straight at the time of the crash. In 10 percent of the accidents, the other vehicle was turning. In 9 percent, either the truck or the other vehicle was negotiating a curve. In 8 percent, either the truck (6 percent) or the other vehicle (2 percent) was stopped or parked in a traffic lane. A new ruling by the Federal Motor Carrier Safety Administration (FMCSA) mandated that by June 1, 2001, motor carriers must install reflectors or reflective tape on their older trailers, to increase their visibility at night.

Drivers of large trucks were less likely to have a previous license suspension or revocation than were passenger car drivers involved in accidents. However, almost one of three truck drivers involved in fatal accidents had at least one prior speeding conviction, compared to one of five passenger car drivers involved in fatal crashes. (See Figure 6.4.)

In 1999, only 1 percent of drivers of large trucks involved in fatal crashes were intoxicated (blood alcohol levels of 0.10 grams per deciliter or greater). Drivers of these large trucks have shown the highest drop in intoxication rates since 1989, a 63 percent decrease. In 1999, the intoxication rate for drivers of passenger cars in fatal collisions was 17 percent; for light trucks, 20 percent; and 28 percent for motorcycles.

Driver Fatigue

The National Transportation Safety Board estimates that truck drivers who fall asleep at the wheel are a factor in 750 to 1,500 deaths on roads each year, and that fatigue contributes to as many as 40 percent of all heavy-truck accidents. In the United States, drivers are not supposed to drive longer than 10 hours at a time, and then they must have 8 hours to rest.

Nonetheless, the 1997 "Commercial Motor Vehicles Driver Fatigue and Alertness Study," an eight-year, $4.45 million examination of 80 American and Canadian truck drivers, sponsored by the Department of Transportation, reported that truck drivers are still sleep-deprived. Under study conditions, nighttime truck drivers averaged about four-and-one-half hours of sleep daily; daytime drivers got fewer than six hours of sleep.

In 2000, the Federal Motor Carrier Safety Administration drafted a rule limiting hours of service for truck

TABLE 6.3

Fatalities and injuries in crashes involving large trucks, 1998

Type of Fatality	Number	Percentage of Total
Occupants of Large Trucks	728	14
Single-Vehicle Crashes	481	9
Multiple-Vehicle Crashes	247	5
Occupants of Other Vehicles in Crashes Involving Large Trucks	4,212	78
Nonoccupants (Pedestrians, Pedalcyclists, etc.)	434	8
Total	**5,374**	**100**

Type of Injury	Number	Percentage of Total
Occupants of Large Trucks	29,000	23
Single-Vehicle Crashes	14,000	11
Multiple-Vehicle Crashes	14,000	11
Occupants of Other Vehicles in Crashes Involving Large Trucks	97,000	76
Nonoccupants (Pedestrians, Pedalcyclists, etc.)	2,000	2
Total	**127,000**	**100**

SOURCE: "Fatalities and injuries in crashes involving large trucks," in *Traffic Safety Facts 1998: Overview*, U.S. Department of Transportation, National Highway Traffic Safety Administration, Washington, D.C.

TABLE 6.4

Persons killed in crashes involving a large truck, by person type and crash type, 1994–99

Year	Person Type					
	Large Truck Occupants by Crash Type					
	Single Vehicle	Multiple Vehicles	Total	Other Vehicle Occupants	Nonmotorists	Total
1994	451	219	670	4,013	461	5,144
1995	425	223	648	3,846	424	4,918
1996	412	209	621	4,087	434	5,142
1997	499	224	723	4,223	452	5,398
1998	486	256	742	4,215	438	5,395
1999	480	279	759	4,180	441	5,380

SOURCE: "Persons killed in crashes involving a large truck, by person type and crash type, 1994–99," in *Fatality Analysis Reporting System (FARS)*, U.S. Department of Transportation, National Highway Traffic Safety Administration, Washington, DC, 1999

FIGURE 6.4

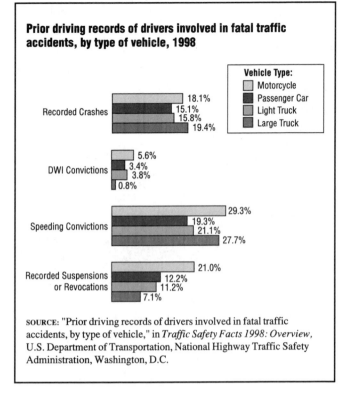

Prior driving records of drivers involved in fatal traffic accidents, by type of vehicle, 1998

SOURCE: "Prior driving records of drivers involved in fatal traffic accidents, by type of vehicle," in *Traffic Safety Facts 1998: Overview,* U.S. Department of Transportation, National Highway Traffic Safety Administration, Washington, D.C.

TABLE 6.5

Air pollutant emissions from mobile sources

Nitrogen oxide emissions	
Cars & light-duty trucks	49.0%
Off-highway equipment - diesel	27.7%
Heavy-duty trucks/buses - diesel	18.5%
Heavy-duty trucks/buses - gasoline	3.1%
Off-highway equipment - gasoline	1.3%
Particulate oxide emissions	
Off-highway equipment - diesel	50.3%
Heavy-duty trucks/buses - diesel	27.2%
Cars & light-duty trucks	14.6%
Off-highway equipment - gasoline	6.5%
Heavy-duty trucks/buses - gasoline	1.4%

SOURCE: "Air pollutant emissions from mobile sources," in *Trucks and Clean Air: Meeting the Challenges of the Future,* American Trucking Association, Alexandria, VA, 1997

ing between lanes. The lane tracker watches the road and beeps if the driver is not steering a relatively straight course. Such devices must, of necessity, be able to warn drivers subtly, since a loud, distracting alarm could cause an accident on its own.

drivers, and mandating the length of rest time. The rule went through the public comment process, and the American Trucking Associations sponsored their own study by the National Economic Research Association, a private entity. This study disputed the DOT study figures for hours of driving and argued that the DOT had understated the costs of the proposed rule to the trucking industry and overstated the benefits. The proposed rule did not go into effect and its future is uncertain.

HELP FOR DROWSY DRIVERS. Some truck drivers turn to coffee, short periods of exercise, naps in the back of their cabs, or even amphetamines (illegal stimulants) to wake themselves up when they start to feel tired. Others do nothing and may finally fall asleep at the wheel. In an effort to remedy this situation, the Department of Transportation (DOT) is testing some moderately priced devices that can keep track of a driver's sharpness and give a warning before weariness overcomes the driver.

One such device is a pen-sized infrared camera mounted on the dashboard that would shine infrared light into the driver's eyes. People cannot see the light, but it can measure the amount of light reflected off the retina of the eye. If the light level becomes too low (because of closing eyelids), the camera would emit a sound, or shake the seat, or release a peppermint spray into the cab and rouse the driver. This device would work only at night, because daylight makes the measurement unreliable.

The lane tracker is another mechanism currently being evaluated that could alert drivers if they are weav-

TRANSPORTATION OF HAZARDOUS MATERIALS

The federal government has set standards for the transportation of hazardous materials by interstate carriers and continues to update these standards. In 2000, the Hazardous Materials Program Plan further specified requirements for handling hazardous materials by motor carriers. As of 2001, FMCSA requires that interstate trucking operators carrying hazardous materials register annually with FMCSA and follow specific federal regulations for describing, packaging, handling, labeling, and shipping of any hazardous materials. In 1997, 4 percent of trucks involved in crashes were carrying hazardous materials (HM). Hazardous materials were released from the cargo compartment in about one-third of these crashes.

Transporting nuclear waste material by truck or by train is particularly controversial. Congress has long debated the location of temporary and permanent disposal sites for spent nuclear material, and part of the debate involves the transportation of the material across states. Although there have already been more than 2,500 shipments of radioactive waste, with no death or injury due to the radioactive nature of the cargo, many people are fearful of transportation of nuclear material.

The transportation of spent nuclear fuel is chiefly a federal responsibility, but the states are also involved. The U.S. Department of Transportation and the Nuclear Regulatory Commission are responsible for packaging regulations, certifications of container safety, regulations governing sabotage, escorts, routing, and employee training. The states are responsible for regulatory mechanisms, such as permits, liability rules, inspections, notification, and emergency training to ensure safe transportation of spent fuel and other hazardous materials.

Safety Measures

All states are part of the Commercial Vehicle Safety Alliance, an organization of truck inspectors that has developed rigid safety rules for trucks carrying nuclear cargo. In addition, 10 states have stipulated certain routes that can be used for nuclear shipments; according to federal guidelines, these are the safest highways. Eighteen states require truckers to get permits before they are allowed to haul spent fuel. Prior to issuance, the trucking company's operations are analyzed, and its past conformity with safety regulations must be approved.

TRUCKS AND THE ENVIRONMENT

The Clean Air Act of 1970 (CAA; PL 91-604) and the Clean Air Act Amendments of 1990 (CAAA; PL 101-549) called for reduction in air pollutants from truck engines. Since then, the heavy-duty diesel truck engine has become far less threatening to the environment. Engine manufacturers have totally redesigned their motors to reduce emissions of the six major pollutants—carbon monoxide, lead, oxides of nitrogen, hydrocarbons, particulates, and sulfur dioxide. A truck engine manufactured in 1997 gave off nearly 70 percent fewer nitrogen oxides and 90 percent fewer particulates than a truck engine manufactured in 1987.

In 1997, diesel trucks accounted for less than 2 percent of hydrocarbon emissions in the United States and only about 5 percent of carbon monoxide emissions. On the other hand, heavy-duty diesel trucks and buses gave off 18.5 percent of all nitrogen oxide emissions and 27.2 percent of all particulate oxides from mobile sources. (See Table 6.5.)

CHAPTER 7

AIRLINES AND AIR TRAVEL

From ancient times, people have dreamed of flying. Greek mythology tells the story of Icarus, who strapped on primitive wings, attached them with wax, and tried to fly. Soaring through the sky, he flew too close to the sun. His wings melted, and he plummeted to his death.

Not until 1783, when two Frenchmen—the Montgolfier brothers—sent a hot-air balloon aloft, did manned flight seem a real possibility. Benjamin Franklin, then U.S. ambassador to France, witnessed the flight and was asked what good it was. Seeing the beginning of a limitless new era of flight, he replied, "What good is a newborn baby?"

The prototype of today's airplanes finally rose into the air on December 17, 1903, when Orville Wright took off from a beach near the town of Kitty Hawk, North Carolina, flew for 59 seconds, and landed half a mile away from the take-off point. Just eleven years after the Wright brothers' first flight, the combatants of World War I enlisted airplanes for military use. In 1918, the first U.S. airmail postal delivery began, with regular service between Washington, D.C. and New York. Air flight was no longer experimental. By 1919, a "flying boat" (an airplane that takes off from and lands on water) was the first plane to cross the Atlantic Ocean, flying from Newfoundland, Canada to Lisbon, Portugal. In that same year, KLM Airlines was founded in the Netherlands, beginning regular, scheduled passenger service from Amsterdam to London in 1920.

In 1925, two airline companies were established in the United States, companies that would later become Trans World Airlines and Northwest Airlines. At about the time Charles Lindbergh made his celebrated solo flight across the Atlantic in 1927, Pan American Airways also started up business. That year, U.S. airlines flew six million miles and carried 37,000 passengers. Commercial airline travel had begun.

The 1930s were years of expansion of the airline industry. The Civil Aeronautics Act of 1938 created the Civil Aeronautics Authority, largely to regulate safety provisions and aid in the modernization of airports. By 1939, U.S. airlines transported passengers all over the globe. Pan American's glamorous Clippers (large flying boats) flew routes across the Atlantic and Pacific, and featured passenger cabins, sleeping berths, and full-service dining rooms.

During the years of World War II, the airlines, like all other U.S. industries, were enlisted in the war effort, and put few resources into development of their own industry. But after the hostilities ended, new technology developed during the war and a booming economy paved the way for explosive airline growth. In the 1950s, jet aircraft joined the air fleets. Planes got bigger and faster, and air travel became more common. With increased demand airlines developed more and more routes to cover more destinations. Eventually, they connected even more destinations through use of hub-and-spoke networks. Under this system, passengers boarding at many different locations arrive at one of the nation's 24 large hub airports. (See Figure 7.1.) Connecting flights then transport them, through the spokes, to their final destinations (see below for more on the hub-and-spoke system).

FEDERAL LEGISLATION

Unlike the railroads, the airline industry was heavily regulated almost from its beginning. The rapid growth of airplanes and air services in the early 1920s prompted legislation both to support and to control the growing industry. The transport of mail, initially the province of the federal government, was opened to private operators by the Kelly Air Mail Act of 1925 (45 Stat. 594). The U.S. government used air mail contracts to subsidize commercial airlines. The Air Commerce Act of 1926 (44 Stat. 568) promoted air safety. It authorized the Secretary of Commerce to register aircraft and certify pilots, established air traffic rules, and required the government to supply and maintain lighted runways.

FIGURE 7.1

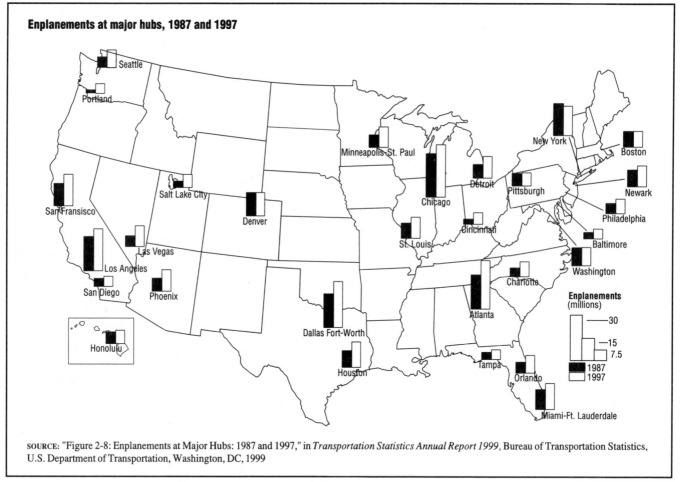

Enplanements at major hubs, 1987 and 1997

SOURCE: "Figure 2-8: Enplanements at Major Hubs: 1987 and 1997," in *Transportation Statistics Annual Report 1999,* Bureau of Transportation Statistics, U.S. Department of Transportation, Washington, DC, 1999

The Civil Aeronautics Act of 1938 (72 Stat. 731) created the Civil Aeronautics Authority (CAA) to provide economic regulation, investigate accidents, and administer airport construction and maintenance. The CAA would eventually become the Federal Aviation Administration (FAA). Economic regulation and safety functions were turned over to the newly formed Civil Aeronautics Board (CAB) in 1939. The Federal Airport Act of 1946 (60 Stat. 170) provided financial assistance for airport development.

The Airways Modernization Board was formed to study a national air navigation and traffic control system. The Federal Aviation Act of 1958 (PL 85-726) brought its work under the jurisdiction of the new Federal Aviation Agency. It became part of the Department of Transportation (DOT) in 1966 when DOT was created, and the agency was given its present-day name, the Federal Aviation Administration (FAA). Air safety functions were taken over by the new National Transportation Safety Board (NTSB).

The Airport and Airway Development Act of 1970 (PL 91-258) provided increased financial support for airport development. Taxes and fees on air travelers and airlines have been accruing in a trust fund. To make federal budget deficits appear smaller, Congress appropriated these dedicated funds far slower than the FAA or the air-

lines would like, thus delaying the improvement of the air traffic system.

AIRLINE DEREGULATION

Prior to 1978, an airline company needed government approval to enter the market, merge with another company, engage in foreign commerce, establish a new route, abandon an existing route, or set or change fares. While this regulation of airlines ensured service to almost all cities, it discouraged competition on the basis of low prices. Airlines, instead, vied for market share by attempting to provide the best service.

Many Americans think that government intervention in any industry restricts free competition and is thus detrimental to the public interest. Critics of airline regulation had pointed out during the 1970s that airlines operating entirely within one state, thereby escaping Civil Aeronautics Board (CAB) regulation, charged far lower fares for routes of the same distance than CAB-regulated carriers. In 1978 these critics convinced the federal government to pass the Airline Deregulation Act, which eliminated many government restrictions on airline behavior, allowed competition between airlines, and led to the elimination of CAB in 1984. The act was intended to increase competition in the domestic airline industry by easing the requirements for new airlines entering the market, reducing 40 years of restrictions on routing and scheduling, and eliminating price controls. Its supporters believed that competition and "free market forces" would benefit both the industry and the public with more choices, lower fares, better service, and increased passenger loads.

The Airline Deregulation Act had far-reaching and surprising effects on the airline industry, determining its shape for decades to come. While fares did drop, service did not improve, and the expected boom in new airlines did not materialize. Advocates of deregulation apparently did not foresee how effectively the largest airlines would use their size advantage to thwart the smaller airlines and the numerous newcomers to the market. They also did not predict that intense fare competition would make it difficult for new entrants to finance their growth, or even for some of the established airlines to maintain their profits. Instead of expanding, the industry concentrated, with only a small number of major carriers able to survive in such a competitive environment. While there have been a few successes, most notably the expansion of Southwest Airlines across much of the country, a number of major airlines, including Braniff, Pan American, and Eastern, have gone out of business since deregulation.

By 2000, deregulation had produced an air travel system dominated by a relatively small number of carriers. Of the 614.2 million passengers who flew in the United States in 1999, 48 percent flew on Delta, United, and American, and 78 percent flew on the six largest airlines. With most of the industry operating under the hub-and-spoke system, many airports were served primarily by a single airline. Many people complained that this lack of choice meant that airlines could get away with high prices and poor service.

TYPES OF CARRIERS

Traffic at an airport falls broadly into three categories: (1) large commercial airlines and cargo haulers, (2) commuter, or regional, airlines and air taxis, and (3) general aviation. In general, *commercial* airlines are very large operations that fly between the major "hub" cities and have fleets consisting mainly of large jets. *Regional,* or *commuter,* airlines provide regularly scheduled service from the hubs to smaller, outlying communities and have fleets predominantly composed of aircraft with 60 or fewer seats. *General aviation* refers to airplanes, almost all of them very small aircraft, owned and operated by individuals or companies for their private use.

Due to the dramatic growth of the regional airlines and the scramble to claim a share of the different market segments following deregulation in 1978, these categories are no longer clear cut. The Federal Aviation Administration

(FAA), which regulates airlines, refers to the larger airlines as "commercial air carriers" and to the smaller airlines as "regionals" or "commuters," even though the regionals are, in fact, commercial airlines that operate for profit.

Large commercial airlines are sometimes referred to as scheduled airlines, because they usually fly only on regular, fixed schedules. Again, regional airlines also offer scheduled services. In some cases, the term "scheduled" refers to both types of carriers. In addition, both types of carriers may provide charter, or "unscheduled," services.

THE AIR TRAVEL INDUSTRY TODAY

Most Americans have flown in an airplane. A 1997 Gallup survey found that more than 80 percent of adults in the United States had traveled by air, and 45 percent of Americans had flown in the previous 12 months. In 1999, 635.4 million passengers flew on more than 8.6 million flights on major U.S. airlines. (See Table 7.1 and Table 7.2.)

The Air Transport Association reported that 1999 was the fifth consecutive year of strong growth for the commercial aviation industry. Increases in both domestic and international markets continue to be driven by a generally strong U.S. economy. The 1997–1998 financial crises in Southeast Asia, Latin America, and Eastern Europe did not seriously harm U.S. commercial airlines' financial performance, although orders for new planes were down, and enplanements (airplane boardings) to both Southeast Asia and Latin America decreased.

Between 1991 and 1999, U.S. commercial air carrier passenger enplanements rose 40 percent, and U.S. commercial air carrier revenue passenger miles (RPMs) grew 45 percent. (A revenue passenger mile is one fare-paying passenger transported one mile.) The financial performance of commercial airlines has shown considerable improvement over the past five years. In 1999, U.S. carriers reported operating revenues of $118.2 billion and net profits of $5.6 billion for the year. See Table 7.1 for the general statistics on the nation's scheduled airlines.

The large commercial airlines continue to restructure (develop new organization plans) and cut costs to facilitate future growth and finance new aircraft. It is vital for the airlines to set fares that will attract enough passengers and still provide a profit. In addition, the major airlines are under pressure from start-ups with lower expenses, such as Western Pacific and Frontier, and expanding regional operators, like Southwest, with efficient operations and lower overhead. Major airlines have asked for concessions from the pilots' and flight attendants' unions in order to cut costs.

The Crowded Skies

In 1998, the privately owned fixed-wing fleet (airplanes with wings fastened to the fuselage, as distin-

TABLE 7.1

Summary of scheduled airlines, 1989–99

In millions, except when noted	1989	1990	1991	1992	1993	1994	1995	1996	1997	1998	1999
Traffic - scheduled service											
Revenue passengers enplaned	453.7	465.6	452.3	475.1	488.5	528.8	547.8	581.2	599.1	612.9	635.4
Revenue passenger miles	432,714	457,926	447,955	478,554	489,684	519,382	540,656	578,663	605,574	618,086	651,597
Available seat miles	684,376	733,375	715,199	752,772	771,641	784,331	807,078	835,071	860,803	874,090	917,849
Passenger load factor (%)	63.2	62.4	62.6	63.6	63.5	66.2	67	69.3	70.3	70.7	71
Average trip length (in miles)	954	984	990	1,007	1,002	982	987	996	1,011	1,008	1,025
Freight & express revenue ton miles	10,275	10,546	10,225	11,130	11,944	13,792	14,578	15,301	17,959	18,131	19,346
Aircraft departures (in thousands)	6,622	6,924	6,783	7,051	7,245	7,531	8,062	8,230	8,192	8,292	8,617
Financial											
Passenger revenues	$53,802	$58,453	$57,092	$59,828	$63,945	$65,422	$69,594	$75,286	$79,471	$80,986	$84,167
Freight & express revenues	6,893	5,432	5,509	5,916	6,662	7,284	8,616	9,679	10,477	10,697	11,239
Mail revenues	955	970	957	1,184	1,212	1,183	1,266	1,279	1,362	1,708	1,734
Charter revenues	2,052	2,877	3,717	2,801	3,082	3,548	3,485	3,447	3,575	3,821	3,706
Total operating revenues	69,316	76,142	75,158	78,140	84,559	88,313	94,578	101,938	109,568	113,465	118,245
Total operating expenses	67,505	78,054	76,943	80,585	83,121	85,600	88,718	95,729	100,982	104,138	110,342
Operating profit (loss)	1,811	-1,912	(1,785)	-2,444	1,438	2,713	5,860	6,209	8,586	9,327	7,903
Interest expense	1,944	1,978	1,777	1,743	2,027	2,347	2,424	1,981	1,733	1,742	1,825
Net profit (loss)*	$128	($3,921)	($1,940)	($4,791)	($2,136)	($344)	$2,314	$2,804	$5,170	$4,903	$5,576
Revenue per passenger mile (in cents)	12.4	12.8	12.7	12.5	13.1	12.6	12.9	13	13.1	13.1	12.9
Rate of return on investment (%)	6.3	-6	-0.5	-9.3	-0.4	5.2	11.9	11.5	14.7	12	11.5
Operating profit margin (%)	2.6	-2.5	-2.4	-3.1	1.7	3.1	6.2	6.1	7.8	8.2	6.7
Net profit margin (%)	0.2	-5.1	-2.6	-6.1	-2.5	-0.4	2.4	2.8	4.7	4.3	4.7
Employees (Average full-time equivalent)	506,728	545,809	533,565	540,413	537,111	539,759	546,987	564,425	586,509	621,058	646,410

*Excludes fresh-start accounting extraordinary gains of Continental and Trans World in 1993.

SOURCE: "1989–1999 Summary U.S. Selected Airlines," in *Air Transport Association 2000 Annual Report,* Air Transport Association of America, Inc., Washington, DC, 2000

TABLE 7.2

Airline traffic

in millions, except when noted	1998	1999	Percent Change
Revenue passengers enplaned	612.9	635.4	3.7
Domestic service	559.7	582.3	4.0
International service	53.2	53.1	(0.2)
Revenue passenger miles	618,086	651,597	5.4
Available seat miles	874,090	917,849	5.0
Passenger load factor (%)	70.7	71.0	
Aircraft departures in thousands	8,292	8,617	3.9
Cargo revenue ton miles	20,496	21,641	5.6
Freight & express Revenue ton miles	18,131	19,346	6.7
Mail revenue ton miles	2,365	2,295	(3.0)
Total revenue ton miles	82,305	86,801	5.5

SOURCE: "Traffic," in *Air Transport Association 2000 Annual Report,* Air Transport Association of America, Inc., Washington, DC, 2000

guished from helicopters) numbered approximately 175,200, with turbine-powered engines accounting for about 12,000 of that number, split roughly half turboprop, half turbojet. The rest of the fleet had piston engines turning propellers. Individuals or companies privately own almost all of these aircraft. The 5,335 planes owned by major airlines are powered by jet turbines, as are the vast majority of the approximately 2,000 aircraft belonging to regional carriers. Other types of aircraft include helicopters, balloons, gliders, and blimps.

A License to Fly

In 1998, 618,298 people had licenses to fly in the United States, down from 622,261 in 1996. Of that number, 97,736 held student licenses and were learning to fly. Approximately 247,000 had private licenses that permitted them to fly small planes. Another 122,053 had commercial licenses that allowed them to fly smaller commercial airplanes owned by the airlines. More than 134,000 pilots held airline transport licenses, which permit them to fly the big jets owned by the airline companies. Nearly 7,000 had licenses for helicopters, and 9,402 for gliders.

THE TOP AIRLINES

As shown in Table 7.3, Delta Airlines led the industry in 2000 in number of passengers carried (105 million). Second was United (nearly 87 million), then American (81 million). Federal Express carried, by far, the largest number of freight ton kilometers (FTKs), followed by Lufthansa Cargo and United Parcel Service (UPS). American Airlines, Federal Express, Delta, and United had the most operating planes (fleet size).

Yield—or fares per passenger per mile—has remained relatively steady in recent years after inching up in the early 1990s. In 1989, airlines received an average yield of 12.4 cents per passenger mile. In 1998, the yield was 13.1 cents per passenger mile. In 1999, it declined to 12.9 cents per passenger mile. (See Table 7.4.)

TABLE 7.3

Top 25 airlines worldwide, by various characteristics

In RPKs

Rank	Airline	RPKs (000,000)
1	United	201,873
2	American	177,334
3	Delta	168,596
4	Northwest	119,336
5	British Airways	117,463
6	Continental	93,367
7	Air France	83,736
8	Japan Airlines	82,904
9	Lufthansa	81,401
10	US Airways	66,875
11	Singapore	64,529
12	KLM	58,903
13	Southwest	58,695
14	Qantas	58,134
15	All Nippon	56,725
16	TWA	41,945
17	Cathay Pacific	41,503
18	Air Canada	39,005
19	Thai Int'l	38,534
20	Alitalia	36,689
21	Korean	36,662
22	Iberia	35,379
23	Swissair	34,670
24	Malaysia	32,238
25	America West	28,497

In operating revenue

Rank	Airline	Op. revenue (000)
1	UAL Corp.	$18,027,000
2	AMR Corp.	17,730,000
3	Japan Airlines Group	15,150,000
4	Delta	15,051,000
5	FedEx	14,508,367
6	British Airways	14,304,000
7	Lufthansa Group	12,847,527
8	All Nippon Group	11,305,112
9	Northwest	10,276,000
10	Air France Group	9,922,299
11	Continental	8,639,000
12	US Airways	8,460,000
13	SAirGroup	8,135,351
14	KLM Group	6,050,888
15	Qantas	5,584,591
16	SAS Group	4,868,888
17	Singapore Airlines	4,773,680
18	Southwest	4,735,587
19	Air Canada	4,480,145
20	Korean	4,218,794
21	Iberia	3,877,980
22	Cathay Pacific	3,693,947
23	TWA	3,308,712
24	Airborne Express	3,140,226
25	Thai	2,833,000

In operating profit

Rank	Airline	Op. profit (000)
1	UAL Corp.	$1,391,000
2	Delta	1,356,000
3	AMR Corp.	1,156,000
4	Lufthansa Group	1,016,532
5	FedEx	909,914
6	Southwest	781,576
7	Northwest	714,000
8	Continental	600,000
9	Singapore Airlines	475,727
10	Qantas	463,890
11	Thai	452,000
12	Japan Airlines	425,439
13	SAirGroup	421,722
14	Cathay Pacific	363,191
15	Air Canada	346,215
16	Air France Group	345,008
17	SAS Group	324,335
18	All Nippon Group[1]	294,944
19	China Southern	223,400
20	America West	197,901
21	Atlas	187,500
22	Alaska Airlines	176,300
23	Korean	158,739
24	US Airways	139,000
25	British Airways	134,400

In net profit

Rank	Airline	Net profit (000)
1	Delta	$1,285,000
2	UAL Corp.	1,235,000
3	AMR Corp.	985,000
4	Singapore Airlines	737,452
5	Lufthansa Group	632,971
6	Southwest	474,378
7	Continental	455,000
8	FedEx	442,063
9	Air France Group	340,173
10	KLM Group	324,022
11	Northwest	300,000
12	Cathay Pacific	281,982
13	Qantas	278,678
14	US Airways	273,000
15	Korean	226,374
16	SAS Group	216,536
17	America West	200,974
18	Alaska Airlines	196,400
19	Japan Airlines	187,096
20	SAirGroup	170,816
21	Iberia	153,576
22	Air Canada	146,608
23	Thai	140,000
24	Air New Zealand	113,782
25	Ansett Group	103,645

In passengers

Rank	Airline	Pass. (000)
1	Delta	105,534
2	United	86,580
3	American	81,507
4	Southwest	57,500
5	Northwest	56,114
6	US Airways	55,812
7	Continental	44,012
8	All Nippon	42,743
9	Lufthansa	38,872
10	Air France	37,028
11	British Airways	36,346
12	Japan Airlines	32,933
13	TWA	25,854
14	Iberia	24,274
15	Alitalia	24,048
16	SAS	22,225
17	Japan Air System	20,597
18	Korean	20,537
19	America West	18,704
20	Qantas	16,692
21	Thai Int'l	16,593
22	Malaysia	15,659
23	Air Canada	15,200
24	China Southern	15,112
25	Swissair	14,501

In FTKs

Rank	Airline	FTKs (000)
1	FedEx	10,312,379
2	Lufthansa Cargo	7,072,000
3	UPS	6,019,476
4	Korean	5,962,143
5	Singapore	5,481,708
6	Air France	4,726,604
7	British Airways	4,536,000
8	Japan Airlines	4,423,157
9	KLM	4,149,000
10	Cathay Pacific	3,769,616
11	United	3,580,863
12	China Airlines	3,381,658
13	Cargolux	3,246,555
14	EVA Air	3,152,180
15	Northwest	3,016,405
16	American	2,511,439
17	Nippon Cargo	2,215,933
18	Martinair	2,060,400
19	Delta	1,984,966
20	Swissair	1,948,724
21	LanChile	1,737,300
22	Thai Int'l	1,672,801
23	Air China	1,641,625
24	Alitalia	1,611,287
25	Emery	1,576,229

In employees

Rank	Airline	No. of employees
1	UPS	308,000
2	FedEx	150,000
3	United	96,675
4	American	86,100
5	Delta	72,000
6	Lufthansa	66,207
7	DHL Airways	60,000
8	Air France	55,199
9	British Airways	53,060
10	Northwest	51,823
11	Continental	44,091
12	US Airways	41,636
13	Iberia	29,079
14	Southwest	27,653
15	KLM	27,302
16	SAS	25,754
17	Thai Int'l	24,121
18	Qantas	23,411
19	Air Canada	22,991
20	Malaysia	22,800
21	Indian	21,990
22	TWA	20,972
23	EgyptAir	20,067
24	Japan Airlines	18,974
25	Alitalia	18,825

In fleet size

Rank	Airline	No. of aircraft
1	American	697
2	FedEx	650
3	United	594
4	Delta	584
5	Northwest	423
6	US Airways	398
7	Continental	370
8	Southwest	318
9	British Airways	283
10	Lufthansa	240
11	American Eagle	240
12	Air France	234
13	UPS	231
14	Iberia	172
15	Air Canada	157
16	America West	153
17	SAS	152
18	Alitalia	152
19	Continental Express	149
20	All Nippon	141
21	TWA	138
22	Japan Airlines	138
23	Mesa Airlines	135
24	Aeroflot Russian	121
25	Comair	109

SOURCE: "The World's Top 25 Airlines" in "The World Airline Report," *Air Transport World,* Penton Media, Cleveland, OH, 2000

Employment

The major U.S. airlines employed 646,410 people in 1999, a 4 percent increase from 1998, when airlines employed 621,058 people, and up 28 percent from 1989 (Table 7.5.) Most of these employees work on the ground, servicing and maintaining aircraft and running the business side of the airlines. Only about 30 percent of airline employees serve on the flights themselves, one-third of them pilots or copilots.

When jet airplanes became part of the air passenger industry in 1958, pilots were largely recruited from the armed forces. These were men (exclusively) with prior military flight training and experience. Although pilots

TABLE 7.4

Airline passenger yields

Passenger yield			
Revenue per Passenger Mile (in cents)	1989	1998	1999
Domestic	13.1	14.1	14.0
International	10.4	10.4	10.0
Total	12.4	13.1	12.9

SOURCE: "Passenger Yield," in *Air Transport Association 2000 Annual Report,* Air Transport Association of America, Inc., Washington, DC, 2000

TABLE 7.5

Airline industry employment

U.S. Scheduled Airlines	1989	1998	1999
Pilots & copilots	43,671	64,099	68,209
Other flight personnel	8,070	11,060	14,300
Flight attendants	77,771	97,574	105,366
Mechanics	57,282	69,927	73,675
Aircraft & traffic service	225,166	290,109	294,549
Office employees	42,717	40,944	41,033
All other	52,051	47,345	49,278
Total employment	506,728	621,058	646,410
Average compensation per employee			
Salaries & wages	$36,694	$50,523	$52,124
Benefits & pensions	6,299	9,821	9,629
Payroll taxes	2,729	3,557	3,588
Total compensation	$45,722	$63,901	$65,341

SOURCE: "Employment," in *Air Transport Association 2000 Annual Report,* Air Transport Association of America, Inc., Washington, DC, 2000

are private employees of the airline for which they fly, they are subject to mandatory FAA-imposed retirement at age 60. The pool of military pilots has shrunk in recent years, and the rising cost of private pilot training has discouraged many would-be students. Many pilots now begin their careers with regional or cargo airlines in order to get enough required flying hours, hoping to move to the major airlines as vacancies appear.

Some pilots have tried to overturn the mandatory retirement age. The ruling, made over 30 years ago, was intended to reduce the danger of an older pilot suffering a heart attack or stroke while flying. Opponents of the ruling cite recent medical advances that greatly reduce this risk. They argue that older pilots have accumulated a vast store of experience during their many years of flying that classroom training cannot duplicate. The FAA, however, has stood by its decision and indicates that it intends to maintain the age limit. The Ninth Circuit Court of Appeals agreed in *Western Air Lines, Inc. v. Criswell et al.* (709 F.2d 544, 1984), when it decided that the airlines could retire pilots at age 60.

Jumbo Jets

Many experts are debating the future of jumbo jets, the huge, 600-passenger, four-engine aircraft that airlines use for high-volume routes. Major international carriers are building hubs in cities that do not generate enough traffic to fill these giant planes. Instead, smaller two-engine jumbo planes, such as the 767, are increasingly being used, because their 176 to 230 seats are more easily filled, making them more efficient. While overseas flights, particularly to Asia, still use the larger aircraft, the fragmentation of air routes (dividing long routes into shorter ones) has created demand for smaller planes carrying between 300 and 400 passengers. In 1995, Boeing introduced its two-engine giant, the 777 (350 to 475 seats). Boeing also builds the MD-11, which carries 231 to 350 passengers. (The MD-11 was originally built by McDonnell Douglas, now part of Boeing.) Airbus Industries, a European consortium, offers two competitor planes, the A330 and the A340 (253 to 485 seats). In June 1998, the FAA awarded the Russian Ilyushin IL-96T cargo plane an

air-worthiness certificate. A passenger version, the Ilyushin IL-96M, which carries 436 passengers, will be introduced soon, although it is debatable whether this aircraft will find a market in the United States.

The opening of China and the potential for lucrative routes there, which would attract overseas Chinese visiting the homeland, still motivates Airbus and the now-merged Boeing and McDonnell Douglas to propose 600–800 passenger craft. Forecasts show that the demand for jumbo jets will probably increase through at least 2010, and could eventually account for as much as 70.7 percent of equipment expenditures. Asia/Pacific-headquartered airlines will account for most of the larger airplane purchases.

Yield Management

Deregulation produced a dizzying array of new fare categories. Fares now swing sharply from season to season and, sometimes, day to day. Even the most sophisticated traveler can become confused by the multitude of ticket prices offered. These prices result from the airlines' efforts to obtain maximum revenue from each planeload.

The increasing power and sophistication of computer systems have allowed the airlines to develop a strategy called "yield management" or "revenue control." The point is to sell the mix of low-, medium-, and high-priced coach tickets that will earn the most money from each flight. Yield management leads the major airlines to introduce many discount fare categories, each with its own set of restrictions.

Business travelers are the airlines' favorite customers, since they must travel and tend to leave for trips on short notice, and since companies usually pay full fare. Business travelers, however, usually buy seats at the last minute, and there are not enough of them to fill airplanes.

Airlines attempt to fill the remaining seats at lower prices with leisure travelers. An estimated 41 percent of passengers fly for business and 59 percent for pleasure. The point of yield management is to charge business travelers, who have the least flexibility, the highest fares. Having maximized their profits with these business travelers, the airlines can then discount fares to fill their remaining seats, which would go empty if they insisted on the high prices. This is because serving one more passenger, even at a deep discount, costs little more than the price of a small meal, the ticket taxes, and a slight amount of additional fuel.

Discount fares attract vacation travelers. Restrictions that apply to reduced fares, such as advance-purchase requirements and travel extending through Saturdays, inhibit the use of these fares by business travelers, and thus serve to maintain profit margin. Fully refundable tickets, standard before deregulation, are now less common. Most tickets include a charge for refund or exchange.

Frequent-Flier Plans—Wooing the Travelers

The intense competition resulting from deregulation caused major changes in airline marketing strategies. One technique, aimed primarily at the higher-paying business traveler, is the so-called frequent-flier (mileage bonus) program. Such plans offer future free tickets as a reward for accumulating trip mileage on a specific airline, encouraging brand loyalty among those who fly often. Frequent-flier plans also offer seasonal discounts and coupons that the passenger can use to upgrade from a coach seat to the more desirable first-class or business-class sections, as well as other promotions. Since the larger carriers, with their extensive number of routes, offer the most attractive destinations for flyers when they cash in their mileage bonus points, this marketing tool gives them a special edge in the era of deregulation.

The first frequent-flier plan was started by American Airlines in 1981 as the American AAdvantage program and was intended to be temporary. The program was a huge marketing success, however. The airline found that passengers were choosing to stay with an air carrier in order to accumulate miles, and soon other airlines started their own plans. *Inside Flyer* magazine estimated total frequent-flier membership in the United States and Canada at about 60 million in 1999. After many planes became too full to make room for frequent flyers, airlines tightened up the rules, raising redemption levels and combining them with expiration deadlines. In July 1999, American Airlines announced that it would do away with expiration deadlines and that AAdvantage program members would have 36 months for their account to show any activity—from booking a flight to simply making a purchase on an AAdvantage credit card—to keep the miles indefinitely. United Airlines made similar changes to its program.

REGIONAL AND COMMUTER AIRLINES

In response to deregulation in the late 1970s, the regional, or commuter, airlines underwent dramatic changes. Previous restrictions to planes with fewer than 12 seats severely hampered growth, and deregulation freed the regional airlines to increase passenger capacity and passenger revenue-miles. As the major airlines converted to larger turbojets suitable for high-capacity, long-haul flights, the regionals moved into the gap left in the low-density, short-haul market.

Since 1969, when the commuter lines received formal industry recognition, more than 600 different carriers have been in operation at one time or another. However, the consolidation that occurred among the major airlines also affected the regionals. In 1998, there were 102 operating U.S. carriers, down from a high of 246 in 1981. Passenger enplanements on commuters, including Alaska and foreign territories, totaled almost 66.1 million in 1998, a gain of 7.2 percent over 1997.

The regionals and the commuter industry have created niches in the market tailored to the specific needs of their customers. While the fleet once consisted of a variety of small general-aviation aircraft, the planes are increasingly state-of-the-art, including a growing number of small, but comfortable, jet aircraft, and the airlines now offer services similar to those of the commercial carriers.

The regional airlines became an essential element of the hub-and-spoke structure of the major airlines. Many regionals have routes and schedules designed to mesh with major carriers at hub cities. They funnel passengers from smaller cities to flights outbound from the hub and relay arriving passengers to their final destinations. The regional airlines have become an important component in the airline industry, leading some of the majors to buy their connecting regionals to ensure continued operation and cooperation. The regionals also provide a training ground for pilots with backgrounds in military or general aviation who hope to fly for one of the major airlines.

The regional/commuter industry is growing faster than the larger commercial carriers. Table 7.6 illustrates the forecasted passenger growth through the year 2011. The regional/commuter airlines are expected to have more seats per plane and carry more passengers farther.

Regional/commuter air carriers are separated into two groups. One group operates commuter aircraft of 60 seats or fewer and reports traffic data to the U.S. Department of Transportation's (DOT) Office of Airline Information on DOT Form 298-C. These carriers are known as Form 298-C carriers. The second group operates both large aircraft over 60 seats and smaller commuter aircraft and reports traffic data to the DOT Office of Airline Information on Form 41. These carriers are known as Form 41 carriers. In 1998, a total of eight carriers (Atlantic Southeast, Conti-

TABLE 7.6

Regionals/commuters forecast assumptions

	Average seats per aircraft			Average passenger trip length			Average passenger load factor		
Fiscal Year	298-C carriers (Seats)	Form 41 carriers (Seats)	All carriers (Seats)	298-C carriers (Miles)	Form 41 carriers (Miles)	All carriers (Miles)	298-C carriers (Percent)	Form 41 carriers (Percent)	All carriers (Percent)
Historical									
1994	27.1	35.8	29.1	205.9	210.5	207.2	49.6	52.3	50.4
1995	27.7	36.1	30.3	215.2	211.0	213.6	48.6	50.4	49.3
1996	27.8	35.0	30.5	224.3	220.7	222.7	51.5	53.4	52.3
1997	28.3	37.3	31.4	234.0	226.0	230.6	52.9	54.6	53.6
1998	28.9	40.8	33.2	248.7	237.6	243.5	54.9	58.4	56.5
1999E	31.3	42.8	36.0	265.7	255.2	260.2	55.5	59.7	57.6
Forecast									
2000	32.5	44.0	37.3	275.0	265.5	270.1	56.0	60.5	58.2
2001	33.5	45.0	38.3	282.0	273.0	277.3	56.5	61.0	58.7
2002	34.2	46.0	39.2	287.0	280.0	283.4	57.0	61.3	59.1
2003	34.9	46.5	39.9	291.0	285.0	287.9	57.3	61.6	59.4
2004	35.6	47.0	40.5	295.0	290.0	292.4	57.6	61.9	59.8
2005	36.2	47.5	41.1	299.0	295.0	296.9	57.9	62.2	60.1
2006	36.7	48.0	41.7	303.0	300.0	301.4	58.2	62.4	60.3
2007	37.2	48.5	42.2	307.0	305.0	305.9	58.5	62.6	60.6
2008	37.7	49.0	42.7	311.0	310.0	310.5	58.8	62.8	60.8
2009	38.2	49.5	43.3	315.0	315.0	315.0	59.1	63.0	61.1
2010	38.7	50.0	43.8	319.0	320.0	319.5	59.4	63.2	61.4
2011	39.2	50.5	44.3	323.0	325.0	324.1	59.7	63.4	61.6

SOURCE: "Table 23: U.S. Regionals/Commuters Forecast Assumptions," in *FAA Aerospace Forecasts, Fiscal Years 2000–2011*, Federal Aviation Administration, Washington, DC, 2000

FIGURE 7.2

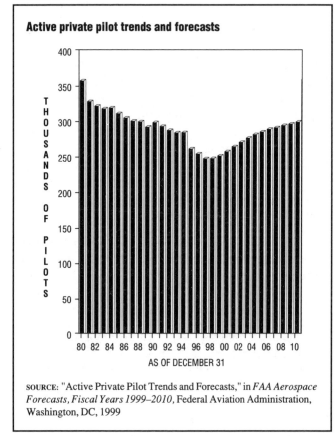

Active private pilot trends and forecasts

SOURCE: "Active Private Pilot Trends and Forecasts," in *FAA Aerospace Forecasts, Fiscal Years 1999–2010*, Federal Aviation Administration, Washington, DC, 1999

nental Express, Executive, Horizon, Mesaba, Trans States, United Feeder Service, and American Eagle—including Flagship, Simmons, and Wings West) reported their data on DOT Form 41.

GENERAL AVIATION

Since flights by individuals in privately owned airplanes produce no revenue, the state of general aviation is reported in terms of numbers of private pilots, hours flown, fleet composition, and aircraft shipments by the manufacturers of general aviation aircraft. The total number of private pilots has decreased from 360,000 in 1980 to 247,226 in 1998. Figure 7.2 shows, however, that the number of private pilots is expected to increase to about 300,000 by 2010.

For FAA reporting purposes, the active general aviation fleet consists of those private airplanes that have been flown at least one hour during the previous year. As of 1999, the active fleet numbered 219,464 aircraft (See Table 7.7.) up from 192,414 airplanes in 1997.

Since 1978, the total number of shipments of new general aviation aircraft has been declining. In 1978, almost 18,000 general aviation aircraft were shipped; in 1994, fewer than 1,000 general aviation aircraft were shipped. The major cause for this decline was manufacturer liability. Up to that time, any time a general aviation plane crashed, no matter how old or poorly maintained, and regardless of the ability of the pilot, the manufacturer

TABLE 7.7

Active general aviation and air taxi aircraft by type and primary use, 1999
(Excluding Commuters)

Aircraft type	Active GA aircraft	Public use	Corporate	Business	Personal	Instruc-tional	Aerial applica-tion	Aerial observa-tion	Aerial other	Sight-Seeing	External load	Air Tours	Air taxi	Medical	Other
All aircraft –Total	219,464	4,138	10,804	24,543	147,085	16,081	4,254	3,240	366	832	190	290	4,279	834	2,363
Piston–Total	171,923	2,104	2,635	21,794	120,678	14,458	3,146	2,491	207	150	5	37	2,223	255	1,582
One-Engine	150,886	1,723	902	15,559	111,574	13,213	3,121	2,096	143	131	5	37	615	187	1,427
Two-Engine	20,930	364	1,733	6,216	9,087	1,245	25	395	38	8	0	0	1,607	68	137
Other Piston	108	17	0	19	17	0	0	0	25	11	0	0	0	0	18
Turboprop–Total	5,679	242	2,368	1,061	516	46	337	7	20	7	0	0	935	82	60
One-Engine	1,018	20	121	288	159	0	337	0	12	0	0	0	75	6	0
Two-Engine	4,641	201	2,246	773	357	46	0	7	8	0	0	0	860	76	60
Other Turboprop	21	0	0	0	0	0	0	0	0	7	0	0	0	0	0
Turbojet–Total	7,120	79	5,170	676	430	36	106	15	18	0	0	0	496	16	79
Two-Engine	6,387	79	4,633	621	412	36	0	15	18	0	0	0	496	9	69
Other Turbojet	733	0	537	56	17	0	106	0	0	0	0	0	0	7	9
Rotorcraft–Total	7,448	1,622	482	368	1,206	836	603	617	102	145	166	138	608	435	119
Piston	2,564	173	20	159	878	525	423	203	43	64	39	0	10	8	19
Turbine	4,884	1,449	462	209	327	312	179	414	59	80	127	138	598	428	100
One-Engine	4,045	1,404	287	202	304	312	174	409	31	80	68	109	453	182	31
Two-Engine	839	45	176	7	23	0	5	5	28	0	59	30	145	246	69
Gliders–Total	2,041	0	0	0	1,707	256	0	0	0	63	0	0	0	0	15
Lighter-than-air–Total	4,725	0	30	19	3,751	205	0	6	0	445	0	102	0	0	166
Experimental–Total	20,528	91	119	625	18,797	244	63	104	20	22	19	12	18	46	343
Amateur	16,858	13	0	406	16,027	157	0	77	0	5	0	12	0	6	149
Exhibition	1,999	0	0	55	1,780	17	0	0	0	12	0	0	0	0	136
Other	1,671	78	119	164	990	70	63	27	20	5	19	0	18	40	58

Note: Row and column summation may differ from printed totals due to estimation procedures, or because some active aircraft did not report use.

SOURCE: "Number of Active General Aviation and Air Taxi Aircraft By Type and Primary Use—1999," in *General Aviation 2000 Statistical Databook*, General Aviation Manufacturers Association, Washington, DC, 2000

was at least partly responsible. It became too financially risky to manufacture aircraft. In 1994, following a virtual shutdown of the general aviation industry, Congress passed the General Aviation Revitalization Act (PL 103-298), limiting the manufacturers' liability and the amount of time during which they could be held legally liable.

The act states that "no civil action for damages for death or injury to persons or damage to property arising out of an accident involving a general aviation aircraft may be brought against the manufacturer of the aircraft or the manufacturer of any new component, system, sub-assembly, or other part of the aircraft, in its capacity as a manufacturer" if the accident occurred after an agreed-upon, specified time, which starts on the date of delivery to the original buyer or lessee. Similarly, if the aircraft is delivered to a sales person or company, no civil action for damages may be brought against the manufacturer if the accident occurs beyond an agreed-upon, specified time after that sales person or company receives the aircraft. The same conditions hold true for any new or replacement component, system, subassembly, or other part which was added to or replaced on the aircraft and which is alleged to have caused death, injury or damage.

The passage of the General Aviation Revitalization Act meant that aircraft manufacturers could now buy more reasonably priced insurance. Helped along by the new law and an improving economy, aircraft shipments slowly began to increase. A total of 1,549 planes were shipped in 1997, 2,200 in 1998, and 2,504 in 1999. (See Figure 7.3.) Table 7.8 shows the number of purchases of single-engine and multi-engine piston, turboprop, and jet planes between 1962 and 1999.

ROTORCRAFT

As of December 31, 1997, the FAA reported a total of 6,785 active civil rotorcraft (helicopters and gyrocopters) in the United States. Jet-powered (turbine) helicopters accounted for 66.7 percent of the active helicopters, while piston engines powered the rest. Most rotorcraft are used for sightseeing; agricultural applications; law enforcement; fire-fighting; personal transportation; emergency medical services; transporting personnel and supplies to offshore oil rigs; traffic reporting; news gathering; corporate or business transportation; and heavy lifting for the oil, utility, and lumber industries.

AIRPORTS

Orville Wright's runway was a sand dune; Charles Lindbergh's, an open field. The first airline passengers walked to hangars or fields to board the parked planes.

FIGURE 7.3

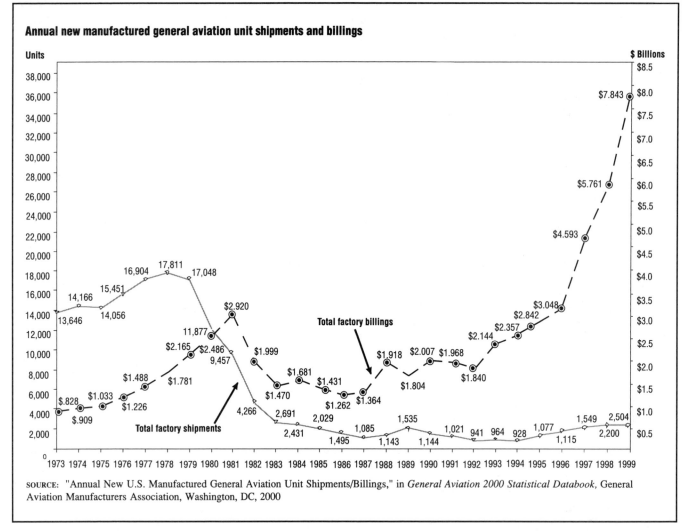

Annual new manufactured general aviation unit shipments and billings

SOURCE: "Annual New U.S. Manufactured General Aviation Unit Shipments/Billings," in *General Aviation 2000 Statistical Databook,* General Aviation Manufacturers Association, Washington, DC, 2000

These arrangements soon proved inadequate. Larger planes, heavier loads, and increased traffic required paved runways and lighting for night flights and a more orderly system for loading passengers onto planes.

Government interest in airport development lagged behind its support for the industry as a whole. Federal aid was eventually granted under the Federal Airport Act of 1946 (60 Stat. 170), the 1970 Airport and Airways Development Act (PL 91-258) (which, like the Highway Trust Fund after which it was patterned, levied taxes on airline users), and the 1982 Airport and Airway Improvement Act (PL 97-248). Most airports are now owned and operated by the cities or municipalities in which they are located, with funding provided locally and, to a lesser extent, by the federal government.

In 2000, planes could take off and land at 19,119 airports, heliports, and seaplane bases in the United States. Most of these airports are not big international airports with towers and multiple runways. Many are privately located in remote rural areas and may be only unlit grass strips. (See Table 7.9.) Table 7.10 shows the busiest U.S.

airports in 1999. Atlanta, with nearly 78 million passengers, Chicago O'Hare (72.6 million), Los Angeles (63.9 million), and Dallas/Fort Worth (60 million), served the largest number of passengers in the United States. The route with the most passengers in the United States is from New York to Los Angeles. Nine of the 10 busiest routes originate or end in New York City. (See Table 7.11.)

Local Impact

An airport has an enormous effect on the communities in its vicinity and can be a major benefit to the local economy. Quick, direct access to a city increases business activity. Many companies are attracted to cities with large airport facilities. An airport may employ hundreds and even thousands of people. Local industries, from the food industry to real estate, benefit by serving the needs of both the airport and its employees.

Ideally, an airport is located reasonably close to a community's business district, but far from its residential areas. Often, this is not the case. Population growth can overtake an airport that was once "out in the country."

TABLE 7.8

Annual new manufactured general aviation airplane shipments by type of airplane

Year	Grand total	Single-engine	Multi-Engine	Total piston	Turboprop	Jet	Total turbine
1962	6,697	5,690	1,007	6,697	0	0	0
1963	7,569	6,248	1,321	7,569	0	0	0
1964	9,336	7,718	1,606	9,324	9	3	12
1965	11,852	9,873	1,780	11,653	87	112	199
1966	15,768	13,250	2,192	15,442	165	161	326
1967	13,577	11,557	1,773	13,330	149	98	247
1968	13,698	11,398	1,959	13,357	248	93	341
1969	12,457	10,054	2,078	12,132	214	111	325
1970	7,292	5,942	1,159	7,101	135	56	191
1971	7,466	6,287	1,043	7,330	89	47	136
1972	9,774	7,913	1,548	9,446	179	134	313
1973	13,646	10,788	2,413	13,193	247	198	445
1974	14,166	11,579	2,135	13,697	250	202	452
1975	14,056	11,441	2,116	13,555	305	194	499
1976	15,451	12,785	2,120	14,905	359	187	546
1977	16,904	14,054	2,195	16,249	428	227	655
1978	17,811	14,398	2,634	17,032	548	231	779
1979	17,048	13,286	2,843	16,129	639	282	921
1980	11,877	8,640	2,116	10,756	778	326	1,104
1981	9,457	6,608	1,542	8,150	918	389	1,307
1982	4,266	2,871	678	3,549	458	259	717
1983	2,691	1,811	417	2,228	321	142	463
1984	2,431	1,620	371	1,991	271	169	440
1985	2,029	1,370	193	1,563	321	145	466
1986	1,495	985	138	1,123	250	122	372
1987	1,085	613	87	700	263	122	385
1988	1,143	628	67	695	291	157	448
1989	1,535	1,023	87	1,110	268	157	425
1990	1,144	608	87	695	281	168	449
1991	1,021	564	49	613	222	186	408
1992	941	552	41	593	177	171	348
1993	964	516	39	555	211	198	409
1994	928	444	55	499	207	222	429
1995	1,077	515	61	576	255	246	501
1996R	1,115	524	67	591	290	233	523
1997R	1,549	898	86	984	223	342	565
1998R	2,200	1,434	94	1,528	259	413	672
1999	2,504	1,634	114	1,748	239	517	756

R=Revised

SOURCE: "Annual New U.S. Manufactured General Aviation Airplane Shipments By Type of Airplane," in *General Aviation 2000 Statistical Databook,* General Aviation Manufacturers Association, Washington, DC, 2000

Smaller airports, built before the advent of jets in 1958, may have been able to coexist with suburban neighbors, but more flights and bigger planes have led to major complaints about noise and concerns about safety in populated areas. The FAA limits the noise which airliners can produce. Some airports impose additional restrictions on noise emissions, operating hours, or flight paths to reduce the discomfort of nearby residents.

The Hub-and-Spoke Network System

The major airlines gradually developed the hub-and-spoke system over the years in order to increase efficiency and thereby maximize their profits. Rather than flying people directly from where they are to where they want to go, in a hub-and-spoke network the airlines fly people from all over the country to one of their major hub airports. Once there, the passengers transfer to flights going to their actual destination. This system enables airlines to send passengers from any airport they service to any other airport they service. Yet it does not require them to schedule flights to and from every airport in the country, a system that would require many more flights and planes to carry the same number of passengers.

Approximately two-thirds of all air travelers go through a hub to reach their destinations. (See Figure 7.1.) Many low-demand routes are no longer served by nonstop flights. On the one hand, travelers benefit, since the hub systems allow them to travel to more destinations and have a wider choice of arrival and departure times. However, the time required for getting a connecting flight at the hub means flight times are longer than for direct flights. Airline consultant Theodore P. Harris estimates that the average trip of under 2,000 miles now takes twice as long as it did prior to deregulation and the use of the hub system.

The hub-and-spoke system can also cause frequent and long flight delays. Most of the major airlines schedule hub departures and arrivals during the peak time periods—

TABLE 7.9

Civil and joint use airports, heliports, stolports, and seaplane bases on record, January 2000

| | | Total Facilities, By Ownership | | Airports Open to the Public | | | | |
| FAA Region and State | Total Facilities | Public | Private | Paved Airports[1] | | Unpaved Airports[1] | | Total Airports |
				Lighted	Unlighted	Lighted	Unlighted	
Grand Total	19,119	5,145	13,974	3,634	256	402	763	4,934
United States—Total[2]	19,058	5,110	13,948	3,616	254	402	762	4,913

[1] Includes all airports open to the public, both publicly and privately owned.
[2] Excludes Puerto Rico, Virgin Islands, and South Pacific.

SOURCE: "U.S. Civil and Joint Use Airports, Heliports, Stolports, and Seaplane Bases On Record By Type Of Ownership—January, 2000," in *General Aviation 2000 Statistical Databook,* General Aviation Manufacturers Association, Washington, DC, 2000

early morning and early evening. When too many jets are scheduled to leave at the same time, the airplanes are forced to line up on the tarmac and wait. Bad weather at a large hub can cause long delays throughout the network. The problems of congestion and delays at the hubs have displeased many passengers. The Air Transport Association of America, which represents the airline industry, estimates that these long waits at major hubs cost the nation's air travelers about $2 billion a year in lost time.

For the airlines, the hub system, along with the introduction of sophisticated air traffic control systems (see below) and a booming economy, has allowed a dramatic increase in passenger load factor. Passenger load factor (the percentage of passengers relative to the number of seats available) increased from 62.4 percent in 1990 to 71 percent in 1999. (See Table 7.1.) Relatively speaking, this is a huge increase, which was reflected in the elevated airline profits of the late 1990s. Fuller planes have also generated consumer complaints, however, as flights become more crowded.

Demand Exceeds Capacity

Air traffic is reaching critical levels as passenger numbers increase. The FAA expects that by the year 2010, the number of airline passengers will reach 931.1 million, more than the existing system can handle. Additional airports, or expansion of existing airports, may be part of the solution, but building or expanding a major airport requires enormous capital expenditures and large areas of land. Further investment is also needed for operation of the facility. The airports must hire personnel for customer relations, maintenance, and security.

The popularity of air travel means that cutting back the number of flights is unlikely, even though this would relieve crowding of the nation's air space. Some restrictions, however, have been made at O'Hare Airport in Chicago, Ronald Reagan Washington National Airport in Washington, DC, and at both La Guardia and Kennedy Airports in New York City. The authorizations to land and

take off at peak times have become valuable commodities at these airports and are bought and sold among carriers.

After the airline industry was deregulated in 1978, no major new airports were built in the United States until 1992, when Pittsburgh International Airport opened its new terminal building. The $1.06 billion facility, the nation's most expensive airport at that time, represented a new age of efficiency and convenience. Designed to accommodate the increased traffic of the hub-and-spoke system, it was equipped with innovative security checkpoints, automated baggage handling, and "smart" computer terminals for ticket information, in order to avoid the congestion typical of older airports.

Denver International, which opened in 1995, stirred controversy because of its $4 billion price tag, its two-year delay in completion, its 23-mile distance from the city, and doubts whether traffic volumes would justify its cost. Initial difficulties with the baggage-handling system only compounded the problems. Other hubs have undergone expansion. Lindbergh Field, San Diego's International Airport, was expanded in 1997, and there is already talk of another expansion. Detroit is completing construction on a $1.2 billion new terminal, Midfield Terminal, that will offer more than 80 additional gates, an automated people mover, a parking lot with a capacity of 11,000 automobiles, and an electric generating plant. It is expected to open in late 2001. Chicago O'Hare, already one of the largest U.S. airports, is working on a $1 billion expansion. Atlanta's airport and Washington, D.C.'s Dulles International Airport are both adding new runways.

THE FEDERAL AVIATION ADMINISTRATION AND AIR TRAFFIC SERVICES

Created by Congress in 1938, the Federal Aviation Administration (FAA) oversees airlines operating in the United States. The FAA certifies all pilots and aircraft mechanics. It also tests and certifies all aircraft designs built or flown in the United States, and establishes regula-

TABLE 7.10

Top 20 airports, 1999

Passengers (arriving & departing)		In thousands
1	Atlanta	77,940
2	Chicago O'Hare	72,568
3	Los Angeles	63,877
4	Dallas/Ft. Worth	60,000
5	San Francisco	40,387
6	Denver	38,034
7	Minneapolis/St. Paul	4,216
8	Detroit	34,038
9	Miami	33,899
10	Las Vegas	33,669
11	Newark	33,623
12	Phoenix	33,533
13	Houston	33,089
14	New York Kennedy	31,708
15	St. Louis	30,189
16	Orlando	29,173
17	Seattle	27,700
18	Boston	26,965
19	New York La Guardia	23,927
20	Philadelphia	23,786
Cargo metric tonnes (enplaned & deplaned)		
1	Memphis	2,413
2	Los Angeles	1,952
3	New York Kennedy	1,905
4	Anchorage	1,677
5	Miami	1,651
6	Chicago O'Hare	1,532
7	Louisville	1,486
8	Newark	1,206
9	Indianapolis	1,108
10	Dayton	894
11	Atlanta	883
12	San Francisco	845
13	Dallas/Ft. Worth	844
14	Oakland	685
15	Philadelphia	551
16	Toledo	490
17	Honolulu	479
18	Denver	467
19	Seattle	449
20	Boston	444

SOURCE: "Top 20 U.S. Airports—1999," in *Air Transport Association 2000 Annual Report,* Air Transport Association of America, Inc., Washington, DC, 2000

TABLE 7.11

Top 30 domestic airline markets, 1999

Passengers - Outbound plus Inbound for twelve months ended December 1999, in thousands

1	New York	Los Angeles	3,728
2	New York	Chicago	2,982
3	New York	Boston	2,821
4	New York	Miami	2,800
5	New York	Orlando	2,777
6	New York	San Francisco	2,743
7	Honolulu	Kahului, Maui	2,691
8	New York	Washington	2,551
9	New York	Atlanta	2,546
10	New York	Ft. Lauderdale	2,386
11	Los Angeles	Las Vegas	2,304
12	Dallas/Ft. Worth	Houston	2,219
13	Los Angeles	San Francisco	2,006
14	New York	San Juan	1,988
15	Chicago	Los Angeles	1,772
16	Honolulu	Lihue, Kauai	1,749
17	Chicago	Detroit	1,509
18	Chicago	Atlanta	1,498
19	Los Angeles	Oakland	1,493
20	New York	Dallas/Ft. Worth	1,475
21	New York	West Palm Beach	1,468
22	Honolulu	Kona, Hawaii	1,459
23	Boston	Washington	1,425
24	Atlanta	Washington	1,424
25	Chicago	Dallas/Ft. Worth	1,415
26	Los Angeles	Honolulu	1,389
27	Los Angeles	Phoenix	1,383
28	New York	Houston	1,345
29	New York	Las Vegas	1,320
30	New York	Detroit	1,315

SOURCE: "Top 30 Domestic Airline Markets," in *Air Transport Association 2000 Annual Report,* Air Transport Association of America, Inc., Washington, DC, 2000

tions on their required maintenance. Airports are another area of responsibility for the FAA. It manages federal funds for the improvement and construction of airports, and sets the official regulations for airport security.

Air Traffic Control

In addition to regulating the air travel industry, the FAA plays a crucial role in its success by providing a nationwide network of air traffic control (ATC) systems. It is the ATC that controls the movements of airplanes over in the United States allowing safe, orderly, and efficient air travel. (See Figure 7.4.) However, the increase in air traffic in the 1980s and 1990s has put a strain on the ATC system. To correct this problem, in 1981, the FAA began to modernize its hardware, software, and communications equipment. The $34 billion program has over 200 separate projects and will be completed by the year 2003.

All four aviation system user groups—air carriers, commuter/air taxi, general aviation, and military—use the ATC to maintain the flow and safety of aviation traffic. The ATC system is made up of five types of facilities:

- Flight service stations—usually used by private aircraft for flight plan filing and weather report updates

- Air traffic control towers—control aircraft on the ground, before landing and after take-off within five nautical miles of the airport and up to 3,000 feet above the ground

- Terminal radar approach control (TRACON) stations—communicate with pilots to line up and separate aircraft as they approach and leave busy airports, 5 to 50 miles from the airport, up to 10,000 feet above the ground

- En route centers—control aircraft while in flight over the continental United States. The 20 en route centers usually control commercial aircraft above 18,000 feet

- Oakland and New York (oceanic) en route centers—control in the same way as the other 20 en route centers, but also control aircraft over the ocean, using radar for up to 225 miles offshore. For aircraft farther

FIGURE 7.4

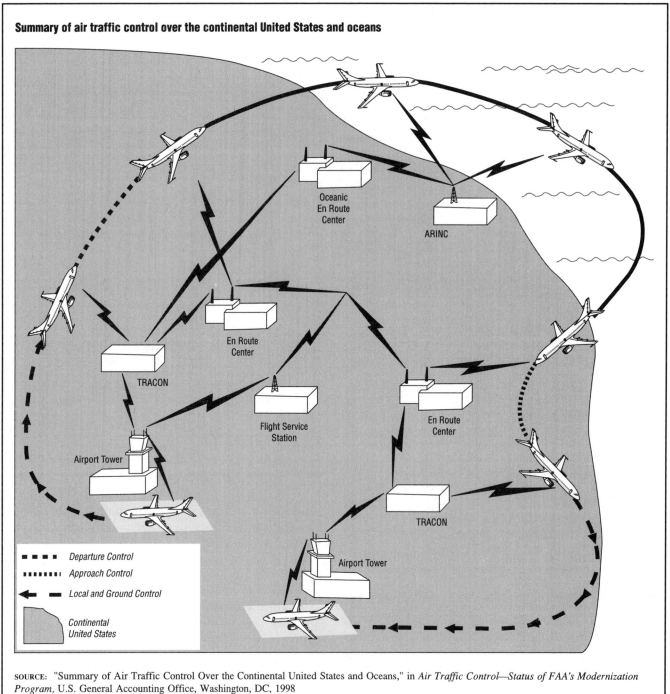

Summary of air traffic control over the continental United States and oceans

Oceanic En Route Center

ARINC

En Route Center

TRACON

Flight Service Station

En Route Center

TRACON

Airport Tower

Airport Tower

■ ■ ■ ■ Departure Control

▪▪▪▪▪▪ Approach Control

◀━ ━   Local and Ground Control

Continental United States

SOURCE: "Summary of Air Traffic Control Over the Continental United States and Oceans," in *Air Traffic Control—Status of FAA's Modernization Program,* U.S. General Accounting Office, Washington, DC, 1998

away than that, they use radio contact to learn aircraft location over the ocean.

AIR TRAFFIC CONTROLLERS. Air traffic controllers are FAA employees specially trained to safely manage air traffic. They work at airport control towers and FAA facilities throughout the country. In 1981, a strike by air traffic controllers was broken when President Ronald Reagan fired 11,400 striking controllers. Their number has since returned to pre-strike levels, but there is still a shortage of experienced controllers, especially in busy East Coast air-

ports. Training new controllers takes two-and-a-half to three years. Congress sets the controllers' salaries, and neither the FAA nor union negotiations can change them.

The growing number of aircraft and flights makes an air traffic controller's job very stressful, but some relief may be on the way. New technological developments, in various stages of planning or testing, include advanced computer automation, navigation, and landing systems. These new technologies use the Defense Department's highly accurate global positioning system satellites, microwave landing systems, and on-board anticollision devices. Whether they can completely solve existing problems remains to be seen.

Congress often reduces or delays expenditures from the Airport and Airway Trust Fund to help reduce the federal deficit, thus postponing improvements in the air traffic control system. In the mid-1990s, air traffic controllers reported that their equipment (technology and computers) was so outdated it was dangerous. Computers at major hubs such as Chicago's O'Hare International were 30 years old. In July 1995, Chicago's computers broke down, requiring use of the back-up system, which, controllers claimed, was inadequate and a safety risk. Since that time, FAA has set about replacing aging computer systems in major hubs as part of its program to modernize the National Airspace System infrastructure. In 1999, the new computer system was installed in New York, Chicago, Miami, Washington, D.C., Atlanta, Denver, Boston, Oakland, Fort Worth, and Albuquerque.

In January 1994, the FAA reported that an increasing number of aircraft were flying too close to other planes because of errors made by air traffic controllers. The required distances of separation were breached 757 times in 1993, the year of the study. Controllers attribute the increase in plane separation errors to increased air traffic, overburdened airports, and stressed and tired controllers. In New York and other crowded airports where there are chronic shortages of air traffic personnel, flights are often delayed for lack of controllers, and many controllers work massive amounts of overtime. Officials in those airports are attempting to recruit controllers from other parts of the country where crowding is less of a problem. Some observers, however, believe that the required distances between planes, established many years ago when planes were much less sophisticated, are much too great and could be reduced.

For the most part, since the early 1990s, the number of pilot-reported near-midair collisions have decreased. In 1997 there were 239 near-midair collisions, up from 194 in 1996, but down significantly from the 311 that occurred in 1992.

Proposals for Free Flight

In response to the crisis in air traffic control, some experts have proposed a method known as "free flight" to replace the existing system. Free flight is exactly what the term implies—pilots take off and land when they want and fly to their destinations by whatever routes they desire. The system is based on the assumption that most aircraft will be equipped with flight management systems that can guide them on a four-dimensional track. That is, the systems can predict where the aircraft will be at any given time until it reaches its destination. The on-the-ground component of the free flight system is a "conflict probe," a software package that examines all tracks within its sector and detects any possible contact that would result between two aircraft. Advocates of the system believe free flight will yield massive savings for airlines and reduce congestion and delays. FAA is already testing such a system. The technology essentially provides a "safety bubble" around each plane.

A REMARKABLE SAFETY RECORD—LARGER IS SAFER

The crash of a jumbo jet is a major disaster. Hundreds of lives may be lost in a single incident. Nonetheless, flying on a scheduled air carrier is one of the safest ways to travel, and the risk of death or injury is far less than when riding the same distance in a car.

Consumer advocates are concerned that deregulation has created intense competition that has led to dangerous cost cutting. Airline mechanics complain of an erosion of maintenance standards. Some airline critics believe that the old direct-route system was less dangerous than the hub-and-spoke system, because the latter involves more takeoffs and landings, when most accidents occur.

Despite statistics that find it safer than most forms of transportation, the American public sometimes feels that air travel has become less safe. Some recent airplane accidents have been attributed to flight or ground crew failures. These include, for example, failure to de-ice airplanes properly, improper setting of flaps and slats, misjudgment of weather (including "wind shear"), poor navigation, pilot fatigue, and improper maintenance or parts replacement. Airlines are working with the FAA to improve the training and teamwork of both flight and ground crews. Table 7.12 shows the accident and fatality figures for scheduled aircraft from 1994 through 1999.

General and Commuter Aviation Accidents

In 1994, after several crashes of small commuter planes known as ATRs, the National Transportation Safety Board called for study of those aircrafts and the crashes in order to determine if commuter planes should be held to the same safety requirements as the larger aircraft. It concluded that the commuter airlines' rapid expansion has outpaced regulation. Original regulation of commuter aircraft dated from the 1950s, when small planes were not a major segment of the transportation system.

As Table 7.12 illustrates, the commuter airlines' safety record has swung between one and five fatal accidents per year since 1994, when there were three fatal accidents and 25 fatalities. In 1998, there were no fatal commuter aircraft crashes. In 1999, there were five fatal accidents in which 12 people died—a rate of 1.86 deaths per 100,000 hours flown. (In that same year, 12 passengers died in two

TABLE 7.12

Total system accident data by segment

Segment	Year	Flight Hours	Total	Accidents		Accident Rate	
				Fatal	Fatalities	Total	Fatal
Large Air Carrier	1994	13,124,315	23	4	239	0.175	0.030
	1995	13,505,257	36	3	168	0.267	0.022
	1996	13,746,112	38	5	380	0.276	0.036
	1997	15,838,109	49	4	8	0.309	0.025
	1998	16,846,063	50	1	1	0.297	0.006
	1999	17,428,000	52	2	12	0.298	0.011
Commuter	1994	2,784,129	10	3	25	0.359	0.108
	1995	2,626,866	12	2	9	0.457	0.076
	1996	2,756,755	11	1	14	0.399	0.036
	1997	982,764	16	5	46	1.628	0.509
	1998	353,765	8	0	0	2.261	0.000
	1999	269,000	13	5	12	4.833	1.859
Air Taxi	1994	1,854,000	85	26	63	4.585	1.402
	1995	1,707,000	75	24	52	4.394	1.406
	1996	2,029,000	90	29	63	4.436	1.429
	1997	2,250,000	82	15	39	3.644	0.667
	1998	2,538,000	77	18	48	3.034	0.709
	1999	2,809,000	76	12	38	2.706	0.427
General Aviation	1994	22,235,000	1994	403	725	8.968	1.812
	1995	24,906,000	2053	412	734	8.243	1.654
	1996	24,881,000	1908	360	632	7.669	1.447
	1997	25,464,000	1853	353	643	7.277	1.386
	1998	26,796,000	1909	365	623	7.124	1.362
	1999	27,080,000	1908	342	628	7.046	1.263

Rates are per 100,000 hours flown

SOURCE: "Total System Accident Data by Segment," in *Aviation Safety Statistical Handbook*, Federal Aviation Administration, Washington, DC, 1999

fatal accidents on large air carriers—an accident rate of only 0.011 fatalities for every 100,000 hours flown.)

The accident and fatality rates of the general aviation fleet are far worse than that of large jets. General aviation aircraft are mostly small, single-engine piston planes, and pilot training and testing are less stringent. As shown in Figure 7.5, the rate of accidents and fatalities in general aviation fell sharply from 1978 to 1979, and then declined much more slowly over the past two decades. Figure 7.6 shows the number of fatal accidents in U.S. general aviation between 1975 and 1999.

Wearing Out

No matter how well designed, properly handled, and carefully maintained, machines eventually wear out, and airplanes are no exception. The FAA increased its inspection staff by almost 75 percent between 1985 and 1993. In 1994 and 1995, the FAA suffered a $600 million budget reduction, which led to cutbacks of 5,000 non-safety positions. The DOT appropriations bill for 1997 provided funds for hundreds of new controllers, maintenance technicians, inspectors, and safety personnel.

Meanwhile, their workload has continued to grow. More planes are in the air, and a large number are growing very old. Adding to the problem are the slow delivery and expense of new airplanes, which has forced some airlines to buy and fly used, usually older, aircraft. In addition, many new airlines have chosen to buy older aircraft.

Although not as efficient as the newer planes, their low purchase price makes them very attractive. It is not unusual for a plane to be more than 25 years old.

Accidents attributed to structural failure appear to be on the rise. Both the airline industry and government agencies are seeking solutions. Proposals include more frequent and thorough inspections, stepped-up preventive maintenance, and a scheduled program of mandatory repairs or parts replacement.

In 1988, the average age of commercial airplanes was approximately 13 years. In 2000, it was nearly 16 years, and it is expected to be 18 to 20 years within a decade. FAA officials feel that improved maintenance techniques have made it safer to fly older planes.

CUSTOMER DISSATISFACTION

The modern, deregulated, airlines have received mixed reviews from consumers. After an initial period of extremely low fares, ticket prices have risen on many routes, especially to areas served by only one or two carriers. Ridership has, nonetheless, increased, suffering only a slight setback in the early 1980s. Many observers believe that current prices are near the ceiling of consumer tolerance and that further increases may result in reduced passenger travel.

The airlines counter that airline ticket prices have lagged well behind the Consumer Price Index and are a good buy. In addition, fare wars, ticket sales, Internet pro-

FIGURE 7.5

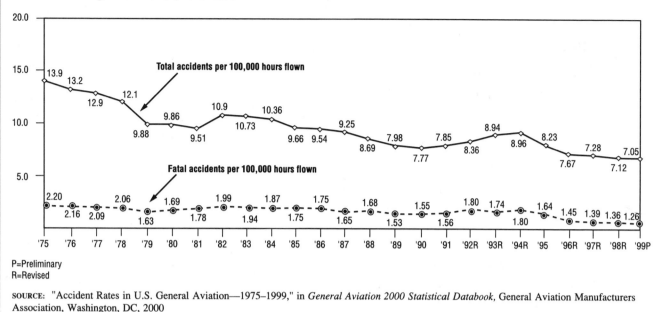

Accident rates in general aviation, 1975–1999

FIGURE 7.6

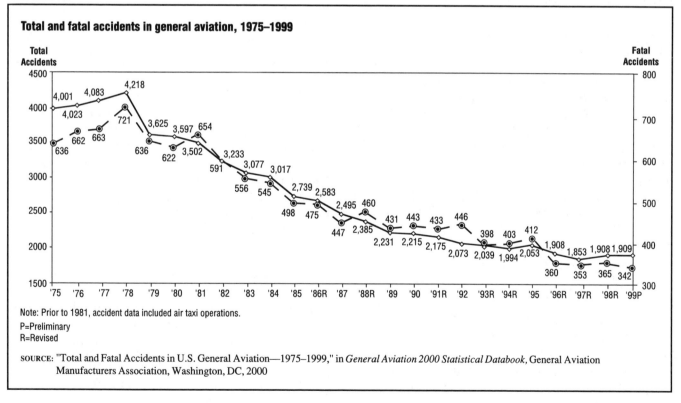

Total and fatal accidents in general aviation, 1975–1999

Note: Prior to 1981, accident data included air taxi operations.
P=Preliminary
R=Revised

motions, and advance purchase tickets allow passengers with time to plan a trip to get greatly reduced price tickets. In fact, it is possible that one passenger, who bought a bargain advance purchase ticket, may be sitting next to a business traveler who paid four times as much for her last-minute ticket on the same flight.

After deregulation, customer complaints about flight delays and cancellations, overbookings (flights with more tickets sold than seats actually available), bad airline food, cramped seating conditions, and lost luggage skyrocketed as new carriers entered the market and airlines began to experience cost pressures and cut corners on service. Pas-

FIGURE 7.7

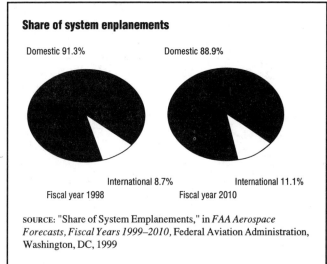

Share of system enplanements

Domestic 91.3%   Domestic 88.9%

International 8.7%   International 11.1%

Fiscal year 1998   Fiscal year 2010

SOURCE: "Share of System Emplanements," in *FAA Aerospace Forecasts, Fiscal Years 1999–2010,* Federal Aviation Administration, Washington, DC, 1999

ment, some of which is decades old and in the process of being replaced.

GOING GLOBAL—FOREIGN MARKETS

Under the Carter Administration, Congress passed the International Air Transportation Competition Act of 1979 (PL 96-192), intended to create a more competitive international system of airline travel. Despite concern among many foreign governments about the new law, a few governments—mainly those that realized their national airlines had more to gain than to lose—edged toward the U.S. "open skies" objective (the easing of market restrictions between the United States and other countries).

In 1995, the United States signed an open-skies agreement with Canada for full open-sky service, after a three-year phase-in period. The value of the agreement to the economy has been estimated at about $15 million per year. Bilateral open-skies agreements, enabling each country to provide increased air service to and from the other, have also been reached with 53 countries in Europe, Asia, Latin America, and the Middle East. On May 1, 2000, the U.S., Brunei, Chile, New Zealand, and Singapore signed a new Multilateral Agreement to replace the bilateral agreements between them. The United States has talked to other countries about easing the market restrictions as well. More agreements over the next few years could significantly increase the level of activity between United States carriers and foreign flag carriers.

The International Market

Most long-term economic indicators are positive for the industry. Global passenger traffic is projected to grow at an average annual rate of 5.9 percent in the first decade of the 21st century. The FAA forecasts that international enplanements will grow at a faster rate than domestic enplanements. In 1998, 91.3 percent of enplanements were domestic. This will likely drop to 88.9 percent in 2010. (See Figure 7.7.)

Passenger capacity requirements are expected to rise by 5.6 percent annually. In order to satisfy those projected needs, it will be necessary to expand the world's passenger jet fleet to nearly 18,600 aircraft by 2014, roughly doubling today's active fleet. At the same time, approximately 4,800 active jetliners will be permanently retired. Most of these will be short- and medium-range narrow-body aircraft.

Of the more than 635.4 million U.S. domestic and international passengers enplaned on U.S. scheduled airlines in 1999, more than 53 million were on international routes. International freight (revenue ton miles) surpassed domestic shipments, reflecting the increasing importance of international air cargo and foreign trade.

International aviation is increasingly important to U.S. airlines. In 1998, the FAA estimated that U.S. and

sengers today are flying on more crowded airplanes, waiting in more congested hub airports, facing more delayed take-offs, and putting up with more stopovers en route to their destinations than ever before. These aggravations have contributed to cases of "air rage," when out-of-control passengers have fought with flight crews and endangered the lives of everyone on the plane. The Association of Flight Attendants reported in 2001 that there were approximately 4,000 cases of air rage each year, and they complained that, although air rage is a felony, few cases are prosecuted. Air rage most often involves passengers who drink alcohol excessively, smoke in lavatories, or continue to use their electronic devices when told to turn them off.

Air passengers have also endured long hours strapped into airplane seats on the tarmac, waiting, without being told the reason for the delay. They have arrived at the airport and found their flights cancelled. They have sat for long flights in narrow seats, with the passenger in front leaning back, inches from their face. They have arrived at their destination, only to find that their luggage went elsewhere. With record numbers of airline delays in 2000, and a 16 percent increase in consumer complaints, Congress has considered a "Bill of Rights" for airline passengers, which would ensure passengers' rights and regulate how the airlines treat their customers. Such a measure was introduced in the Senate in 1999, and again in 2001.

The problems can not all be attributed to deregulation. From 1980 to 1998, the number of domestic passenger miles more than doubled from 204.4 billion to an estimated 459.7 billion and is forecast to reach 737 billion by 2010. Also, the number of aircraft used by certified air carriers more than doubled from 2,818 to 5,961. These are huge increases in a short period of time. While airports have expanded, they have not kept up with this rapid growth. Furthermore, the FAA, which controls the movement of these aircraft, still works with outdated equip-

foreign flag carriers conveyed a total of 126.1 million passengers between the United States and the rest of the world, a number that is expected to increase to 230.2 million in 2010, an average annual growth rate of 5.1 percent. Passenger traffic is forecasted to increase by 6.3 percent annually in Latin American markets, 5.8 percent in Pacific markets, 4.4 percent in Atlantic markets, and 3.3 percent between the United States and Canada.

EUROPE. With nearly 50 million passengers flying between the United States and Europe annually (according to DOT statistics in 2000), trans-Atlantic service is the largest international market for U.S. airlines. Teaming up, or forming alliances, is emerging as one way American and European airlines can gain footholds on each other's continents, in spite of continuing governmental controls that hamper foreign competition. Although airlines claim these unions will produce smoother, "seamless" travel for passengers, the greatest benefit for the airlines is a financial one—greater access to markets. Under such pacts, the two airlines operate as one to avoid foreign ownership limitations.

The FAA expects the industry to continue toward globalization through agreements. The number of alliances has recently increased. Northwest and KLM have formed an alliance; Delta has made agreements with Air France, AeroMexico, Air Jamaica, China Southern, Czech Airlines, Korean Air, Malaysia, Singapore Airlines, and South African Airways; and United, Lufthansa, SAS, Thai Airlines, Air Canada, and Varig formed the Star Alliance. Alliances also offer shared frequent flier benefits to passengers.

Despite the fact that Europe's population is larger than that of the United States, intra-Europe air travel accounts for just 8.5 percent of the world's scheduled airline traffic, compared to 41 percent within North America. Air travel in Europe is complicated by certain structural factors. An outdated air traffic control system limits capacity. Restrictions on over-flights (the right to fly over another country's territory) mean that some flights between countries in Europe use more time and fuel than would otherwise be necessary. Many European airports are at capacity, thus discouraging new service. Most Europeans prefer to travel by train, particularly for shorter distances. Train fares are often much lower than air fares, and seating on European trains is more comfortable than the typical coach seat on any jumbo jet. In addition, trains generally drop the passenger off downtown in their destination city.

CHAPTER 8

BUSES AND MASS TRANSIT

BUSES FROM CITY TO CITY

Buses, also called motorcoaches, have played a significant role in the U.S. transportation system, connecting small towns that do not have railway or airline service with other towns and cities. However, the nation's scheduled intercity (between cities) bus system has been in decline since the end of World War II.

Growing Competition

In the early 1950s, buses saw competition on a number of fronts. After World War II, automobiles began to be more readily available to the public, and America's love affair with the automobile began. The construction of the national highway system, which began in earnest in the 1950s, enabled people to drive long distances. At the same time, airline fares became less expensive, and more travelers could enjoy the convenience, speed, and comfort of air travel. The 1971 creation of Amtrak, the national passenger railroad system, also posed a threat to commercial bus carriers—because the federal government supported the new rail company, it could offer cheaper fares to its riders. In addition, Americans began leaving rural areas—best served by buses—for the cities and suburbs.

By the late 1960s and early 1970s, bus ridership had dwindled to about 400 million riders annually. In subsequent years, the number of people using buses continued to drop. Between 1987 and 1997, scheduled intercity bus traffic did increase 5.3 percent, from 333 million to 351 million riders, but bus ridership declined in relation to the overall passenger transportation market. Bus passengers represented 30.7 percent of intercity passengers in 1987 and 27.3 percent in 1997. (See Figure 8.1.)

The number of locales served by intercity buses also fell, from 17,000 locations in 1968 to 5,690 in 1991. By the spring of 1996, intercity buses served or stopped at only 4,274 cities. In 1997, intercity buses accounted for 29.6 billion passenger-miles (the cumulative sum of the distances

ridden by each passenger), just 1.2 percent of domestic intercity miles traveled. (See Figure 8.2.) About half (52 percent) of interstate bus companies own six or fewer buses; only one percent (161) own 100 or more buses.

GREYHOUND LINES

Greyhound Lines, Inc., is the largest of all the private bus companies and is the only remaining nationwide provider of scheduled, regular-route intercity bus service. During 2000, Greyhound reported that it carried 25.4 million passengers, with service to 2,600 destinations across North America.

The decades of industry decline, along with the pressures of union wage disputes, culminated in Greyhound's filing for bankruptcy protection in 1991. Although it emerged from the bankruptcy intact, Greyhound has continued to struggle for survival and has undergone major restructuring. In 1998, Greyhound reported net income of $35.2 million, or $0.50 per share—the first full-year profit realized by the company since 1993.

Struggling with years of declining ridership, bankruptcy, and a poor image, Greyhound has taken measures to attract the public back to bus service. It has renovated bus stations and increased security at terminals. In addition, Greyhound has instituted airline marketing techniques such as mail delivery of tickets and computerized reservations. A smoking ban keeps the air fresher; express routes between big cities decrease travel time; and plans are underway to make rental cars available at terminals, as they are at airports.

New services being offered by Greyhound include casino trips to popular gambling destinations around the country and other specialized travel tours. In 1998, its casino ridership contributed over $30 million to the company's revenues. Bus-to-air travel service is a recent option offered by Greyhound. Initiated in the mid-1990s at Hartsfield Airport in Atlanta, Greyhound now serves 13 airports

FIGURE 8.1

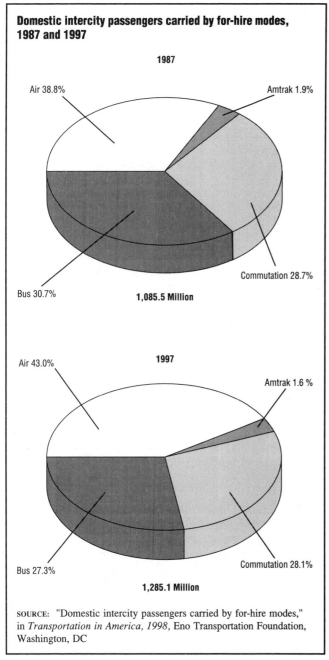

Domestic intercity passengers carried by for-hire modes, 1987 and 1997

1987

Air 38.8%

Amtrak 1.9%

Commutation 28.7%

Bus 30.7%

1,085.5 Million

1997

Air 43.0%

Amtrak 1.6 %

Commutation 28.1%

Bus 27.3%

1,285.1 Million

SOURCE: "Domestic intercity passengers carried by for-hire modes," in *Transportation in America, 1998,* Eno Transportation Foundation, Washington, DC

FIGURE 8.2

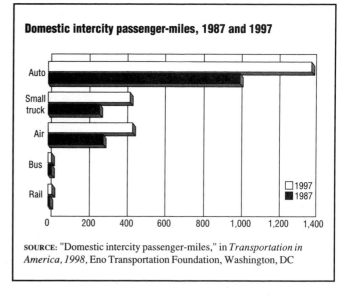

Domestic intercity passenger-miles, 1987 and 1997

SOURCE: "Domestic intercity passenger-miles," in *Transportation in America, 1998,* Eno Transportation Foundation, Washington, DC

around the country. The bus company provides pickup and drop-off service to terminals at selected airports. A similar service is available to various Amtrak stations.

Changes at Greyhound

In 1998, Greyhound formed joint ventures with several Mexican bus carriers to create Autobuses Americanos and Autobuses Amigos. The two new companies, operating under a Greyhound subsidiary, Sistema Internacional Transporte de Autobuses, Inc. (S.I.T.A.), provides cross-border bus service between five southwestern states and several cities in Mexico.

In 1999, Greyhound began to test a new communications system on 250 buses. Called On-Guard Tracker Sys-

tem, it is a satellite/cellular personal security and vehicle tracking system. The two-way communication and tracking system allows drivers to contact an emergency center or a Greyhound dispatcher by pushing a button. If the test run is successful, Greyhound will install the system on all its 2,400 buses.

Greyhound has been in the shipping business since 1930. In February 1999, Greyhound expanded its shipping services when it acquired On Time Delivery, a Minnesota-based courier company. In June 1999, the company further expanded shipping in the Midwest with the acquisition of Larson Express, a Chicago-area courier. The two courier companies will provide Greyhound with pickup and delivery services for its shipping customers and allow Greyhound to rebuild its package express service in the Midwest. Today, shipping constitutes only 4 percent of the company's total revenues.

In March 1999, Greyhound became a wholly owned subsidiary of Laidlaw, Inc., based in Burlington, Ontario, Canada. The merger makes Laidlaw the largest provider of school and intercity bus, municipal transit, patient transportation, and emergency department management services in North America.

REGULATORY REFORM

Congress had hoped to reverse the downward trend in the bus industry by enacting the Bus Regulatory Reform Act (PL 97-261) in 1982. This act deregulated the bus industry, diminishing the role of the federal Interstate Commerce Commission (ICC) (since replaced by the Office of Motor Carriers) and state agencies and giving bus firms greater freedom to set rates and determine routes. Despite the act, bus companies continued to face declining profits.

The Intermodal Surface Transportation Act of 1991 (PL 102-240) was an attempt to further improve bus transportation. The law required the states to use 15 percent of certain federal transportation grants to help promote intercity bus traffic. For fiscal years 1992 through 1997, the act set aside about $122 million in federal grant funds for states to use specifically for intercity bus service. A state does not have to use the funds, however, if the governor certifies that the state's bus needs are met by local funding or passenger revenues.

In 1998, Congress passed the Transportation Equity Act for the Twenty-first Century (TEA-21; PL 105-178). It included funding for improved rural (city to city) bus service and for new buses that operate on cleaner fuel, such as natural gas. The Blue Bird Corporation, of Macon, Georgia, has already begun manufacturing school buses that run on natural gas. Motorcoaches using natural gas engines are currently in operation in Los Angeles, San Diego, Atlanta, Phoenix, Tampa, Miami, Washington, D.C., New York, and numerous other cities, mainly in city transit systems. In 1999, in fact, 65 per cent of city transit systems had at least some natural gas buses. Some city fleets have changed over entirely to natural gas buses. These alternative fuel vehicles have not yet made a mark on the intercity bus industry, however.

WHO RIDES INTERCITY BUSES?

According to a 1996 Greyhound survey, 49 percent of riders traveled 200 miles or less on the bus; 56 percent traveled for pleasure. Most travelers were alone (73 percent) and did not own an automobile (64 percent). Most of the passengers were female (56 percent) and single (70 percent). The ages of travelers were spread fairly evenly from 18 to 65 years and older. Thirty-six percent of riders were employed full time, 22 percent were high school graduates, and 33 percent had some college education. Nearly 30 percent lived alone, 51 percent were white, 24 percent were African-American, and 11 percent were Asian.

CHARTER OR TOURIST BUSES

A charter bus is rented for a special reason. If, for example, a student group plans to attend a museum or special event, it may rent—or charter—a bus for a day. If the students are visiting a distant city, they might choose to buy a ticket on a sightseeing bus that will show them city landmarks and sights. A bus used for this purpose is called a tourist bus.

Charter and tourist buses have become an increasingly large part of the bus system as intercity passenger traffic has declined. In the 1990s, scheduled buses carrying people from town to town represented only a small slice (10.9 percent) of all bus traffic. The remaining traffic consisted of charter (66.6 percent) and tourist (22.5 percent)

buses. At a time when most intercity passenger carriers are losing money, charter and tourist bus companies are often quite profitable.

BUILDING BUSES

There are seven manufacturers of buses in the United States (MCI, Dina, Neoplan, Eagle, Prevost, Van Hool, and Setra), none of which are American-owned. In 1996, the most recent year for which figures were available, 2,650 intercity coaches were either built or sold in North America, a 25 percent increase over 1995.

Buses built today are not necessarily made for commercial bus companies. Many buses are now custom built for private use. These vehicles may be very luxurious, with comfortable chairs and beds for sleeping. Some buses are built to be used as mobile medical clinics for delivering vaccinations, performing health screenings, or taking blood donations. Entertainers and performers who tour from city to city also use customized buses.

In addition, manufacturers build buses as recreational homes for people who want to live in the bus and travel the country. These buses often have many features of home, such as bathrooms and kitchens, televisions, and compact disk (CD) players. Some very expensive motorhome buses can cost over a million dollars. Industry sources estimate that there are more than 5,000 of these recreational buses traveling the roads of the United States.

Until the mid-80s, buses were also often seen on the political campaign trail, but fell out of favor when candidates decided they needed faster modes of transportation. Recently, however, some candidates for public office have turned once more to buses in order to visit small cities and towns and appear more accessible to voters. These campaign buses are equipped with multiple telephone lines, faxes, and satellite phones.

Cost

According to the Motorcoach Census 2000, prepared by research firm R.L. Banks & Associates for the American Bus Association, the average cost of a new 45-foot motorcoach (more than 90 percent of motorcoaches are 40 feet or longer) is more than $350,000. For fuel economy, buses average 5.8 miles per gallon of fuel, but, if they are carrying an average of 30 passengers, that is said to be equivalent to 165 passenger-miles per gallon. In 1999, the operating cost for a motorcoach was figured to be $1.46 per mile, including driver and fuel. This figure varies with fuel price changes.

Hybrid Buses

Hybrid buses are buses designed to use less energy and run on cleaner or more efficient fuels than traditional buses. A new hybrid bus is being used as a shuttle

TABLE 8.1

Urban mass transit active fleet and infrastructure, 1997

	Urbanized areas over 1 million	Urbanized areas under 1 million	Total
Vehicles			
Buses	43,169	20,088	63,257
Heavy rail	10,273	0	10,273
Light rail	1,216	46	1,262
Self-propelled commuter rail	2,520	0	2,520
Commuter rail trailers	2,757	0	2,757
Commuter rail locomotives	624	0	624
Vans	12,620	8,662	21,282
Other (including ferryboats)	145	138	283
Rural service vehicles	0	17,879	17,879
Special service vehicles	4,400	24,931	29,331
Total active vehicles	**77,723**	**71,745**	**149,468**
Infrastructure			
Track mileage			
Heavy rail	2,148	0	2,148
Commuter rail	6,845	104	6,949
Light rail	780	23	803
Other rail	21	2	23
Total track mileage	**9,794**	**129**	**9,922**
Stations			
Heavy rail	997	0	997
Commuter rail	1,103	8	1,111
Light rail	493	37	530
Other rail	36	7	43
Total transit rail stations	**2,629**	**52**	**2,681**
Maintenance facilities			
Heavy rail	53	0	53
Light rail	23	3	26
Commuter rail	41	0	41
Ferryboat	6	1	7
Buses	272	235	507
Demand response	28	55	83
Other	9	3	12
Rural transit maintenance facilities	0	450	450
Total maintenance facilities	**433**	**746**	**1,179**

SOURCE: "Exhibit 2-18. Urban mass transit active fleet and infrastructure, 1997," in *1999 Status of the Nation's Surface Transportation: Conditions and Performance Report,* Department of Transportation, Federal Highway Administration, Washington, DC

between terminals at Logan Airport in Boston. The vehicle hums at a constant tone, never emits visible exhaust, and runs on about half the horsepower used by a compact car. The bus is 30 feet long, is powered by two electric motors—one for each rear wheel—and has a natural gas engine. The bus, made of more fiberglass than steel, is two-thirds as heavy as a regular bus. The prototype cost about $1 million, while a comparably sized bus costs between $225,000 and $275,000. The cost of the hybrid model is expected to drop, however, as other bus designers move in the same direction.

New York City has been using five hybrid buses with conventional steel bodies since September 1998 and plans to purchase 10 more. The New York City hybrid bus has two electric motors powered by batteries charged continuously by a generator, which in turn is powered by the small natural gas engine. According to a spokesman for New York City Transit, the hybrid buses afford a great reduction in energy use; when the bus stops, the brake pedal turns the drive motors into generators, slowing the bus and converting the energy into electricity that flows back into the battery. A conventional New York City bus the same size as the hybrid would require a 190-horsepower diesel engine, while the hybrid uses a 68-horsepower engine.

URBAN MASS TRANSIT

The term "mass transportation" encompasses a wide range of vehicles and systems but generally includes transport by bus, rail, or other conveyance, either publicly or privately owned, which provides service to the public in a particular region on a regular, frequent, and continuing basis. However, mass transportation can also include less formal arrangements known as "ridesharing," the voluntary association of individuals in a variety of conveyances including vanpools, carpools, and shared-ride taxis. It differs from intercity buses, railroads, and other forms of transportation because it is designed to carry large numbers of people over relatively short distances, such as their commute from home to work.

While the motor bus is the most widely used mass transit vehicle, a variety of fixed-guideway modes (steel wheels or rubber tires on a set path) operate in U.S. cities. These modes include rapid rail, light rail, commuter rail, subway, trolleys, cable cars, ferryboats, and tramways. Table 8.1 shows the array of vehicles and types of infrastructures that make up the U.S. transit system.

A HISTORY OF MASS TRANSIT RIDERSHIP

In 1827, a 12-passenger horse-drawn carriage began carrying passengers along Broadway in New York City, marking the debut of what would become mass transportation. Horses continued to pull most passenger cars for most of the nineteenth century, but in 1887, Frank Sprague built and profitably ran an electric streetcar (trolley) company in Richmond, Virginia. Cars moved through streets with the help of electric current, delivered by overhead trolley lines connected to a central power source.

Sprague's success led to a veritable explosion in electric car lines, and by 1895, approximately 850 electric car lines were running over 10,000 miles of track. In 1897, Boston officials came up with the innovative idea of putting the electric cars underground, creating the country's first subway line. In 1904, New York City inaugurated its subway service.

In such cities as New York, Chicago, and Boston, the electric streetcar and subway offered a major advance in comfort and relatively pollution-free transportation. Previously, these cities had built overhead railroads or "els," for elevated railways. These "els," however, were expensive to construct and blocked out light to the streets underneath. Furthermore, the small steam engines that usually pulled three or four cars proved to be hazardous, because they dropped soot and hot coals on the pedestrians below.

FIGURE 8.3

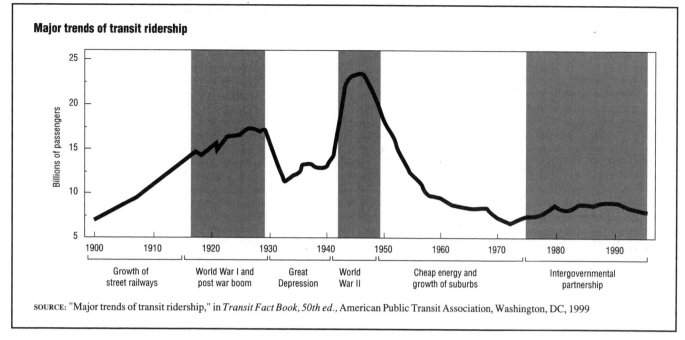

Major trends of transit ridership

SOURCE: "Major trends of transit ridership," in *Transit Fact Book, 50th ed.,* American Public Transit Association, Washington, DC, 1999

By comparison, electric trains were far cleaner and safer. Many cities introduced cable cars during the latter part of the nineteenth century, but only San Francisco's cable car system remains active today, both amusing tourists and transporting the city's citizens. In 1905, the first motorized bus company began operating in New York City.

Transit ridership has gone through several major cycles of growth and decline over the past century. For the first three decades (1900 to 1929), mass transit grew steadily in popularity. By the late 1920s, more than 1,000 cities and towns had trolley systems operating nearly 63,000 streetcars over about 40,000 miles of track. During the Great Depression (from 1929 through the 1930s), there was a steep decline in the number of transit riders. Unemployed people were no longer traveling to work, and money was scarce, making pleasure trips infrequent.

World War II (1939–1945) brought about another surge of interest in mass transit, because gasoline and rubber tires were strictly rationed and automobile manufacturers built fewer cars and more military equipment, such as jeeps and tanks. During the war years, employment was high, especially among the growing female labor force, and public ridership shot up 80 percent. The number of transit passengers peaked at an all-time high of over 23 billion in 1946.

Following the war, a number of factors contributed to the decline in ridership on transit systems. Low-cost, tax-deductible mortgages, a growing number of highways, and inexpensive fuel prices made suburban living and car ownership extremely attractive. The returning soldiers began buying the newly available cars, starting families, and purchasing houses in less congested areas. The rapid growth of suburban living contributed to a decentralization of housing, employment, shopping, and recreation.

The popularity and affordability of the automobile and the increasing development of new highways led many Americans to rely more heavily on their personal cars. Cars promised a wonderful world of speed, freedom, and convenience, taking drivers and passengers in comfort and privacy wherever and whenever they wanted to travel. Americans' love affair with the car has never waned.

Government officials began seeing public transportation as a relic from an earlier time and, consequently, gave it less support. As a result of these changing American attitudes, private transit systems were faced with a deadly spiral of increasing costs, deferred maintenance, rising fares, declining ridership, shrinking profits, deteriorating equipment, and decreasing quality of service. Mass transit became an increasingly unappealing alternative to the private automobile. These factors combined to produce a steep decline in the public's interest in using mass transit. In 1973, transit ridership reached an all-time low of seven billion passengers. (See Figure 8.3.)

A Renewed Interest—The Government Becomes Involved

Not until the 1960s and 1970s did serious interest again develop in mass transit. Urban and suburban growth led to frequent traffic jams. Noise and air pollution became an increasing worry. Rising fuel prices provided further incentive to seek alternatives to cars. In 1961, Congress included a $25 million mass transit pilot demonstration grant in the Housing and Urban Development Act (PL 87-117). Three years later, in 1964, Congress approved the

TABLE 8.2

Operating Funding Sources, 1984–1999

Year	Directly generated funds[c]			Government funds				Total Public Funds[e]	Total
	Pasenger Fares[a]	Other	Total	Local[c]	State	Federal	Total		
1984	4,447.70	780.5	5,228.20	5,399.1 (b)	(b)	995.8	6,394.90	6,394.90	11,623.10
1985	4,574.70	701.8	5,276.50	5,978.5 (b)	(b)	939.6	6,918.10	6,918.10	12,194.60
1986	5,113.10	737.3	5,850.40	4,244.50	2,305.60	941.2	7,491.30	7,491.30	13,341.70
1987	5,114.10	776.6	5,890.70	4,680.60	2,564.60	955.1	8,200.30	8,200.30	14,091.00
1988	5,224.60	840.7	6,065.30	4,893.10	2,677.10	905.1	8,471.30	8,471.30	14,536.60
1989	5,419.90	836.7	6,256.60	4,995.40	2,796.30	936.6	8,728.30	8,728.30	14,984.90
1990	5,890.80	895	6,785.80	5,326.80	2,970.60	970	9,267.40	9,267.40	16,053.20
1991	6,037.20	766.8	6,804.00	5,373.40	3,199.50	955.9	9,728.80	9,728.80	16,532.80
1992[d]	6,152.50	645.9	6,798.40	5,268.10	3,879.50	969.1	10,116.70	10,116.70	16,915.10
1993	6,350.90	764	7,114.90	5,490.60	3,704.20	966.5	10,161.30	10,161.30	17,276.20
1994	6,756.00	2,270.60	9,026.60	4,171.20	3,854.40	915.6	8,941.20	10,570.30	17,967.80
1995	6,800.90	2,812.20	9,613.10	3,980.90	3,829.60	817	8,627.50	10,171.70	18,240.60
1996	7,416.30	2,928.20	10,344.50	4,128.50	4,081.80	596.4	8,806.70	10,502.10	19,151.20
1997	7,545.70	3,308.40	10,854.10	4,095.10	3,918.70	647	8,660.80	10,524.40	19,514.90
1998	7,969.60	3,684.70	11,654.30	4,376.90	4,279.40	751.2	9,407.50	11,360.90	21,061.80
1999 P	8,282.40	3,647.60	11,930.00	4,539.80	4,878.60	871.8	10,290.20	12,574.70	22,220.20
1999 % of Total	37.30%	16.40%	53.70%	20.40%	22.00%	3.90%	46.30%	56.60%	100.00%

P = Preliminary
[a] Includes fares retained by contractors; beginning 1991 includes fare subsidies formerly included in "other".
[b] "Local" and "state" combined.
[c] "Local" includes taxes levied directly by transit agency and other subsidies from local government such as bridge and tunnel tolls and non-transit parking lot funds. Beginning 1994, such funds reclassified from "local" to "other".
[d] Beginning 1992, "local" and "other" declined by about $500 million due to change in accounting procedures at New York City Transit Authority.
[e] Includes "Total Government Funds" plus that portion of "Other Directly Generated Funds" included in "Local Government Funds" beginning in 1994 consisting of transit agency-raised taxes, tolls, and other dedicated funds.

SOURCE: "Table 17. Operating Funding Sources, millions of dollars," in *Public Transportation Fact Book,* American Public Transportation Association, Washington, DC, 2001

Urban Mass Transportation (UMT) Act (PL 88-365). Passed mainly to help public authorities take over ailing private transit systems, the bill also called for improved mass transit. The UMT Act established federal matching grants (two-thirds federal, one-third local) for repairing, improving, or developing mass transit. A 1966 amendment to the UMT Act directed the Secretary of Transportation to establish a comprehensive research plan.

The Urban Mass Transportation Act of 1970 (PL 91-453) created the Urban Mass Transportation Administration (UMTA). It also replaced the year-to-year financing for transportation measures with a more reliable 12-year federal funding plan. Other provisions promoted a greater commitment to urban transit construction. The Federal Aid Highway Act of 1973 (PL 93-87) made highway trust monies available for urban mass transit. It increased the matching grant share to 80 percent federal, 20 percent local.

In 1974, transit ridership began to rise again, as price spikes and gasoline shortages caused by the Organization of Petroleum Exporting Countries (OPEC) oil embargo left many motorists either waiting in long lines at gas stations or with empty gas tanks. This crisis prompted the National Mass Transportation Assistance Act of 1974 (PL 95-503), which allocated federal aid for capital expenses and permitted assistance for operating expenses.

The Federal Public Transportation Act of 1978 (PL 95-599) established a $16.4 billion grant and loan program for public transit capital and operating assistance through 1982, the largest commitment ever. Ridership rose until about 1980, and has since leveled off.

The Reagan Administration

The administration of President Ronald Reagan (1981–1989) adopted a policy arguing that it was not the responsibility of the federal government to subsidize mass transit. The use of federal funds, the administration claimed, contributed to local inefficiencies, such as underused routes and unrealistically low fares. Consequently, with every budget proposal, the Reagan Administration tried to phase out operating subsidies, although the Transportation Assistance Act of 1982 (PL 97-424) authorized continued operating subsidies through 1986. Even though President Reagan attempted to reduce the actual authorizations, mass transit continued to receive subsidies for capital purchases (buses, railway cars, stations) because the legislation mandated that one penny of the nickel-a-gallon gasoline tax increase be used for mass transit.

Mass Transportation in the 1990s

Legislators from urban areas most directly affected by the proposed cuts successfully prevented the Reagan

TABLE 8.3

Examples of fuel savings to a person commuting to work on public transportation

Length of trip	Miles traveled per year[a]	Annual fuel savings, gallons based on following fuel efficiencies					
		15 Miles per gallon	20 Miles per gallon	25 Miles per gallon	30 Miles per gallon	35 Miles per gallon	40 Miles per gallon
2 miles	944	62.9	47.2	37.8	31.5	27	23.6
5 miles	2,360	157.3	118	94.4	78.7	67.4	59
10 miles	4,720	314.7	236	188.8	157.3	134.9	118
20 miles	9,440	629.3	472	377.6	314.7	269.7	236
30 miles	14,160	944	708	566.4	472	404.6	354
40 miles	18,880	1,258.70	944	755.2	629.3	539.4	472
50 miles	23,600	1,573.30	1,180.00	944	786.7	674.3	590
60 miles	28,320	1,888.00	1,416.00	1,132.80	944	809.1	708

[a] Based on 472 trips per year based on 365 days minus 52 Saturdays minus 52 Sundays minus 7 holidays minus 10 days vacation minus 8 days sick leave times 2 trips per day.

SOURCE: "Table 68. Examples of fuel savings to a person commuting to work on public transportation," in *Public Transportation Fact Book,* American Public Transportation Association, Washington, DC, 2001

Administration from eliminating federal subsidies. Under the George Bush Administration (1989–1993), Congress passed the Federal Transit Act Amendments, extending transit assistance through 1997 at higher levels than before, to be used for the modes of transportation best suited to individual areas and states.

In 1998, passenger fares and other directly generated funds contributed 55.3 percent to transit revenue. Federal government (3.6 percent), state funding (20.3 percent), and local assistance (20.8 percent) supplied the remaining funds needed to operate the systems. Mass transit is highly subsidized: state and local funding together (41.1 percent) accounted for more revenues than did passenger fares (37.8 percent). (See Table 8.2.)

ADVANTAGES OF MASS TRANSIT

Transit and Basic Mobility

Mass transit offers many advantages and may be the only alternative for many people. It gives mobility to those who cannot afford to purchase or maintain an automobile. It offers greater mobility to the handicapped, the young, and older Americans, freeing family and friends from the obligation of providing transportation for these individuals. It also gives the commuter the opportunity to leave the frustrations of driving in heavy traffic to someone else. Inner city residents use public transportation most often.

Mass transit often provides only minimal service to outlying suburbs, where job growth is the greatest. Therefore, this link between central city residents without cars to possible suburban jobs is weak or, sometimes, nonexistent. The Urban Mass Transportation Administration does not expect this situation to improve.

Fuel and Dollar Comparisons

For many commuters, mass transit can be more economical than driving to work alone. Annual transit costs can range from $236 to $2,077, depending on such factors as the number of miles traveled, transfer fees, and peak-hour surcharges. In 1999, the American Public Transportation Association (APTA) estimated that the cost for a single-occupant driver ranged from $4,661 for a small car to $6,332 for a sport utility vehicle, depending on the number of miles driven. Table 8.3 shows APTA estimates of the annual number of gallons of gasoline saved by a commuter when making a daily trip by public transportation, instead of by car.

Congestion and Land Use

Public transportation reduces congestion on the nation's highways, most notably during the already overcrowded "rush hours." Cities dependent on the automobile must set aside more land for streets, highways, and parking lots. Consequently, they tend to become more spread out. For example, streets and highways take up 68 percent of the land in Los Angeles. In downtown Chicago, which grew up before the automobile and has an extensive bus and rail system, roadways account for only 36 percent of land use. Not only do roadways cause the city to spread out, but they can also lower the tax base, since land used by public highways does not generate taxes.

The Federal Highway Administration (FHWA) reports that during peak driving times anywhere from 47 to 56 percent of all miles driven on urban highways and interstates are under congestion. (See Figure 3.4, Chapter 3.) In other words, during rush hour, up to 56 percent of drivers on major urban roads are experiencing heavy traffic.

Usage of mass transit varies widely from city to city. In the metropolitan area of New York City, more than half the people use mass transit to get to work. More than one-third of workers in Washington, D.C. and San Francisco use mass transit, and about one-fifth in Pittsburgh and Atlanta. Table 8.4 shows other American cities where significant proportions of workers use mass transit.

TABLE 8.4

Cities with highest percentage of workers using public transportation, 1990

City	Percent using public transportation
New York, NY	53.4
Hoboken, NJ	51.0
Jersey City, NJ	36.7
Washington, DC	36.6
San Francisco, CA	33.5
Boston, MA	31.5
Chicago, IL	29.7
Philadelphia, PA	28.7
Atlantic City, NJ	26.2
Arlington, VA	25.4
Newark, NJ	24.6
Cambridge, MA	23.5
Pittsburgh, PA	22.2
Baltimore, MD	22.0
Evanston, IL	20.9
Atlanta, GA	20.0
White Plains, NY	19.1
Camden, NJ	18.1
Oakland, CA	17.9
Hartford, CT	17.1
New Orleans, LA	16.9
Idaho Falls, ID	16.5
Minneapolis, MN	16.0
Seattle, WA	15.9
Berkeley, CA	15.2
Albany, NY	15.1

SOURCE: "Cities with highest percentage of workers using public transportation, 1990," in *Transit Fact Book, 50th ed.*, American Public Transit Association, Washington, DC, 1999

Economic Considerations

Since most downtowns were built before the explosion in automobile ownership and the migration to the suburbs, few can supply enough parking spaces to make shopping convenient. In addition, the growth of the suburbs has meant that downtown shopping districts are miles away from potential suburban shoppers. As a result, downtown stores have lost significant amounts of business to suburban shopping centers and malls. In fact, the so-called "Main Streets" of 50 years ago have been replaced in most suburbs by malls. Teenagers, young mothers, workers, and the elderly go the local malls to shop, eat, and see movies.

Effective public transport has helped to support some downtown business or, as in the case of BART (Bay Area Rapid Transit) in San Francisco, to revitalize it, but this is the exception, not the rule. Many systems have not met their original projections for ridership. Those who support mass transit claim that to simply add up direct financial costs and compare them with revenues does not give the full picture. A simple profit and loss statement does not take into account benefits to society, such as increased mobility for those without automobiles, increased employment opportunities, less congestion, better land use, increased downtown economic growth, and less pollution and energy use. These factors not only benefit society gen-

FIGURE 8.4

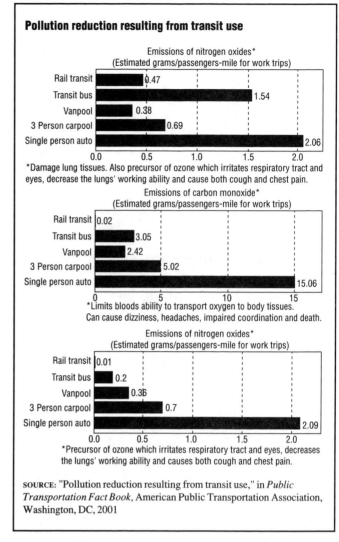

Pollution reduction resulting from transit use

Emissions of nitrogen oxides*
(Estimated grams/passengers-mile for work trips)

Rail transit	0.47
Transit bus	1.54
Vanpool	0.38
3 Person carpool	0.69
Single person auto	2.06

*Damage lung tissues. Also precursor of ozone which irritates respiratory tract and eyes, decrease the lungs' working ability and cause both cough and chest pain.

Emissions of carbon monoxide*
(Estimated grams/passengers-mile for work trips)

Rail transit	0.02
Transit bus	3.05
Vanpool	2.42
3 Person carpool	5.02
Single person auto	15.06

*Limits bloods ability to transport oxygen to body tissues. Can cause dizziness, headaches, impaired coordination and death.

Emissions of nitrogen oxides*
(Estimated grams/passengers-mile for work trips)

Rail transit	0.01
Transit bus	0.2
Vanpool	0.36
3 Person carpool	0.7
Single person auto	2.09

*Precursor of ozone which irritates respiratory tract and eyes, decreases the lungs' working ability and causes both cough and chest pain.

SOURCE: "Pollution reduction resulting from transit use," in *Public Transportation Fact Book,* American Public Transportation Association, Washington, DC, 2001

erally, but also have a real financial value that can justify considerable public support through financial subsidies.

Environmental Pollution

Half of all air pollution comes from transportation sources, most from automobiles. Proponents of mass transit point out that hydrocarbons and carbon monoxide emissions are reduced dramatically (more than 99 percent) on a trip by rail compared to the average trip by car, while nitrogen oxide emissions are reduced more than 77 percent. Riding the bus also promotes cleaner air, even with diesel buses. Taking the bus to work instead of driving a car cuts hydrocarbon emissions by almost 90 percent and reduces carbon monoxide fumes by about 80 percent. (Figure 8.4 shows a comparison of emissions by various modes of transportation.)

Energy Use

If more people used mass transit, the nation would use less energy. According to the federal Energy Information Agency, 66 percent of all oil and 27 percent of all the energy used by the United States in 1999 went towards transportation. Most of the energy used for transportation is consumed by cars and light trucks. Mass transit consumes far less energy per person carried. The APTA believes that one answer to the nation's energy problems and dependence on foreign sources lies in encouraging a move back to mass transit. For every commuter who uses mass transit instead of a car, the APTA estimates that 200 gallons of gasoline would be saved every year.

TRANSIT SYSTEMS—A VARIETY OF TYPES

In 1997, 5,975 transit agencies were transporting passengers in the United States. (See Table 8.5.) The following is a list of the most common types in service today.

- Transit Bus—a generic term for a rubber-tired vehicle with front and center doors and a rear-mounted diesel engine, usually designed for frequent-stop service. It is not equipped with luggage storage or restroom facilities. Many newer buses are fueled by natural gas, which significantly reduces emissions.

- Heavy Rail—an electric transit railway with the capacity for a heavy volume of traffic and character-

ized by multi-car trains, high speed, rapid acceleration, and exclusive rights-of-way. Heavy rail systems

TABLE 8.5

Number of transit agencies by mode

Mode	Number
Aerial tramway	1
Automated guideway transit	6
Bus	2,250
Cable car	1
Commuter rail	18
Demand response	5,214
Ferryboat (b)	25
Heavy rail	14
Inclined plane	5
Light rail	22
Monorail	2
Trolleybus	5
Vanpool	55
Total (a)	5,975

(a) Total is not sum of all modes since many agencies operate more than one mode.
(b) Excludes international, rural, rural interstate, island, and urban park ferries.

SOURCE: "Number of transit agencies by mode," in *Transit Fact Book, 50th ed.*, American Public Transit Association, Washington, DC, 1999

FIGURE 8.5

Denver's regional transportation district streetcars are a good example of a light rail system. Like most such systems, it relies on government funding to cover its expenses. *(AP/Wide World Photos. Reproduced by permission.)*

TABLE 8.6

Unlinked passenger trips by mode, 1984–1999
Millions

Year	Bus	Commuter rail	Demand response	Heavy rail	Light rail	Trolley bus	Other	Total
1984	5,908	267	62	2,231	135	165	61	8,829
1985	5,675	275	59	2,290	132	142	63	8,636
1986	5,753	306	63	2,333	130	139	53	8,777
1987	5,614	311	64	2,402	133	141	70	8,735
1988	5,590	325	73	2,308	154	136	80	8,666
1989	5,620	330	70	2,542	162	130	77	8,931
1990	5,677	328	68	2,346	175	126	79	8,799
1991	5,624	318	71	2,172	184	125	81	8,575
1992	5,517	314	72	2,207	188	126	77	8,501
1993	5,381	322	81	2,046	188	121	78	8,217
1994	4,871	339	88	2,169	284	118	80	7,949
1995	4,848	344	88	2,033	251	119	80	7,763
1996	4,887	352	93	2,157	261	117	81	7,948
1997	5,013	357	99	2,430	262	121	92	8,374
1998	5,399	381	95	2,393	276	117	89	8,750
1999 P	5,648	396	100	2,521	292	120	91	9,168
1999 % of Total	61.60%	4.30%	1.10%	27.50%	3.20%	1.30%	1.00%	100.00%

P = Preliminary

SOURCE: "Table 26. Unlinked passenger trips by mode, millions," in *Public Transportation Fact Book,* American Public Transportation Association, Washington, DC, 2001

TABLE 8.7

Passenger miles by mode of travel, 1984–1999
Millions

Year	Bus	Commuter rail	Demand response	Heavy rail	Light rail	Trolley bus	Other	Total
1984	21,595	6,207	349	10,111	416	364	382	39,424
1985	21,161	6,534	364	10,427	350	306	439	39,581
1986	21,395	6,723	402	10,649	361	305	369	40,204
1987	20,970	6,818	374	11,198	405	223	360	40,348
1988	20,753	6,964	441	11,300	477	211	434	40,580
1989	20,768	7,211	428	12,030	509	199	458	41,603
1990	20,981	7,082	431	11,475	571	193	410	41,143
1991	21,090	7,344	454	10,528	662	195	430	40,703
1992	20,336	7,320	495	10,737	701	199	453	40,241
1993	20,247	6,940	562	10,231	705	188	511	39,384
1994	18,832	7,996	577	10,668	833	187	492	39,585
1995	18,818	8,244	607	10,559	860	187	533	39,808
1996	19,096	8,351	656	11,530	957	184	604	41,378
1997	19,604	8,038	754	12,056	1,035	189	663	42,339
1998	20,360	8,704	735	12,284	1,128	182	735	44,128
1999 P	21,205	8,766	813	12,902	1,206	186	779	45,857
1999 % of Total	46.30%	19.10%	1.80%	28.10%	2.60%	0.40%	1.70%	100.00%

P = Preliminary

SOURCE: "Table 30. Passenger miles by mode, millions," in *Public Transportation Fact Book,* American Public Transportation Association, Washington, DC, 2001

are also known as "subways," "elevated railways," or "metropolitan railways" (metros).

- Light Rail—a type of electric transit railway with a "light volume" of traffic compared to "heavy rail." Generally, light rail includes streetcars (trolley cars) and tramways. (See Figure 8.5.)

- Commuter Railroad—a "main line" railroad (not electric) that involves passenger train service between a central city and adjacent suburbs. Commuter railroad service typically is characterized by multi-trip tickets, specific station-to-station fares, and normally only one or two main stations in the central business district. It is also known as a "suburban railroad."

- Demand Response Service—a type of non-fixed-route bus or van service that typically picks up and drops off passengers at any location within the transit provider's

TABLE 8.8

Ethnicity and race of public transportation riders by population group, 1992

Population of Urbanized Area/ Urban Place	White	Black	Hispanic	Other
Under 50,000	82%	6%	9%	3%
50,000-199,999	63%	24%	8%	5%
200,000-500,000	48%	34%	14%	4%
500,000-999,999	45%	41%	9%	5%
1 million and more	45%	31%	18%	6%
National average	45%	31%	18%	6%

SOURCE: "Table 33. Ethnicity and race of public transportation riders by population group," in *Public Transportation Fact Book,* American Public Transportation Association, Washington, DC, 2001

TABLE 8.9

Age of public transportation riders by population group, 1992

Population of Urbanized Area/ Urban Place	18 and under	19-64	65 and over
Under 50,000	21%	61%	18%
50,000-199,999	19%	68%	13%
200,000-500,000	15%	70%	15%
500,000-999,999	9%	77%	14%
1 million and more	10%	84%	6%
National average	10%	83%	7%

SOURCE: "Table 31. Age of public transportation riders by population group," in *Public Transportation Fact Book,* American Public Transportation Association, Washington, DC, 2001

TABLE 8.10

Gender of public transportation riders by population group, 1992

Population of Urbanized Area/ Urban Place	Male	Female
Under 50,000	36%	64%
50,000-199,999	43%	57%
200,000-500,000	39%	61%
500,000-999,999	38%	62%
1 million and more	49%	51%
National average	48%	52%

SOURCE: "Table 35. Gender of public transportation riders by population group," in *Public Transportation Fact Book,* American Public Transportation Association, Washington, DC, 2001

service area. The vehicles provide services at times requested by the passengers.

• Ridesharing—an informal and voluntary association of individuals in a variety of vehicles, including van-pools, carpools, and shared-ride taxis.

About 8.7 billion trips were made in 1998. The largest number of mass transit riders took the bus (61.7 percent); 27.3 percent traveled by heavy rail; 4.4 percent by commuter rail; 3.2 percent by light rail; and approximately 1 percent each by demand response and trolley bus. (See Table 8.6.) About 54 percent of these trips were for work; 15 percent for school; 9 percent, shopping; 9 percent, social; and 5.5 percent, medical.

In 1998, mass transit passengers traveled more than 44 billion miles. Nearly half (46 percent) was by bus; 27.8 percent by heavy rail; 19.7 percent, commuter rail; 2.5 percent, light rail; and the rest by demand response and trolley bus. (See Table 8.7.)

By 2000, 81 percent of all buses were wheelchair accessible, as were 93.1 percent of demand response vehicles. Nearly two-thirds (64 percent) of commuter rail cars

could accommodate wheelchairs, as could 98.5 percent of heavy rail cars and 76.7 percent of light rail cars.

A LOOK AT TRANSIT RIDERS

The American Public Transportation Association reports that in 2000, riders took approximately 9.4 billion trips on public transit in the United States. This reflects an increase of 3.5 percent over the 1999 figures and a 21 percent growth over the preceding five years.

APTA considered characteristics of mass transit users based on the size of the city where they lived. It found that approximately 55 percent were non-white. (See Table 8.8.) It also found that young people and those over 65 years of age made up nearly equal portions (10 percent and 7 percent, respectively) of transit users in cities with populations under 500,000 persons. (See Table 8.9.)

Women were more likely to use public transportation, especially in cities under one million people. (See Table 8.10.) Poorer Americans—those with incomes under $15,000—were the heaviest users of mass transit in cities under one million people. However, in cities of one million people or more, people with incomes of $15,000 or more made up a majority of public transport users, a fact that may be related to the overall higher cost of living in these regions. (See Table 8.11.)

In smaller cities with populations under 200,000, people used public transportation for many reasons, including work, school, going to the doctor, and social activities. In the larger cities, however, people used mass transit mainly to get to work or school. (See Table 8.12.)

In an effort to lure commuters to mass transit, cities are considering innovations—unusual design including futuristic architecture, use of artwork, and decoration with color murals and lighting—color, fantasy, and whimsy that planners hope will be "magnets" to commuters. Some cities that have experienced loss of riders on subways and buses, such as New York City, are proposing restructuring fare schedules to allow riders to transfer from subway to bus and are planning better connecting routes for such transfers.

SUBURBAN COMMUTING

As families headed to the outlying areas in the 1950s and 60s, many businesses followed. Between 1960 and 1980 alone, the growing suburbs doubled in size and received approximately two-thirds of all job growth. This explosion and shifting of growth is a major factor in the future of commuting.

A closer balance between the number of work opportunities and employees in a given suburb does not necessarily mean that there will be less commuting to work. Many workers still have to commute many miles from one suburb to another in large metropolitan areas. In fact, the most common commuter pattern now is the trip from one suburb to another. Suburb-to-suburb trips represent about 33 percent of all metropolitan commuting and the largest work trip growth over the last 20 years. About twice as many workers commute from suburb to suburb than commute from suburb to downtown.

Commuting to and from suburbs heavily favors the use of the private automobile. (Auto commuting refers not only to cars, but also to light trucks, vans, and sport utility vehicles.) The number of cars per household has risen steeply since 1960, and the number of available vehicles per person has almost doubled. In fact, the majority of households of every size have more vehicles than workers. The Federal Highway Administration (FHWA) reported in 1995 that 40 percent of American households owned two vehicles, while those households owning three or more vehicles totaled nearly 20 percent. (See Figure 8.6.) The doubling of the number of cars available for travel has meant that car commuting increased at the same time that mass transit use declined.

In contrast, according to FHWA, the number of households with no access to private transportation shrank to 8.1 percent in 1995. (See Figure 8.6.) Two-thirds of the households without vehicles also had no workers, and another 28 percent had only one worker. Zero-vehicle households are usually very small and are located in large central cities. The New York City area leads the list, with 20 percent of its households having no personal vehicle.

Carpooling

Despite energy issues, pollution, and traffic congestion, most motorists shun carpooling. Campaigns to persuade people to carpool or vanpool have generally failed. Among the reasons motorists prefer to drive alone are the ability to come and go at will, freedom to run errands with their own autos, and the ability to depart immediately in the case of family emergencies. Also cited are the choice of radio stations, privacy, and, most importantly, an unfettered, go-as-you-please American individualism.

When Congress passed the Clean Air Act Amendments of 1990 (PL 101-549), it intended to address such issues. In certain polluted regions, such as New York, Southern California, and the Chicago area, companies employing more than 100 people at a single site must develop plans to increase the number of employees using mass transit or carpooling. The amendments include fines against companies that have not drawn up such plans.

TABLE 8.11

Annual family income of public transportation riders by population group, 1992

Population of Urbanized Area/ Urban Place	Under $15,000	$15,000-$50,000	Above $50,000
Under 50,000	61%	36%	3
50,000-199,999	55%	39%	6
200,000-500,000	54%	38%	8
500,000-999,999	52%	42%	6
1 million and more	25%	57%	18
National average	28%	55%	17

SOURCE: "Table 32. Annual family income of public transportation riders by population group," in *Public Transportation Fact Book*, American Public Transportation Association, Washington, DC, 2001

TABLE 8.12

Purpose of public transportation trips by population group, 1992

Population of Urbanized Area/ Urban Place	Work	School	Shopping	Medical	Social	Other
Under 50,000	20%	9%	8%	34%	27%	2%
50,000-199,999	39%	22%	12%	6%	9%	12%
200,000-500,000	46%	19%	13%	5%	8%	9%
500,000-999,999	51%	15%	11%	5%	6%	12%
1 million and more	55%	15%	9%	5%	9%	7%
National average	54%	15%	9%	5%	9%	8

SOURCE: "Table 34. Purpose of public transportation trips by population group," in *Public Transportation Fact Book,* American Public Transportation Association, Washington, DC, 2001

GOVERNMENTAL ATTEMPTS TO CHANGE COMMUTER BEHAVIOR

Urban traffic congestion imposes large costs on society. Time spent in traffic results in lower productivity, excess fuel consumption, and increased pollution. The federal government, under mandate of the Clean Air Act Amendments of 1990 (PL 101-549), the Intermodal Surface Transportation Efficiency Act (ISTEA; PL 102-240) of 1991, the Transportation Equity Act for the Twenty-first Century, which reauthorizes ISTEA (TEA-21; PL 105-178), and other state and local regulations, has attempted to discourage drive-alone commuting.

The ISTEA (through September 1997) and TEA-21 (from 1998 through 2003) authorize special funding for projects likely to reduce vehicle miles traveled, decrease fuel consumption, or otherwise reduce congestion and improve air quality. The Clean Air Act requires employers in 11 states (Arizona, California, Connecticut, Georgia, Maryland, Minnesota, New Jersey, Oregon, Texas, Virginia, and Washington) to reduce drive-alone commuting among employees by providing incentives to employers. Some of the efforts include:

- Transit voucher programs—employers provide employees with vouchers for free or reduced fare to use for mass transit

- Taxing employers for parking space

- Zoning changes—changing zoning laws to encourage transit use and reduce the supply of parking spaces

- Cash returns for the value of parking spaces—offering employees cash equivalent to the market value of a parking space in lieu of the use of that space

- Higher gasoline taxes

- Congestion pricing—charging drivers for the use of congested roads

TEA-21 retains the basic structure of the federal transit programs authorized under ISTEA. TEA-21 provides $41 billion, $36 billion of which is guaranteed, in transit funds between 1998 and 2003. (The guaranteed amount is protected in the budget process and can only be allotted for transit uses, subject to annual appropriation by Congress.) The money will be spent in both rural and urban areas. New transportation systems will be built, and existing ones will be improved and modernized. The Rail Modernization Program will increase the proportion of new funds for newer fixed-guideway (steel wheel or rubber tires on a set path) systems.

Another benefit of TEA-21 is a $100 per month tax-exempt employee allowance that will be available for workers who use public transit, effective December 31, 2001. Prior to TEA-21, the maximum benefit was $65 per month.

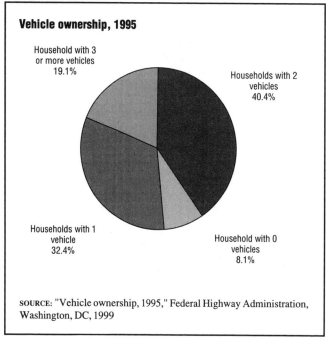

FIGURE 8.6

Vehicle ownership, 1995

Household with 3 or more vehicles 19.1%

Households with 2 vehicles 40.4%

Households with 1 vehicle 32.4%

Household with 0 vehicles 8.1%

SOURCE: "Vehicle ownership, 1995," Federal Highway Administration, Washington, DC, 1999

Two new programs were also created under TEA-21. The Clean Fuels Formula Grant program provides funds for adoption of clean fuel technologies, including purchase or lease of clean fuel buses and facilities. The Job Access and Reverse Commute Program funds projects designed to help welfare and low-income families and others who do not own cars get to and from higher-paying jobs in suburbs without bus service, or to travel to and from off-hour jobs, when other forms of public transportation have stopped running. The program authorized $50 million for 1999, of which $10 million was set aside for "reverse commuting" projects. Funding up to $150 million annually for five years may become available.

TRANSIT SAFETY

The U.S. Department of Transportation monitors U.S. mass transit workers for drug and alcohol use. Congress mandated the testing program, the largest of its kind in the United States, in 1991 in response to a series of accidents involving alcohol. Among them were the *Exxon Valdez* oil spill in 1989, which was partly attributed to the captain's drinking, and the derailment of a subway train that killed five people in New York City in 1991, in which the motorman's drinking was blamed.

The regulations apply to truck drivers, school bus drivers, railroad employees, pilots and air traffic controllers, merchant mariners, and others involved in "safety sensitive" jobs. New employees will be tested, and random tests of those already employed will be conducted.

The transportation industry had long held that testing was an invasion of privacy, but federal courts, in *Skinner,*

TABLE 8.13

Light-rail lines in comparable metro areas, 1998

	Length of line	Open	Cost	Average weekly ridership
Dallas	20 miles	1996 and 1997	$860 million	35,000
Denver	5.3 miles	1994	$116.5 million	16,000
Portland	15 miles	1986	214 million	33,000
Scramento	18 miles	1987	$176 million	27,500
Salt Lake City	15 miles (under construction)	2000 (projected)	$322 million	20,000 expected
St. Louis	17 miles	1993	$464 million	44,000

SOURCE: "Light-rail lines in comparable metro areas, 1998," in *Minneapolis Star Tribune,* March 29, 1998

Secretary of Transportation et al. v. Railway Labor Executives' Association et al. (839 F.2d 575, Ninth Circuit, 1989), decided that safety considerations can override privacy concerns, as in the decision to require drug testing of transportation employees.

Drug and alcohol abuses are not the only causes of accidents. Sometimes, trains are not equipped with the latest safety features. Following a February 1997 accident that took three lives in New Jersey when a transit train ran a red light and collided with another train, New Jersey Transit was ordered to install Automatic Brake Control (an automatic braking system) on every transit train.

The braking system automatically stops trains that run a red light. The system was designed to prevent the type of human error that was blamed for the crash in 1997. Automatic Brake Control is expensive; it can cost over $100 million, depending on the size of the rail network. However, a spokesman for a network that has installed the system claims that results are nearly guaranteed, since the Automatic Brake Control enables the train to stop itself.

Overly long work shifts are often responsible for contributing to fatigue and human error. Split shifts—extended work periods of up to fourteen and one-half hours with only a four-hour break in the middle—have been blamed for several accidents. One such case involved a shift that began at 6 p.m. and finished at 8:30 a.m. the following day, with a four-hour break during the night. In this accident, three people were killed and more than 160 were injured.

THE FUTURE OF MASS TRANSPORTATION

Light Rail Systems

Many U.S. cities have successfully introduced light-rail lines. Although such systems are expensive to build and to operate, and most do not make a profit, ridership is higher than expected, and six major cities have recently begun expanding their systems. (See Table 8.13.)

Portland, Oregon has extended its original 15-mile track by adding another 18 miles. The system's usage has grown even faster than they expected, with about 70,000 rides per day, as of early 2001. Voters in Denver, Colorado rejected a system-wide expansion in 1997, so the city has instead begun to extend its 5.3-mile light-rail system piece by piece. Average weekly ridership on Denver's light-rail system is 16,000. Sacramento, California, where 27,500 persons use the light-rail system weekly, plans to increase its 18 miles of track to 39 miles by 2002. In Salt Lake City, Utah a 15-mile line is currently being built, and another line is being planned for the 2002 Winter Olympic Games. Weekly ridership on the completed system is expected to amount to 20,000. Dallas, Texas recently added light-rail to its existing bus routes, and now has 20 miles of track and an average weekly ridership of 35,000 people.

Not all systems run smoothly, however. St. Louis, Missouri's ridership has grown from 44,000 per week in 1998 to 1.4 million commuters in fiscal year 2000, and the city plans to build another light-rail line. Unfortunately, the rail line has not come close to covering its operating expenses. A half-cent sales tax is helping to pay the cost of the light rail system. Los Angeles, California built too many rail lines too quickly and soon had a $50 million deficit. The system has gained some ground, however, and now averages 216,400 weekday riders on nearly 60 miles of track in the Los Angeles Metropolitan Area.

Light Rail in the Grand Canyon

In 1901, visitors to the Grand Canyon in Arizona took the Santa Fe Railroad to see the south rim of the canyon. Now, nearly 100 years later, mass transit is once again planned to reduce congestion in the park. Ground was broken recently on a $100 million light-rail system, the first to service a national park. The system is designed to cut vehicle traffic by 80 percent.

IMPORTANT NAMES AND ADDRESSES

Air Traffic Control Association, Inc.
2300 Clarendon Blvd., #711
Arlington, VA 22201
(703) 522-5717
FAX: (703) 527-7251
URL: http://www.atca.org

Air Transport Association of America
1301 Pennsylvania Ave. NW, #1100
Washington, DC 20004
(202) 626-4000
FAX: (202) 626-4166
URL: http://www.air-transport.org

American Automobile Association
1000 AAA Drive
Heathrow, FL 32746-5063
(407) 444-7000
FAX: (407) 444-7380
URL: http://www.aaa.com

American Bus Association
1100 New York Ave. NW, #1050
Washington, DC 20005
(202) 842-1645
FAX: (202) 842-0850
URL: http://www.buses.org
E-mail: abainfo@buses.org

American Public Transportation Association
1666 K Street NW, #1100
Washington, DC 20006
(202) 496-4889
FAX: (202) 496-4324
URL: http://www.apta.com

American Trucking Associations
2200 Mill Rd.
Alexandria, VA 22314
(703) 838-1775
FAX: (703) 519-5272
URL: http://www.truckline.com

Association of American Railroads
50 F St., NW
Washington, DC 20001
(202) 639-2100
FAX: (202) 639-2986
URL: http://www.aar.org

Bureau of Transportation Statistics
400 7th St. SW, Rm. 3430
Washington, DC 20590
(202) 366-DATA
FAX: (202) 366-3640
URL: http://www.bts.gov
E-mail: answers@bts.gov

Cargo Airline Association
1220 19th St. NW, #400
Washington, DC 20036
(202) 293-1030
FAX: (202) 293-4377
E-mail: cargoair@aol.com

Eno Transportation Foundation, Inc.
1634 I Street NW, #500
Washington, DC 20006
(202) 879-4700
FAX: (202) 879-4719
URL: http://www.enotrans.com

Federal Aviation Administration
800 Independence Ave., SW
Washington, DC 20591
(202) 267-8521
FAX: (202) 267-5039
URL: http://www.faa.gov

Federal Highway Administration
400 7th St., SW
Washington, DC 20590
(202) 366-0660
FAX: (202) 366-7239
URL: http://www.fhwa.dot.gov

Federal Transit Administration
400 7th St., SW
Washington, DC 20590

(202) 366-4043
FAX: (202) 366-3472
URL: http://www.fta.dot.gov

General Aviation Manufacturers Association
1400 K St. NW, #801
Washington, DC 20005
(202) 393-1500
FAX: (202) 842-4063
URL: http://www.generalaviation.org

Highway Loss Data Institute
1005 N. Glebe Road, #800
Arlington, VA 22201
(703) 247-1600
FAX: (703) 247-1595
URL: http://www.highwaysafety.org

Motorcycle Industry Council, Inc.
2 Jenner St., #150
Irvine, CA 92718
(949) 727-4211
FAX: (949) 727-4217
URL: http://www.mic.org

Motorcycle Safety Foundation
2 Jenner St., #150
Irvine, CA 92718
(949) 727-3227
FAX: (949) 727-4217
URL: http://www.msf-usa.org

National Bicycle Dealers Association
777 W. 19th St., Suite O
Costa Mesa, CA 92627
(949) 722-6909
FAX: (949) 722-1747
URL: http://www.nbda.com
E-mail: info@nbda.com

National Center for Bicycling and Walking
(formerly the Bicycle Federation of America)
1506 21st St. NW, #200
Washington, DC 20036

(202) 463-6622
FAX: (202) 463-6625
URL: http://www.bikefed.org
E-mail: info@bikefed.org

National Highway Traffic Safety Administration
400 7th St. SW, #5232
Washington, DC 20590
(202) 366-9550
(800) 424-9393
FAX: (202) 366-5962
URL: http://www.nhtsa.dot.gov

National Railroad Passenger Corporation (Amtrak)
60 Massachusetts Ave., NE
Washington, DC 20002
(202) 906-3860
(800)-USA-RAIL
FAX: (202) 906-3306
URL: http://www.amtrak.com
E-mail: service@sales.amtrak.com

National Safety Council
1121 Spring Lake Dr.
Itasca, IL 60143-3201
(630) 285-1121
FAX: (630) 285-1315
URL: http://www.nsc.org

National Transportation Safety Board
490 L'Enfant Plaza East SW, 6th floor
Washington, DC 20594
(202) 314-6000
FAX (202) 314-6148
URL: http://www.ntsb.gov

Recreational Vehicle Industry Association
1896 Preston White Dr.
P.O. Box 2999
Reston, VA 20195-0999
(703) 620-6003
FAX: (703) 620-5071
URL: http://www.rvia.org

Regional Airline Association
2025 M Street, NW
Washington, DC 20036-3309
(202) 367-1170
FAX: (202) 367-2170
URL: http://www.raa.org
E-mail: raa@dc.sba.com

U.S. Army Corps of Engineers
441 G Street, NW
Washington, DC 20314
(202) 761-0010
FAX: (202) 761-1803
URL: http://www.usace.army.mil

U.S. Department of Transportation
400 7th St., SW
Washington, DC 20590
(202) 366-5580
FAX (202) 366-5583
URL: http://www.dot.gov

RESOURCES

The U.S. Department of Transportation (DOT) is an excellent source of information about all types of transportation. DOT prepared the *1999 Status of the Nation's Surface Transportation System: Conditions and Performance,* which provides current data on transportation and projects transportation needs for the future. The Bureau of Transportation Statistics, another DOT agency, publishes several excellent annual compendia, including *Transportation Statistics Annual Report* (1999) and *National Transportation Statistics* (1998).

The Federal Highway Administration (FHWA), also part of DOT, publishes data on the state of the nation's highways and bridges, including *Our Nation's Highways: Selected Facts and Figures 1998.* FHWA also published *Large Truck Crash Profile: The 1997 National Picture* (1998). The National Highway Traffic Safety Administration, a department of DOT, prepared *Traffic Safety Facts 1999* and many other pamphlets.

The Federal Aviation Administration (FAA), a DOT agency, in its *FAA Aviation Forecasts—Fiscal Years 1999–2010* (1999), provides valuable information on the nation's aviation system, including present conditions and future forecasts. The FAA also published *The Aviation Safety Statistical Handbook* (1999), which reports on accident data.

Air Transport 2000, Annual Report, prepared by the Air Transport Association of America, the airline trade association, is a very useful source for statistics on many facets of the air travel industry. (Call 800-497-3326 [U.S. and Canada], or 301-490-7951 for copies of the annual report.) The General Aviation Manufacturers Association provided its *Statistical Databook* (2000). *Air Transport World* magazine's annual "The World Airline Report " is an invaluable survey of the international airline industry.

The Association of American Railroads, the industry's trade group, furnishes data on the nation's freight trains in its annual *Railroad Facts* (2000). The U.S. General Accounting Office, an investigative agency of the U.S. government, published several reports on the rail industry, including: *Intercity Passenger Rail: Assessing the Benefits of Increased Federal Funding for Amtrak and High-Speed Passenger Rail Systems* (2001); *Intercity Passenger Rail: Amtrak's Progress in Improving Its Financial Condition Has Been Mixed* (1999); *Intercity Passenger Rail: Outlook for Improving Amtrak's Financial Health* (1998); *Intercity Passenger Rail: Financial Performance of Amtrak's Routes* (1998); and *High Speed Rail Projects in the U.S.* (1997).

Waterborne Commerce of the United States (1999), prepared by the Department of the Army Corps of Engineers, reports on the commercial shipping of both foreign and domestic cargo and the condition of the nation's waterways and harbors.

The American Public Transportation Association's *Public Transportation Fact Book* (2001) supplies invaluable data on mass transit. Information Plus appreciates the information on buses received from the American Bus Association and Greyhound Lines.

The *1998 Motorcycle Statistical Annual,* prepared by the Motorcycle Industry Council, Inc., provides information on motorcycles and motorcycle owners. The National Bicycle Dealers Association supplies data on bicycle usage and the U.S. bicycle market. The Recreational Vehicle Industry Association furnishes valuable information on the various types of recreational vehicles and their owners.

Information Plus thanks the American Trucking Associations for allowing the use of information from *American Trucking Trends, 2000 Edition,* which gives the current status of the trucking industry. *Ward's Automotive Yearbook 1999* (Ward's Communications, Southfield, MI, 1999), furnishes complete information on the production and sales of the nation's cars and trucks.

Information Plus would also like to thank the National Safety Council, which prepares the annual *Injury Facts*. The Eno Foundation for Transportation, Inc. publishes *Transportation in America* (1998), an excellent resource for the entire field of transportation.

INDEX

automobile drivers, 52–56, 54*f*, 55*t*
automobiles per household, 112, 113*f*
bicycle riders, 59, 60(*t*5.2), 61(*t*5.3)
bus passengers, 103
motorcycle owners, 63, 64–65, 65(*t*5.6)
pilots, 84, 85–86, 88, 88*f*
recreational vehicle owners, 70
transit riders, 111–112, 111*t*, 112(*t*8.11)
truck drivers, 74–75, 74(*t*6.2), 77–78
Deregulation
air travel, 82–83, 97–98
bus carriers, 102
railroads, 17–18
trucking industry, 75
See also Regulation
Diesel locomotives, 16
Domestic waterborne commerce, 3*f*, 12*t*
Drivers, automobiles, 52–56, 54*f*, 55*t*
Drug use. *See* Alcohol and drug use

E

Electric power
automobiles, 46*t*, 47–48
bicycles, 63
railroads, 16
streetcars, 104
Elevated railways, 104
Employment, airlines, 85–86, 86(*t*7.5)
Energy conservation, 108–109
Enplanements, 82*f*, 83, 84*t*, 93(*t*7.11), 98–99, 98*f*
Environmental issues
alternative fuels, 46–47, 46*t*
bicycles, 61–62
electric vehicles, 47–48, 103–104
energy conservation, 108–109
fuel economy, 44*t*, 45–46, 45*t*
large trucks, 79
railroads, 18
vehicle emissions, all types, 78*t*
Ergonomics, automobiles, 50
Erie Canal, 2
Ethanol, 46, 46*t*
Europe, air travel, 99
EV1 (electric car), 47, *48*
EV Warrior (electric bicycle), 63
Exported goods, 43–44
See also International trade
Extra-long vehicles. *See* Longer combination vehicles (LCV)

F

FAA (Federal Aviation Administration), 82, 92–95
Fares, air, 84, 86–87, 96–97
Farm products industry, 5(*f*1.3), 19, 21(*f*2.4), 21*t*
Fatal accidents
air travel, 95–96, 96*t*, 97*f*
automobiles, 48–51, 49*f*, 50*t*, 53, 54*f*, 55*t*, 65–66, 78*f*
bicycles, 60–61, 60(*t*5.2), 61(*t*5.3)
highways, 32–33, 36*f*
motorcycles, 65–67, 65(*t*5.7), 66(*f*5.4), 67(*f*5.5), 78*f*
trucking industry, 76–77, 77*t*, 78*f*
urban mass transit, 113–114

Fatigue
truck drivers, 77–78
urban mass transit operators, 114
Federal Aid Highway Act (1944), 28
Federal Aid Road Act of 1916, 28
Federal Aviation Administration (FAA), 82, 92–95
Federal government spending, 30–31, 30*t*, 31*f*, 31*t*, 90, 106*t*
See also Government subsidies and support
Federal Maritime Board and the Maritime Administration. *See* Maritime Administration (MARAD)
Federal Motor Vehicle Safety Standards (FMVSS), 63
Federal Railroad Administration (FRA), 17
Finance
air travel, 83, 84, 84*t*, 85*t*, 86
aircraft manufacturing, 90*f*
automobile ownership, 44
bus manufacturing, 103
buses, 101
canals, 2
highways, 28–29, 30–31, 31*f*, 32*f*, 33–34, 73
railroads, 17–20, 19*f*, 20(*f*2.2), 22, 22*f*, 25
recreational vehicle ownership, 67–69, 69*f*
shipbuilding, 2–3, 13–14
trucking industry, 73, 75, 75*f*
urban mass transit, 106*t*, 107, 107*t*
Finland, 62
"Flag of convenience," 7
Fleets (ships)
domestic fleet, 5
foreign fleets, 6*t*
merchant fleet, 2–4
FMVSS (Federal Motor Vehicle Safety Standards), 63
Foreign waterborne commerce, 3*f*
4R (Regional Revitalization and Regulatory Reform Act of 1976), 17
Four-wheel drive automobiles, 51
FRA (Federal Railroad Administration), 17
France, 24
Free flight air traffic system, 95
Freight cars (railroads), 21(*f*2.5), 21(*f*2.6)
Freight transport
buses, 102
Erie Canal, 2
railroads, 16–17, 19–20, 19*f*, 21*f*, 21*t*
trucking industry, 71–73
waterborne, 1–2, 3*f*, 4–7, 4*t*, 5*f*, 12*t*
See also Trucks, trucking industry; Waterborne transportation
Frequent-flier programs, 87
Front-wheel drive automobiles, 51
Fuel cell-powered automobiles, 47–48
Fuel economy, 44*t*, 45–46, 45*t*, 103–104, 107*t*
Fueling stations, 46–47

G

Gas industry. *See* Petroleum industry
Gas stations, 46–47
Gasohol, 46
General aviation, 83, 88–89, 89*t*

General Aviation Revitalization Act (1994), 89
Georgia, 9
Global economy. *See* Transportation worldwide
Good Roads Movement, 28
Government subsidies and support
airports, 90
bicycling, 61–62
highways, 28–29, 30–31, 31*f*, 32*f*, 33–34, 36*t*
railroads, 15–16, 17, 18–19, 22, 25
shipbuilding, 13–14
urban mass transit, 105–107, 106*t*
waterborne transportation, 2–3
Grand Canyon, 114
Great Britain, 62
Great Lakes, 2
Greyhound Lines, Inc., 101–102
Gyrocopters, 89

H

Harbors. *See* Ports and harbors
Hazardous materials, 78–79
Heavy-rail systems, 109–110
Helicopters, 89
Helmets
bicycle, 61, 61(*t*5.4)
motorcycle, 66–67, 67(*f*5.6), 68*t*
Helsinki City Bikes program, 62
High-occupancy vehicle (HOV) lanes, 35–37
High-speed trains, 18, 22–26, 25*f*
Highways, 27–37
See also Traffic congestion
History
air travel, 81–83
automobiles, 39
buses, 101–103
highways and roads, 27–29
railroads, 15–18
urban mass transit, 104–107
waterborne transportation, 1–4
Hub-and-spoke air travel network, 87, 91–92
Hybrid automobiles, 48
Hybrid buses, 103–104
Hydrogen, 46*t*, 47

I

Immigration, 1
Imported goods
automobiles, 43
bicycles, 60
motorcycles, 63–64
See also International trade
Incentive programs, mass transit, 113
Inland waterways, 9, 9*t*, 10*f*–11*f*
Inspection, aircraft, 96
Insurance, automobile, 44, 53
Intelligent Transportation Systems, 34
Intelligent vehicles. *See* Smart cars
Intercity transportation, 102*f*
bus service, 101, 103
trucking industry, 71
Intermodal shipping systems, 8, 13(*f*1.7)
See also Freight transport

V

Van conversions. *See* Recreational vehicles

W

Washington (state), 34
Waterborne transportation, 1–14
Weight controls (trucking industry), 72–73
World War I, 2
World War II, 3, 105
Worldwide economy. *See* Transportation worldwide

Y

Young adults. *See* Teenagers and young adults